The Elizabeth Cady Stanton–Susan B. Anthony Reader
THIRD EDITION

The Elizabeth Cady Stanton–Susan B. Anthony Reader

THIRD EDITION

ELIZABETH CADY STANTON *and*
SUSAN B. ANTHONY

Edited and with Critical Commentary by
Ellen Carol DuBois

McFarland & Company, Inc., Publishers
Jefferson, North Carolina

LIBRARY OF CONGRESS CATALOGUING-IN-PUBLICATION DATA

Names: Stanton, Elizabeth Cady, 1815–1902, author. | Anthony, Susan B. (Susan Brownell), 1820–1906. Works. Selections. | DuBois, Ellen Carol, 1947– editor.
Title: The Elizabeth Cady Stanton–Susan B. Anthony reader / Elizabeth Cady Stanton and Susan B. Anthony ; edited and with critical commentary by Ellen Carol DuBois.
Description: Third edition. | Jefferson, North Carolina : McFarland & Company, Inc., Publishers, 2022 | Includes bibliographical references and index.
Identifiers: LCCN 2022030816 | ISBN 9781476686967 (paperback : acid free paper) ∞
ISBN 9781476646312 (ebook)
Subjects: LCSH: Stanton, Elizabeth Cady, 1815–1902. | Anthony, Susan B. (Susan Brownell), 1820–1906. | Feminists—United States—Correspondence. | Feminism—United States—History—19th century. | BISAC: LITERARY COLLECTIONS / American / General | HISTORY / Women
Classification: LCC HQ1412.S72 2022 | DDC 305.42—dc23/eng/20220728
LC record available at https://lccn.loc.gov/2022030816

BRITISH LIBRARY CATALOGUING DATA ARE AVAILABLE

**ISBN (print) 978-1-4766-8696-7
ISBN (ebook) 978-1-4766-4631-2**

© 2022 Ellen Carol DuBois. All rights reserved

No part of this book may be reproduced or transmitted in any form or by any means, electronic or mechanical, including photocopying or recording, or by any information storage and retrieval system, without permission in writing from the publisher.

On the cover: Elizabeth Cady Stanton, 1815–1902 (left), and Susan B. Anthony, 1820–1906 (both photographs Library of Congress)

Printed in the United States of America

*McFarland & Company, Inc., Publishers
Box 611, Jefferson, North Carolina 28640
www.mcfarlandpub.com*

Table of Contents

Introduction to the Third Edition   1

Part One. 1815–1861

Introduction: Before Seneca Falls   7

DOCUMENT 1. Stanton, "Address Delivered at Waterloo New York about Seneca Falls Convention of July 19, 1848," September 1848   23

DOCUMENT 2. Elizabeth Cady Stanton and Frederick Douglass, First Meeting, c. 1840; Douglass at Seneca Falls Convention, 1848   30

DOCUMENT 3. "Immediate Causes of the Demand for Women's Political Rights" *History of Woman Suffrage, volume 1*, eds., Stanton, Anthony and Matilda Joslyn Gage, 1881   34

DOCUMENT 4. Anthony, Letter on Temperance, August 26, 1852; Stanton, "Appeal for the Maine Law," January 21, 1853   37

DOCUMENT 5. Stanton and Anthony, Letters, 1852–1859   43

DOCUMENT 6. Stanton, "Address to the Legislature of New York on Women's Rights," February 14, 1854   58

DOCUMENT 7. Anthony, Diary of a Lecture Tour with Ernestine Rose to Washington, Baltimore, and Philadelphia, 1854   65

DOCUMENT 8. Stanton, "Speech to the Anniversary of the American Anti-Slavery Society," 1860   71

Part Two. 1863–1878

Introduction 79

DOCUMENT 9. The Woman's National Loyal League, May 1863 92

DOCUMENT 10. Stanton, "Speech at Lawrence, Kansas," 1867 96

DOCUMENT 11. Stanton, "Manhood Suffrage," *The Revolution*, December 24, 1868 100

DOCUMENT 12. Anthony and Frederick Douglass Debate the Fifteenth Amendment at the May 1869 American Equal Rights Association 104

DOCUMENT 13. Anthony, "Constitutional Argument," 1873 107

DOCUMENT 14. Stanton, "Speech to the McFarland-Richardson Protest Meeting," May 1870 117

DOCUMENT 15. Anthony, "Suffrage and the Working Woman," 1871 121

DOCUMENT 16. Stanton, "Home Life," c. 1875 127

DOCUMENT 17. Anthony, "Homes of Single Women," October, 1877 133

Part Three. 1880–1906

Introduction: Anthony and the Consolidation of the Women's Movement 141

DOCUMENT 18. Stanton on Frederick Douglass' Second Marriage; Douglass Response, 1884 156

DOCUMENT 19. Anthony, "Organization Among Women," Columbian Exposition, 1893 160

DOCUMENT 20. Anthony and Ida B. Wells, Friendship, 1894–1895 163

DOCUMENT 21. Stanton, "Address to the Founding Convention of the National American Woman Suffrage Association," February 1890 169

DOCUMENT 22. Stanton, "Educated Suffrage Justified";
Harriot Stanton Blatch, "An Open Letter to Mrs. Stanton,"
1894   173

DOCUMENT 23. Stanton, "The Solitude of Self,"
January 18, 1892   179

DOCUMENT 24. Stanton, "Introduction" and Commentaries
on Genesis, Chapters 1–4, *The Woman's Bible*; Anthony,
Response to the NAWSA Resolution Disavowing
The Woman's Bible; Stanton, Draft of "Criticism of
Bigotry of Women"   185

DOCUMENT 25. Anna Howard Shaw, "The Passing of
Aunt Susan"; Helen Gardener, "Elizabeth Cady Stanton"   199

Chapter Notes   207

Bibliography   215

Index   219

Introduction to the Third Edition

The significance of great historical developments continues to change as we look back on them. Such is the case with respect to the enfranchisement of the female half of the American citizenry. Two dimensions of that history are particularly important: what the impact of women's votes on American politics has been; and how that impact has been reflected in the diversity of the female electorate, especially its racial diversity.

The first edition of this collection of the writings of the two great nineteenth-century pioneers of the suffrage movement, Susan B. Anthony and Elizabeth Cady Stanton, was published in 1981. The field of women's history was then just beginning to develop. Schocken Books included this collection in an early series curated by the great pioneer of the field, Gerda Lerner. By 1980, for the first time since the 1920 ratification of the Nineteenth Amendment, women voters began to register a distinct political impact. They voted at higher percentages, more for the Democratic Party, and more in favor of liberal issues, than male voters. This phenomenon was designated as the "political gender gap" and reflected the obstacles then being faced by two major feminist objectives, passing the Equal Rights Amendment and ensuring constitutional protections of women's reproductive rights.

The issues of women's freedom and racial equality were always intertwined. The women's rights movement was born out of the struggle for abolition, in what Elizabeth Cady Stanton called "the school of anti-slavery." The painful and tragic conflict between the two movements in the Reconstruction years was a turning point for that connection, with woman suffrage breaking away from and leaving behind its connection to Black freedom struggles, becoming in essence an all-white movement. My examination of this complex history in the first edition reflected my own early 1970s experience, when women's liberation was emerging from the shadow of a more visible Black power insurgency.[1] Thus in the 1981 edition of *The Reader* I stressed how Stanton and Anthony broke out of their long alliance with male abolitionists and Republicans and committed themselves to the creation of an independent woman-based movement. The achievement of an autonomous second wave feminist movement had been the seed ground of my own women's history awareness.

In 1992, publication of the second edition having passed on to Northeastern University Press, indicators of women's political impact were growing. Sandra Day O'Connor, the first woman Supreme Court Justice, was about to be joined by Ruth Bader Ginsburg, the second. Senate confirmation hearings of Clarence Thomas for the Court, focused as they were on charges of sexual harassment brought by attorney Anita Hill, highlighted two related issues: disregard of the seriousness of sexual harassment; and the small and the inadequate numbers of women elected to national political office. Nor did it escape attention that the two African American principles fought out their conflict before an all-white, all male Senate audience. In the aftermath, the numbers of Congresswomen and female Senators, though still primarily white, began to rise and to continue to do so steadily thereafter. Public awareness of the plague of sexual violence against women grew.

Also, by the time I was preparing the second edition, the roles and standing of these two movements had been reversed, with feminism now far more prominent than the Black freedom struggle, which had receded into the political background. Simultaneously, the feminist voices of African American women were growing stronger, following in the footsteps of the Boston-based Combahee River Collective. In 1991 the African American legal scholar Kimberlé Crenshaw broke through the assumption that "woman" meant "white woman" by insisting on the concept of "intersectionality."[2] Crenshaw's work taught a whole generation of feminists that "woman" was never a single entity, but always inflected by other identities, none more important in the U.S. than race.

What these developments meant to my own thinking was a reevaluation of the consequences of the 1869 break between the movements for Black and for woman suffrage. To my appreciation for what was gained at that moment I added a new and profound sense of what was lost. In jettisoning their political connection to the champions of Black suffrage, Stanton and Anthony sacrificed their historic connection to Black women.[3] No longer linking the claims of race and sex but now counterpoising (and in the case of Stanton even antagonizing) them, they built a case for woman suffrage that was simultaneously more gender-based and more elitist and racist.

Now, as I prepare this new edition, I work in the context of an even greater shift in the dual contexts of women's political power and the importance of women of color. Even as the hundredth anniversary of the ratification of the Nineteenth Amendment has led to a public celebration of the long struggle for women's enfranchisement, competing political forces struggle to claim that heritage; and attention grows to racism within the suffrage legacy. (What would Susan B. Anthony make of being pardoned by a notorious racist and misogynist for the 1872 crime of voting, of which she was so proud?) Meanwhile "women's votes" had emerged as the crucial lever in the elections of 2016, 2018 and especially 2020, even as that category has been disaggregated to reveal that it is women of color who are in the lead.

Whether women's votes, especially the votes of women of color, will be vigorous and well organized or challenged and suppressed may well tell the future of American democratic politics. In any case, it seems that the power of women's votes and the true diversity of that power may well have come together, as women of color carry the banner of women's political rights and a feminist future. All of this continues to bring forward the meaning and consequences of women's long battle for the vote.

As the suffrage centennial coincided with the Black Lives Matter movement, the racist elements of the history of the woman suffrage movement came under increasing scrutiny. Because they seemed to have betrayed their abolitionist heritage and because of the historic prominence of the Fifteenth Amendment battle, Anthony and especially Stanton became the focal point of this criticism.[4] While I wish to give this critique its due, the third edition of the *Reader* makes it clear that the legacy of these two great pioneers cannot be reduced to this one single aspect of their long history of leadership.

In this edition, I have rewritten the introductory essays to the *Reader*'s three parts to clarify the several phases of this history as reflected in the long careers of Stanton and Anthony. Among new primary source selections are those that highlight their relations to African American suffragists as well as their changing racial politics in the Jim Crow years. These include a fuller account of the 1869 battle over the Fifteenth Amendment, Stanton's advocacy of literacy qualifications for suffrage, and material from Stanton's long relation to Frederick Douglass and Anthony's late-life friendship with Ida B. Wells.

Nonetheless, much of the third edition of the *Reader* has not changed. The *Reader* itself is somewhat of an historic document and I wish to honor that. I note particularly that as I did in the first and second editions, I have continued to use the term "feminism" when referring to the nineteenth-century women's rights/woman suffrage movement, a practice which I would no longer do. Also I have left most of the notes as they were in earlier editions, despite the much greater range of sources and histories that have been published since.

Since the second edition, its publisher, Northeastern University Press, has ceased to exist. I want to thank my new publisher, McFarland Press, for recognizing the importance of this project and joining me to keep it alive.

PART ONE

1815–1861

Introduction
Before Seneca Falls

The 1848 women's rights convention at Seneca Falls was part of a tradition of political thought about women reaching back at least half a century. In general, this tradition involved the extension of natural rights egalitarianism from men to women—especially the principles of individualism, the universal capacity for reason, and political democracy. In the multifaceted debate over the proper position of women in bourgeois society, this tradition, which was called "women's rights," tended to supply more advanced arguments—reaching deeper into the structures of women's subordination, claiming more territory as women's province, going farther in envisioning a totally different sexual order—than other ways of approaching the problem of woman's place.

Mary Wollstonecraft, the Englishwoman who wrote *Vindication of the Rights of Women* (1791), is generally recognized as the first major Anglo-American figure in this tradition. Wollstonecraft wrote in response to the Enlightenment antifeminist Rousseau, who argued that since female nature was different from male, women's rights must be different from men's. Wollstonecraft insisted that women's nature was basically the same as men's—free, rational, and independent—and that, like men, women's "first duty is to themselves as rational creatures," their primary objective being "to obtain a character as a human being regardless of the distinction of sex." Although Wollstonecraft acknowledged that women had "different duties to fulfill" and urged them to become "affectionate wives and rational mothers," her frame of reference for women was not the domestic sphere, but the public world from which they were so largely excluded. "In order to render [women's] private virtue a public benefit," she insisted "they must have a civil existence in the state, married or single." Wollstonecraft believed that education would improve women's position and character, but what distinguished her from more conservative advocates of this reform was her commitment to the kind of education that would narrow the moral and intellectual distance between men and women, and counter the selfish, antidemocratic tendencies of home life. Thus, she specifically advocated coeducation, and a system of public, or "national," schools for all classes "for only by jostling's of equality can we form a just opinion of ourselves."[1]

In the United States, where an energetic debate on women's education was taking place in the 1790s, Wollstonecraft's writings were widely circulated. The publication of the *Vindication* and the clarity and conviction of Wollstonecraft's arguments helped to build sentiment in favor of improving education for women. Yet the larger framework of her thought—her egalitarianism and her belief in the importance of a public role for women—were not well received. Two factors limited Wollstonecraft's influence: her association with the secular radicalism of the French Revolution, which was increasingly in disfavor as a popular ideology after 1800; and—closely related—the revelation that Wollstonecraft had been a free lover and borne a child out of wedlock. The publication of the *Vindication* permitted many American women to speak out more confidently in favor of the intellectual and moral capacities of their sex and at the same time dissociate themselves from Wollstonecraft's larger radicalism. "I confess I admire many of her sentiments," the young Eliza Southgate wrote in 1801, "notwithstanding, I believe should any one adopt her principles, they would conduct [themselves] in the same manner, and upon the whole her life is the best comment on her writings."[2]

Instead, most American proponents of women's education in the early nineteenth century tended to base their arguments on women's special domestic responsibilities and unique moral position rather than on the common human nature and identical social responsibilities of the sexes. Hannah Mather Crocker, writing in 1818, argued that women were the mental and moral equals of men, but her defense of women's education was laced with warnings against "the impropriety of females ever trespassing on masculine ground," or intruding too far into public life. Crocker rested her best hopes for women's education not on the extension of public life and egalitarian principles to women, but on the perfection of "family government" and "a religious course of life." Similarly, Emma Willard, pioneer of women's education in the United States and founder of the Troy Female Seminary (which the young Elizabeth Cady attended) was a staunch advocate of the intellectual equality of the sexes and, at the same time, believed that women's education must be "adapted to that difference of character and duties, to which the softer sex should be formed."[3]

In the 1820s, egalitarian feminism found a brilliant new advocate,

Frances Wright. Wright, a follower of the utopian socialist Robert Owen, settled in the United States as the most likely place to realize her goal of true equality. There were links between Wright and Wollstonecraft, most notably the formative impact of William Godwin, lover and comrade of Wollstonecraft, on Robert Owen. Like Wollstonecraft, Wright believed that girls and boys should be educated in the same way and at the same schools. She was a particularly trenchant critic of the domestic institutions that were emerging to structure nineteenth-century women's lives. She advocated "free and voluntary affection" as an alternative to lifelong, monogamous marriage, and a childrearing system based on state-run coeducational boarding schools instead of the private family.[4]

The attacks on Wright in the American press as a free lover, infidel, and monstrously public woman were very similar to the attacks on Wollstonecraft twenty years earlier. Although the attacks were severe, and Wright's anticlericalism and socialism made her anathema to many, she had an important impact on the American debate on the woman's sphere. Other freethinking radicals took up her ideas that egalitarianism, secularism, and sexual freedom were the basis on which women's true position should be established. Wright's coworker, Robert Dale Owen (Robert Owen's son), and the Polish-born and Jewish feminist and freethinker, Ernestine Rose, were particularly important to later advocates of women's rights.

Egalitarian radicals seem to have played an important part in the early efforts to reform the property laws affecting married women. In New York, a married women's property act was submitted in 1836 by Judge Thomas Herttell, a radical and freethinking member of the state legislature; Ernestine Rose spoke and circulated a petition on behalf of Herttell's bill. In the same year, Robert Dale Owen submitted married women's property legislation in Indiana, where he was a member of the legislature. Owen also worked for reform in the divorce law, in particular to allow women to divorce men who were drunkards, and divorce reform was pursued in conjunction with married women's property legislation in Massachusetts as well.[5] Although not all supporters of the new property laws for women were egalitarian feminists, the opposition was entirely based on conservative ideas about woman's place and the sacred character of the marriage contract. The property law for women was not changed in New York until 1848, which seems to have been an important year for this reform elsewhere: in Pennsylvania, the law was changed in 1848; and in Massachusetts and Vermont, agitation also began in that year.

Despite the efforts of egalitarian feminists, the dominant approach to the improvement of women's position remained the idea of elevating the woman's role in the domestic sphere. Catharine Beecher, a major exponent of what one historian has called "the program of woman's sphere," began to rise to prominence in the early 1830s.[6] Whereas Wright was a critic of monogamous marriage and the private household, Beecher was their staunch defender and placed domesticity at the very center of her strategy for American women. She believed that a woman's influence must be different from a man's and should rest on her ability to inculcate the "spirit of benevolence" into the American character through the children that she raised. Beecher's major innovation was to argue that teaching was a function similar to mothering, and was therefore an appropriate activity for women. Through such womanly efforts, Beecher believed, women could simultaneously secure increased social power for themselves and provide the crucial antidote to the individual ambition and self-striving which seemed to be threatening the very core of American society, especially after the financial panic of 1837. There were many important points of conflict between Wright and Beecher: the former was a militant secularist while the latter advised women to put religious matters before worldly affairs; Wright was a critic of the unequal distribution of property while Beecher defended it as the indispensable "stimulus to industry"; and while Wright criticized the utilitarian dedication to the specialization and professionalization of learning, Beecher urged that it be extended to include housewifery. There were similarities in the thought of the two women—both favored better education and a more active social role for women, and both were committed to elevating a woman's status and winning her new respect—but there were enormous differences of strategy and vision. Beecher explicitly offered her ideas as an alternative to those, like Wright, "who are bewailing themselves over the fancied wrongs and injuries of women in this Nation."[7]

Throughout the 1830s and 1840s, women especially took to heart the notion that their sex gave them the right and capacity to exert a special social influence, and formed networks of local, all-women's organizations to pursue these wider moral obligations. Their concerns ranged from the care of indigents and the education of orphans to the elimination of prostitution and the reform of sexual morality. In the context of these all-women's organizations, women were sometimes able to express their profound resentment of the social and economic power that men had over their lives. In moral reform societies in particular, they attacked the double standard and the sexual and economic exploitation of women with great militancy. Women's barely submerged anger, combined with their conviction of the importance of bringing their special, moral influence to bear on society, led them to the very edges of "woman's sphere." The moral reform societies pursued male licentiousness all the way to the New York legislature, where they petitioned for a law making the sexual seduction of "any unmarried female of previous chaste character" a crime. Believing in the special needs and capacities of women, they nevertheless continued to defer to the authority of men, at least to their institutionalized political and religious power.[8]

When female antislavery activity began in the early 1830s, it was on similar terms. Women abolitionists believed that they had a particular obligation with respect to religious and moral concerns and, on the grounds that slavery was a threat to the moral character of American society, they argued that it was appropriate for women to work for its abolition. Initially they observed the proprieties by meeting separately from men and making their particular concern the women and children who were victims of slavery.[9] Like female moral reformers, they sought to achieve their goals by trying to influence men, both in their private relations and by public petition campaigns.

However, antislavery activity, far more than moral reform or temperance, brought women into conflict with established centers of power, and this in turn helped to lead them beyond the "woman's sphere" way of conceiving their social role. As Elizabeth Stanton explained, slavery was a "question of religion, philanthropy, political economy, commerce, education, and social life, on which depends the very existence of this so called republic" (see Document 8). In 1837, two women abolitionists, Sarah and Angelina Grimké, were attacked by the Congregational clergy of Massachusetts for becoming "public reformers" and speaking to mixed groups of men and women. They responded by embracing the odious tradition of women's rights to defend their abolitionism. Significantly, they were also rebuked by Catharine Beecher, who reminded them that "woman is to win everything by peace and love ... but this is all to be accomplished in the domestic circle ... [by] woman's retaining her place as dependent and defenseless and making no claims and maintaining no rights."[10] Angelina Grimké responded that the antislavery movement had taught her that "human beings have *rights* because they are *moral* beings; ... as all men have the same moral nature, they have essentially the same rights." Applying this "fundamental principle" to women, she realized that sex was a "mere circumstance," falsely "enthroned upon the summit, administering upon rights and responsibilities." Sarah Grimké answered the clerical criticisms of her public activity in a similar fashion. She repudiated "the distinction now so strenuously insisted upon between masculine and feminine virtues" and insisted on the great benefits, to men and women both, of "equality of the sexes."[11]

The Grimkés' defense of women's rights catalyzed a great deal of feminist sentiment among abolitionists. Many other women and a few men supported and encouraged them, and finally, in 1839, antifeminists, finding themselves in the minority, withdrew from the American Anti-Slavery Society (AASS). Abolitionist women subsequently dissolved their separate auxiliaries, took office in the organization, became traveling public lecturers, and generally obliterated all distinctions between men's and women's activity in the AASS. In this atmosphere, feminism and feminists flourished. Elizabeth Cady Stanton, Susan B. Anthony, Lucy Stone, Jane Elizabeth Jones, and other leaders of the women's rights movement in the 1850s were active in the AASS of the 1840s. Thirty years later, when Stanton and Anthony surveyed the influences leading up to the Seneca Falls convention of 1848, they identified three precipitating factors: the radical ideas of Wright and Rose on religion and democracy; the initial reforms in women's property law in the 1830s and 1840s; and "above all other causes," women's experiences in the antislavery movement (see Document 3).

Elizabeth Cady Stanton and Seneca Falls

Elizabeth Cady Stanton bore seven children and lived eighty-seven years in nearly perfect health, mental as well as physical. She was brilliant and learned, and she was also sensuous, defending her own weight (175 pounds in 1860, over 240 when she was an old woman), her propensity to take frequent naps, and the sexuality of all women when none of these things was considered respectable.[12] She had a powerful personality which she used to demolish her enemies and keep her friends at a respectful distance. Above all, she was committed to unearthing and understanding the long history of women's oppression, and to leading women to revolt against it.

She was born in 1815 to one of New York's "blue-blooded first families."[13] Her mother was a Livingston, and this aristocratic background provided her with a tendency to elitism and a special measure of self-confidence that came from generations of landed wealth. She attended Emma Willard's Troy Seminary, where she received the best woman's education available at the time. There, she was caught up in a powerful religious revival, but removed from the pressures of the revival and exposed to secular philosophy, "my religious superstition gave place to rational ideas based on scientific facts, and in proportion as I looked at everything from a new standpoint, I grew more happy day by day."[14] After graduation, she read law in the office of her father, the noted jurist

Daniel Cady, and became a student of legal and constitutional history.[15] Her knowledge of the law and respect for its significance, as well as her hostility to religious enthusiasm and the organized clergy, distinguished her from many other women who believed that religion was a woman's sphere and government and politics were alien, masculine activities.

In this same period, she was introduced into the abolitionist movement by her cousin, Gerrit Smith. Smith was a major figure in the transformation of abolitionism from an evangelical enterprise, which relied on moral suasion and individual conversion to defeat slavery, into a political movement, which focused on the law and the power of the state. In 1839 and 1840, Smith was meeting with other abolitionists convinced of the necessity of political organization, prominent among whom was Henry B. Stanton. Stanton, who had begun his career as a theological student and brilliant abolitionist organizer, had been one of the first abolitionists to recognize the limitations of the moral suasion strategy.

Elizabeth Cady and Henry Stanton met at Gerrit Smith's home. They shared many things, including a belief in the importance of political organization for the achievement of reform. In defense of Henry Stanton's role in the formation of the new, antislavery Free Soil Party, Elizabeth Cady wrote: "I am in favor of political action.... So long as we are to be governed by human laws, I shall be unwilling to have the making and administration of these laws left entirely to the selfish and unprincipled part of the community, which would be the case should all honest men refuse to mingle in political affairs." Political organization, she argued, in this case "a party formed and candidates nominated," "give a reality to antislavery principles."[16] Their courtship was brief and tempestuous, due in part to Judge Cady's opposition and in part to political upheaval within the abolitionist movement, and they married on May 1, 1840.

Marriage to Henry Stanton brought Elizabeth into personal contact with the pioneering feminists of the antislavery movement. The first stop on their wedding trip was the home of Angelina Grimké Weld, Theodore Weld, and Sarah Grimké. "We were very much pleased with Elizabeth Stanton who spent several days with us," Angelina wrote to a friend, "and I could not help wishing that Henry was better calculated to help mould such a mind."[17] From there, the Stanton's went to London to attend the World's Anti-Slavery Convention. The American women delegates, one of whom was Lucretia Mott, were refused admission to the convention. Mott and Elizabeth Stanton spent a great deal of time together in London and, when they returned to the United States, began to correspond.

Meeting Lucretia Mott greatly accelerated Elizabeth Stanton's development as a feminist. "Before meeting Mrs. Mott, I had heard a few men of liberal opinions discuss various political, religious and social theories," Stanton wrote some years later, "but with my first doubt of my father's absolute wisdom, came a distrust of all men's opinions on the character and sphere of women." Mott was the first woman she had met who was as liberal-minded as the men she had known and "who had sufficient confidence in herself to frame and hold an opinion in the face of opposition," especially male.[18] Despite her Quakerism and her piety, Mott was familiar with and sympathetic to the traditions of secular radicalism. Stanton credited her with "banishing religious doubts and fears from my mind."[19] Mott urged her to read Wollstonecraft, Wright, and the Grimkés' writings, which Stanton herself circulated in the early 1840s.[20] "The more I think on the present condition of woman," Stanton wrote to Mott in 1842, "the more am I oppressed with the reality of their degradation."[21] Finally, in 1848, Stanton's feminist apprenticeship was completed. With the help of Mott, her sister Martha Wright, and two other Quaker women, Mary M'Clintock and Jane Hunt, Stanton conceived and organized the first women's rights convention.

There has been considerable historical speculation about the timing of the Seneca Falls convention. Why did it not occur until 1848, especially inasmuch as the two key figures had met and discussed women's rights eight years before? First of all, Stanton's domestic situation had changed, considerably intensifying her personal discontent. By 1848, she was a thirty-three-year-old housewife and mother of three, living in central New York, away from the centers of intellectual and political excitement. Her husband earned only a modest income, was often away from home on political business, and she cared for her children and did most of her housework herself or with the help of one servant.

Larger political influences were also at work. In April, the New York legislature finally passed the law, for which Stanton and others had lobbied, giving married women control over their inherited property. At the same time, revolutionary movements were flaring up all over Europe, demanding the overthrow of despotism, the extension of democratic political rights, and the achievement of full equality. Finally, in the aftermath of the Mexican-American War, both major parties and the national government were committed to the defense and expansion of slavery, and this accelerated political developments among abolitionists. Less than a month after the women's rights convention at Seneca Falls, Henry Stanton played a major role in the organization of an openly antislavery faction within the Democratic Party, and by

November he had been elected to the New York legislature as a Free Soil Democrat.

The Seneca Falls Declaration of Sentiments bore many hallmarks of Stanton's influence (see Document 1). It was shaped by a powerful, eloquent conviction of men's "absolute tyranny" over women, which Stanton infused into everything she said and wrote about women. She also gave the Declaration a sense of great historical significance, almost as if this convention were the first time that women had ever repudiated the false and unequal position into which men had placed them, and demanded the full equality and true freedom that was their right. Finally, she was responsible for the focus on political equality.

In the half century since Mary Wollstonecraft, the debate over sexual egalitarianism had shifted ground. The primary question for feminists was no longer education, but the more distant realms of public activity reserved for men, especially politics. Frances Wright had recognized the importance of political organization, and had spoken and written on "the science of government," but at a time when the principle of political equality had not yet even been won with respect to white men, she did not demand that women be enfranchised. Nor was political equality the focus for feminists in the abolitionist movement, most of whom were suspicious of politics and committed to the strategy of moral suasion.[22] It fell to Elizabeth Stanton, a militant feminist who understood the importance of political organization for reformers, to recognize that feminism, like abolition, had to become a political movement to "give reality" to its principles. This was the basis on which she demanded woman suffrage.

At Seneca Falls, Stanton argued that political equality was the key to women's overthrow of male despotism and the achievement of the "equal status to which they are entitled." The first in the list of grievances in the Declaration of Sentiments was that women were denied their "inalienable right to the elective franchise." From this flowed men's ability to pass laws that deprived women of control over property and wages, subjected them to the authority of their husbands in marriage, deprived them of their children in the case of divorce, and left them "oppressed on all sides." By focusing on the demand for political equality, Stanton gave feminism a clear strategy and set it on firm ground for becoming an organized social movement. She understood that law played a major role in setting men over women. By demanding political power, women could struggle collectively against their degradation, rather than each against her own father or husband. The demand for the vote touched the nerve of woman's subordination by contending that women could have a role in society other than that of wife and mother.

"Depend upon it, this is the point to attack," Stanton wrote prophetically, "the stronghold of the fortress—*the one* woman will find the most difficult to take, *the one* man will most reluctantly give up."[23]

In pressing the demand for political rights, which others attending the Seneca Falls Convention found uncomfortable, either because politics was too male or too corrupt, Stanton was supported by Frederick Douglass, the fugitive slave turned abolitionist orator. Having moved fifty miles west of Seneca Falls to Rochester, Douglass had begun editing *The North Star*, which gave the infant women's rights movement its most regular publicity. Each regarded the other with great appreciation, and both recalled Douglass' intervention at the Seneca Falls Convention as momentous (see Document 2).

Although the Seneca Falls convention was intended to stimulate widespread agitation for women's civil and political equality, it was almost two years before a women's rights convention was held outside New York. Finally, in April 1850, feminists in the abolitionist stronghold of Salem, Ohio, organized a women's rights meeting to exert pressure on the state constitutional convention. Later that year, feminists from seven states met in Worcester, Massachusetts; the leading figure was Paulina Wright Davis, a former moral reformer who had become active in the antislavery movement. The convention set up a rudimentary form of organization: a coordinating committee, a plan for woman suffrage petition campaigns in eight states, and committees to report on women's educational, industrial, legal, and social status.[24] In 1851 Indiana women organized a convention, and the next year Pennsylvania women did the same, even though they remained wary of women becoming involved in "the violence and intrigue which are now frequently practiced by party politicians."[25]

Stanton was unable to attend most of these early women's rights conventions because of the continuing demands of household and children, but nothing kept her from writing. She sent letters of encouragement to those she did not attend and began to plan a book on women's history.[26] Horace Greeley invited her to write occasional articles for *The New York Tribune*, but when another Seneca Falls resident, Amelia Bloomer, began to publish a monthly women's temperance newspaper, Stanton saw the opportunity for a regular outlet for her women's rights ideas. Under her influence, Bloomer's newspaper, *The Lily*, became "the only [medium] in the whole country—for spreading among women accurate news of the women's rights movement."[27]

Feminists of all sorts began to turn to Stanton. "Every article you write hits the nail on the head," wrote Mary Gove Nichols, a health reformer and early proponent of free love. "I like you vastly."[28] The pioneering woman physician, Harriott Hunt, wanted to come to Seneca Falls to meet her. "Our deep interest in the Woman's cause which is opening so wonderfully draws me very near to you my dear Mrs. Stanton and I do not feel as addressing a stranger."[29] There was widespread impatience among feminists to see Stanton released from her domestic responsibilities. "Oh Liz, if you were not tied hand and foot by domestic duties," Sarah Grimké wrote, "what a glorious work you would do for woman. As it is you do much, very much."[30] "When your children are a little more grown, you will surely be heard," Lucy Stone wrote, soon after they met, "for it cannot be possible to repress what is in you."[31]

Susan B. Anthony and Women's Temperance Activity

Stanton's involvement with *The Lily* brought her into contact with a young temperance worker, Susan B. Anthony. Anthony was born in 1820 into an antislavery and liberal Quaker family. Her father had struggled against religious orthodoxy, and so Susan did not have to do so, and she tended to be both more casual and more practical about the power of the established churches than Stanton. In 1837, her father lost his cotton mill during the nation's first major depression, and when the family reached its lowest point economically, Susan and her sisters went out to teach. Within a few years, she had become passionately attached to the idea of self-support and personal independence for women, a conviction which she carried for the rest of her life. She was the only women's rights leader of the first generation to remain unmarried. By 1850, she was looking for a wider field for her labors than teaching, and turned to temperance. She subscribed enthusiastically to the ideas and moral reform perspective of the movement, and became active in the Daughters of Temperance, where her dedicated work and strong personality soon brought her into prominence in western New York.[32]

The temperance movement was undergoing a revival in the early 1850s and had begun to take a turn towards politics.[33] After years of treating intemperance as a sin and moral failing, reformers were beginning to recognize the role that the state played in organizing and facilitating the liquor industry. In Maine, temperance advocates succeeded in getting the legislature to pass a law prohibiting the production or sale of liquor, and agitation grew for a "Maine law" in other states, including New York. Still Anthony believed that the only influence women could bring to bear against alcohol was private, in their homes, and indirectly, "through husband, son, father, or brother."[34] Yet she was very much in favor of bringing the issue into politics, and frustrated because there was no role for women in this work (see Document 2).

Amelia Bloomer introduced Anthony to Stanton sometime in 1851. Perhaps Anthony had expressed a desire to meet the woman who was preaching political equality for women; perhaps Bloomer recognized the affinity between Stanton's ideas about women and the equality of the sexes, and Anthony's drive and capacity. Anthony was immediately drawn to Stanton by the power of her ideas. She was attracted by Stanton's political and secular viewpoint, and her disdain for what Anthony was soon calling the "pharisaical priests" who had considerable control over the temperance movement and in teachers' organizations. Stanton liberated the feminism in Anthony, particularly her anger at the sentimental and trivializing treatment of women by male temperance leaders. When Anthony was prohibited from speaking at a temperance convention because to do so would violate a woman's sphere, she decided to organize a new, independent women's temperance society which would place no such limitations on her. She persuaded Elizabeth Stanton to work with her, and, in April 1852, the New York State Women's Temperance Society held its founding meeting. Five hundred women were present, Elizabeth Stanton was made president, and Anthony became the traveling organizer.[35]

Stanton proposed a women's rights program for the new society, the two most radical elements of which were woman suffrage, "so that woman may vote on this great political and social evil," and a liberalized divorce law, to permit women to divorce drunken husbands (see Document 3). At the first anniversary of the Women's State Temperance Society, Stanton and Anthony were successfully challenged by an alliance of temperance men and conservative women. Once the prohibition against men voting in the Society was overturned, Stanton was deposed from the presidency and the women's rights program of divorce and woman suffrage was repudiated. Although Anthony was re-elected to office, she withdrew in solidarity with Stanton.[36]

The temperance episode solidified the comradeship that Stanton and Anthony had begun to develop. The effect on Stanton was enormous. "In turning the intense earnestness and religious enthusiasm of this great-souled woman into this channel," Stanton wrote, "I soon felt the power of my convert goading me forward to more untiring work."[37] Starting with the temperance movement of the 1850s, Anthony drew Stanton into active reform work among women and kept her there. Anthony was familiar with the network of female benevolent organizations and much more than Stanton appreciated the loyalty to sex that women were beginning to cultivate there. She believed that this sisterhood could be extended into a feminist movement. She was more consistently optimistic about women's development than Stanton, readier to see the signs of developing feminism in them. Although she played a crucial role in this period by relieving Stanton of some of her domestic burdens and acting as her proxy at reform conventions, she may have had an even more important effect in helping her to resist the psychological lure of "narrow family selfishness."[38] Anthony's entire existence was the world of female reform and she provided Stanton with a strong and vital link to that world. "I do believe that I have developed into much more of a woman under her jurisdiction," Stanton wrote thirty-five years later, "than if left to myself reading novels in an easy chair."[39]

Women's Rights and Antislavery in the 1850s

Anthony's conversion from moral reform to political feminism was a total one, and she immediately put her prodigious energies directly in the service of women's rights in New York State. Using the skills and contacts she had acquired while traveling for temperance reform, she organized an ambitious petition campaign for women's rights during the winter of 1853–1854. Sixty women circulated petitions under her direction, and, within a few months, secured more than ten thousand signatures to send to the New York legislature.[40] Women's rights activists had for some time wanted a more systematic approach, but most of them were too attached to the individualistic style of agitation to undertake it. The call to the 1852 national convention had urged "a well digested plan of operation whereby [our] social rights may be secured," but many women's rights leaders found organizations objectionable because they "fettered" and "distorted" the individual spirit.[41] Anthony, fresh from the network of women's benevolent societies, had no such objections to the constraint of organization, and no difficulty disciplining her energies to it. Her willingness to undertake the slow, backbreaking work necessary to teach women the importance of political equality and to force legislatures to grant it proved to be her greatest contribution to feminism. Her total dedication, year after year, eventually won her enormous loyalty from American women and a solid historical reputation as "mother" of the women's movement.

The petition campaign culminated in a grand women's rights convention in Albany in February 1854, the central event of which was Elizabeth Stanton's "Address to the Legislature" (see Document 6). Stanton was unusually nervous about this speech, spent over two months writing it, and consulted several men to make sure that there were no errors in her legal scholarship. The basic premise of her arguments was, as it had been at Seneca Falls, that women's position before the law denied the fundamental truth that "men and women are alike," thus "we ask for no better laws than those you have made for yourself." In three of the four categories in which she surveyed women's legal oppression, the remedies she proposed followed this rule of the identity of men and women before the law: women as citizens must have equal civil status with men, especially the right to vote and sit on juries; women as widows must have equal inheritance rights when their spouses died intestate; and women as wives must have a revised marriage code which subjected marriage "to the same laws which controlled all other contracts" and made it dissolvable at the will of either party. It was only when Stanton considered the unjust laws under which women suffered as mothers that she shifted her philosophical ground, arguing that women had a unique role in "moulding the character of the son" and thus special responsibility for developing "a higher and purer morality." "Thy address to the Legislature we circulate unsparingly," wrote Lucretia Mott. "It gives great satisfaction."[42] "The hearing has confirmed my previous suspicion that you are the head and font of this offence against the oppressors of womanhood," another admirer wrote.[43]

Both Stanton and Anthony went through personal transformations as they developed the skills and sense of self necessary to work for women's rights (see Document 5). After her 1854 speech, Stanton arrived at a "fierce decision" to work for women's rights in earnest, and to "speak when I can do myself credit," but she encountered painful opposition from her father, friends, and husband. "I wish you to consider this letter strictly confidential," she wrote to Anthony in 1855. "Sometimes, Susan, I struggle in deep waters." Anthony faced a different challenge as she began to build the kind of life that would sustain her as an unmarried woman and full-time political reformer. Along with Ernestine Rose, she traveled to slave territory, learning first-hand the human suffering against which she had been protesting as an abolitionist (see Document 7). Above all, she experienced deep loneliness, especially when Lucy Stone and Antoinette Brown, to whom she had looked for companionship and intimacy, each married. "I have *very weak* moments," she wrote to Stanton in despair, "and long to lay my weary head somewhere and nestle my full soul close to that of another in full sympathy. I sometimes fear that I too shall faint by the wayside, and drop out [of] the ranks of the faithful few."

It took more than six years of grueling, sustained work before the New York legislature met any of the women's rights demands. In her 1854 speech Stanton had boldly proclaimed that "the mass speak through us"—"women who support themselves and their children ... the drunkards' wives ... the woman who has worked hard all her days to help her husband to accumulate a large property ... the laboring women ... those women who teach in our seminaries ... the unfortunate ones in our workhouses." But the truth was that it took a long time for women's rights to win any popular support, even among women. The dominant ideology of womanhood continued to be that of separate spheres and female domesticity, and women's rights feminists faced the enormous task of challenging these beliefs. In Washington, D.C., Anthony heard a prominent clergyman preach that "it is ... in the home that ... all women's chiefest duties lie," and she was enraged (see Document 7); when a male reformer, not unfriendly to women's rights, claimed that "women's inherent nature is Love & Man's Wisdom," her "heart sank." Among women, ideas like those of Catharine Beecher continued to be more acceptable than those of women's rights, but slowly, in response to conventions, lectures, articles, and petition campaigns, support began to grow. "In my circle, I hear the movement talked of and earnest hopes for its spread expressed," Mrs. Charles G. Finney, wife of the powerful evangelist minister, told Anthony. "But these women dare not speak out their sympathy." In 1860, after six years of county canvasses, petition campaigns, and memorials to the legislature, New York feminists secured the first comprehensive reform in women's legal status, including full property, parental, and widow's rights, but not enfranchisement.

The major factor affecting the women's rights movement in the late 1850s was the growing intensity of the conflict over slavery. In 1850, Congress passed the Fugitive Slave Law providing federal protection for slave-owners' rights. A series of dramatic conflicts between abolitionists and slave-catchers followed as did heightened antislavery sentiment in the North. Four years later, the Kansas-Nebraska Act inaugurated bloody civil war between proslavery and antislavery settlers in the Kansas Territory. In 1857, the Supreme Court, in its Dred Scott decision, ruled that slavery was fully constitutional. As the power of the federal government was mobilized in favor of slaveholders, antislavery sentiment increasingly moved into national politics, and, in 1855, free-soilers established the Republican Party.

In 1857, Anthony was asked to replace Lucy Stone as a paid organizer for the American Anti-Slavery Society (AASS). For the next four years she traveled tirelessly for abolition, even as she was directing the women's rights campaigns in New York. At first Stanton saw some hope in the Republican Party, in which her husband was active, but the pace of events soon outran the possibility of electoral solutions and she became convinced "that we shall be in the midst of violence, blood, and civil war before we look at it."[44] By 1857 she had identified herself with the AASS because it alone seemed to recognize the enormity of "the monster, slavery."[45] In 1860, she was invited as the foremost representative of American feminism to address the annual meeting of the AASS (see Document 8). Her subject was the link between abolitionism and women's rights, between the Black slave and the white woman. Although her speech was criticized by some for giving too much attention to women's rights, Stanton was herself increasingly caught up in the struggle over slavery.[46] In late 1859, John Brown raided the U.S. Arsenal at Harpers Ferry, Virginia, in an effort to instigate a slave revolt, and was captured, tried and hung. Stanton's cousin Gerrit Smith was a backer of Brown and the episode temporarily drove him mad. Stanton, who loved her cousin and revered Brown, was moved to protest her "dwarfed womanhood," feeling that, "in times like these, every one should do the work of a full grown man." In early 1861, she undertook a short traveling canvass, the first of her life, and joined Anthony in a series of antislavery meetings around western New York. In city after city, they were harassed and physically attacked for demanding that the newly elected Republican president, Abraham Lincoln, commit himself to the abolition of slavery. In April of that year, the federal forces at Fort Sumter were attacked by the secessionist government of South Carolina, and war was declared. From that point on the political life of the North was totally dominated by the war, and the issues of women's rights awaited its end and the ultimate resolution of the slavery issue.

DOCUMENT 1

Stanton, "Address Delivered at Waterloo New York about Seneca Falls Convention of July 19, 1848," September 1848

Despite the title page of its 1870 printing, Stanton's first speech was delivered in the months after the Seneca Falls and Rochester conventions.[47]

Though she claimed to speak with "diffidence," there was nothing timid about this speech, Stanton's first on women's rights. She began by accusing men of the moral crime of assuming that women's nature was different than their own, and criticized not only the ideology of male superiority, but also the idea that the sexes were different but equal. Nor did she hesitate to point out to women the contribution they made to their own degradation, and the "indifference" and "contempt" with which they greeted women's rights. Stanton expected that the remedy she proposed, equality of civil status and political power, would seem "strange to many," and she predicted that it would lead both to domestic upheaval and social reform.

"This is my first lecture. It contains all I knew at the time," Stanton wrote on the manuscript of this speech in 1866 before she handed it over to Harriot and Margaret Stanton. "I give this manuscript to my precious daughters, in the hope that they will finish the work which I have begun."[48]

"Address by ECS on Woman's Rights," excerpted from Gordon et. al, *Selected Letters of Elizabeth Cady Stanton and Susan B. Anthony*, 95–123

... I should feel exceedingly diffident to appear before you having never before spoken in public, were I not nerved by a sense of right and duty, did I not feel the time had fully come for the question of woman's wrongs to be laid before the public, did I not believe that woman herself must do this work; for woman alone can understand the height, the depth, the length, and the breadth of her own degradation and woe. Man cannot speak for us because he has been educated to believe that we differ from him so materially, that he cannot judge of our thoughts, feelings, and opinions by his own. Moral beings can only judge of others by themselves. The moment they assume a different nature for any of their own kind, they utterly fail ....

Among the many important questions which have been brought before the public, there is none that more vitally affects the whole human family than that which is technically called Woman's rights. Every allusion to the degraded and inferior position occupied by women all over the world has been met by scorn and abuse. From the man of highest mental cultivation to the most degraded wretch who staggers in the streets do we hear ridicule, and coarse jests, freely bestowed upon those who dare assert that woman stands by the side of man, his equal, placed here by her God, to enjoy with him the beautiful earth, which is her home as it is his, having the same sense of right and wrong, and looking to the same Being for guidance and support. So long has man exercised tyranny over her, injurious to himself and benumbing to *her* faculties, that but few can nerve themselves against the storm, that she knows not there is a remedy....

As the nations of the earth emerge from a state of barbarism, the sphere of woman gradually becomes wider, but not even under what is thought to be the full blaze of the sun of civilization, is it what God designed it to be. In every country and clime does man assume the responsibility of marking out the path for her to tread. In every country does he regard her as a being inferior to himself, and one whom he is to guide and control. From the Arabian Kerek, whose wife is obliged to steal from her husband to supply the necessities of life; from the Mahometan who forbid pigs, dogs, women and other impure animals, to enter a mosque, and does not allow a fool, madman or woman to proclaim the hour of prayer; from the German who complacently smokes his meerschaum, while his wife, yoked with the ox, draws the plough through its furrow; from the delectable gentleman, who thinks an inferior style of conversation adapted to woman, to the legislator, who considers her incapable of saying what laws shall govern her, is the same feeling manifested ....

Let us consider his intellectual superiority. Man's intellectual superiority cannot be a question until we have had a fair trial. When we shall have had our freedom to find out our own sphere, when we shall have had our colleges, our professions, our trades, for a century, a comparison may then be justly instituted. When woman, instead of being taxed to endow colleges where she is forbidden to enter—instead of forming societies to educate young men, shall first educate herself, when she shall be just to herself before she is generous to others; improving the talents God has given her, and leaving her neighbor to do the same for himself, we shall not hear so much of this boasted superiority....

Let us consider man's claim to moral superiority. Look now at our theological seminaries, our divinity students, the long line of descendants from our Apostolic fathers, the immaculate priesthood, and what do we find there? Perfect moral rectitude in every relation of life, a devoted spirit of self-sacrifice, a perfect union of thought, opinion and feeling among those who profess to worship the one God, and whose laws they feel themselves called upon to declare to a fallen race? Far from it.... It is the moral and religious life of this class what we might expect from minds said to be fixed on such mighty themes? By no means.... The lamentable want of principle among our lawyers, generally, is too well known to need comment. The ever-lasting backbiting and bickering of our physicians is proverbial. The disgraceful riots at our polls, where man, in performing the highest duty of citizenship, ought surely to be sober-minded. The perfect rowdyism that now characterizes the debates in our national Congress, all these are great facts which rise up against man's claim for moral superiority.

In my opinion, he is infinitely woman's inferior in every moral quality, not by nature, but made so by a false education. In carrying out his own selfishness, man has greatly improved woman's moral nature, but by an almost total shipwreck of his own. Woman has now the noble virtues of the martyr, she is early schooled to self-denial and suffering. But man is not so wholly buried in selfishness that he does not sometimes get a glimpse of the narrowness of his soul, as compared with woman. Then he says, by way of an excuse for his degradation, God made woman more self denying than us, it is her nature, it does not cost her as much to give up her wishes, her will, her life, even, as it does us. We are naturally selfish. God made us so."

No, I think not.... God's commands rest upon man as well as woman, and it is as much his duty to be kind, self-denying and full of good works, as it is hers. As much his duty to absent himself from scenes of violence as it is hers. A place or position that would require the sacrifice of the delicacy and refinement of woman's nature is unfit for man, for these virtues should be as carefully guarded in him as in her. The false ideas that prevail with regard to the purity necessary to constitute the perfect character in woman, and that requisite for man, has done an infinite deal of mischief in the world. I would not have woman less pure, but I would have man more so. I would have the same code of morals for both....

Let us now consider man's claim to physical superiority. Methinks I hear some say, surely, you will not contend for equality here. Yes, we must not give an inch, lest you claim an ell, we cannot accord to man even this much, and he has no right to claim it until the fact has been fully demonstrated.... We cannot say what the woman might be physically, if the girl were allowed all the freedom of the boy in romping, climbing, swimming, playing hoop and ball. Among some of the Tartar tribes of the present day, the women manage a horse, hurl a javelin, hunt wild animals, and fight an enemy as well as the men. The Indian women endure fatigues and carry burthens that some of our fair faced, soft handed, moustached young gentlemen would consider quite impossible for them to sustain. The Croatian and Wallachian women perform all the agricultural operations ... in addition to their domestic labors, and it is no uncommon sight in our cities, to see the German immigrant *with his hands in his pockets*, walking complacently by the side of his wife, whilst she is bending beneath the weight of some huge package or piece of furniture upon her head. Physically, as well as intellectually, it is use that produces growth and development.

But there is a class of objectors who say they do not claim superiority, they merely assert a difference, but you will find by following them up closely, that they soon run this difference to be vastly in favor of man....

We, the women of this state have met in convention... to discuss our rights and wrongs. We did not, as some have supposed, assemble to go into the detail of social life alone, we did not propose to petition the legislature to make our Husbands just, generous and courteous, to seat every man at the head of a cradle, and to clothe every woman in male attire, no none of these points, however important they may be considered by humble minds, were touched upon in this convention....

But we did assemble to protest against a form of government, existing without the consent of the governed—to declare our right to be free as man is free, to be represented in the government which we are taxed to support, to have such disgraceful laws as give man the power to chastise and imprison his wife, to take the wages which she earns, the property which she inherits, and, in case of separation, the children of her love; laws which make her the mere dependent on his bounty. It was to protest against such unjust laws as these and to have them, if possible, forever erased from our statute books, deeming them a standing shame and disgrace to a professedly republican, Christian people in the nineteenth century....

And, strange as it may seem to many, we then and there declared our right to vote according to the Declaration of the government under which we live.... We have no objection to discuss the question of equality, for we feel that the weight of argument lies wholly with us, but we wish the question of equality kept distinct from the question of rights, for the proof of the one does not determine the truth of the other. All white men in this country have the same rights, however they may differ in mind, body or estate. The right is ours. The question now is, how shall we get possession of what rightfully belongs to us. We should not feel so sorely grieved if no man who had not attained the full stature of a Webster, Clay, Van Buren, or Gerrit Smith could claim the right of the elective franchise, but to have the rights of drunkards, idiots, horse-racing, rumselling rowdies, ignorant foreigners, and silly boys fully recognized, whilst we ourselves are thrust out from all the rights that belong to citizens, it is too grossly insulting to the dignity of woman to be longer quietly submitted to. The right is ours, have it we must, use it we will. The pens, the tongues, the fortunes, the indomitable wills of many women are already pledged to secure this right. The great truth, that no just government can be formed without the consent of the governed, we shall echo and re-echo in the ears of the unjust judge, until by continual coming we shall weary him....

But what would you gain by voting? Man must know the advantages of voting, for they all seem very tenacious about the right. Think you, if woman had a vote in this government, that all those laws affecting her interests would so entirely violate every principle of right and justice? Had we a vote office holders and seekers propose some change in woman's condition? Might not "woman's rights" come to be as great a question as "free soil"?

"But you are already represented by your Fathers, Husbands, Brothers and Sons." Let your statute books answer the question. We have had enough of such representation. In nothing is woman's true happiness consulted, men like to call her an angel—to feed her with what they think sweet food—nourishing her vanity to induce her to believe her organization is so much finer than theirs, that she is not fitted to struggle with the tempests of public life, but needs their care and protection. Care and protection—such as the wolf gives the lamb—such as the eagle the hare he carries to his eyrie. Most cunningly he entraps her, and then takes from her all those rights which are dearer to him than life itself—rights which have been baptized in blood—and the maintenance of which is even now rocking to their foundations the kingdoms of the old world.

The most discouraging, the most lamentable aspect our cause wears is the indifference, indeed, the contempt, with which women themselves regard our movement. When the subject is introduced among our young ladies, among those even who claim to be intelligent and educated, it is met by the scornful curl of the lip, and by expression of ridicule and disgust. But we shall hope better things of them when they are enlighted in regard to their present position, to the laws and constitutions under which they live, they will not then publish their degradation by declaring ... they have all the rights they want ....

Let woman live as she should, let her feel her accountability to her Maker. Let her know that her spirit is fitted for as high a sphere as man's, and that her soul requires food as pure and refreshing as his. Let her live *first* for God and she will not make imperfect man an object of reverence and idolatry. Teach her her responsibility as a being of conscience and reason, that she will find any earthly support unstable and weak, that her only safe dependence is the arm of omnipotence ... and that true happiness springs from duty accomplished. Thus will she learn the lesson of individual responsibility for time and eternity. That neither Father, Husband, Brother, nor son, however willing they may be, can relieve woman from this weight, can stand in her stead when called into the presence of the searcher of spirits at the last day ....

Let me here notice one of the greatest humbugs of the day, which has long found for itself the most valuable tool in woman. The education society. The idea to me, is monstrous and absurd of woman in her present condition of degradation and ignorance, forming a society for the education of young men, an order of beings above themselves, claiming to be gifted with superior powers of mind and body, having all the avenues to learning, wealth and distinction thrown freely open to them and if they had but the energy to avail themselves of all these advantages, they can easily secure an education. Whilst woman poor and friendless, robbed of all her rights, oppressed on all sides, civilly, religiously and socially, must needs go ignorant herself. Now, is not the idea of such a being working day and night with her needle, stitch, stitch, (for the poor widow always throws in her mite for she is taught to believe that all she gives for the decoration of churches and their black-coated gentry, is unto the Lord. I think a man who under the present state of things has the moral hardihood to take an education at the hands of woman, and at such an expense to her, ought, as soon as he graduates, with all his honours thick upon him, take the first ship for Turkey, and there pass his days in earnest efforts to rouse the inmates of the Harems to a true sense of their degradation, and not, as is his custom, immediately enter our pulpits to tell us of his superiority to us, "weaker vessels,"—his prerogative to command, ours to obey, his duty to preach, ours to keep silence.... The last time when an appeal of this kind was made to me, I told the young lady that I would send her to school a year, if she would go, but I would never again give one red cent to the education society, and I do hope that every christian woman, who has the least regard for her sex, will make the same resolve. We have worked long enough for man, and at a most unjust and unwarrantable sacrifice of self, yet he gives no evidence of gratitude, but has, thus far, treated his benefactors with settled scorn, ridicule and neglect ....

One common objection to this movement is, that if the principles of freedom and equality which we advocate were put into practice, it would destroy all harmony in the domestic circle. Here let me ask, how many truly harmonious households have we now? ... The only happy households we now see are those in which Husband and wife share equally in counsel and government. There can be no true dignity or independence where there is subordination, no happiness without freedom.

Let us then have no fears that the movement will disturb what is seldom found, a truly united and happy family.... There seems now to be a kind of moral stagnation in our midst.... Our churches are multiplying on all sides, our missionary societies, Sunday schools, and prayer meetings are still kept up ... they feel they cannot resist this rushing tide of vice, they feel that the battlements of righteousness are weak against the mighty wicked.... And how shall we account for this state of things? Depend upon it the degradation of woman is the secret of all this woe, the inactivity of her head and heard. The voice of woman has been silenced, but man cannot fulfill his destiny alone, he cannot redeem his race unaided. There are deep and tender chords of sympathy and love in the heart of the down-fallen and crushed that woman can touch more skillfully than man. The earth has never yet seen a truly great and virtuous nation, for woman has never yet stood the equal with man ... God, in his wisdom, has so linked the whole human family together that any violence done at one end of the chain is felt throughout its length....

... We do not expect our path will be strewn with the flowers of popular favour ... upon our banner will beat the dark storm cloud of opposition from those who have entrenched themselves behind the strong bulwark of might, of force and who have fortified their position by every means holy and unholy, but we steadfastly abide the result. Unmoved we will bear it aloft. Undaunted we will unfurl it to the gale, for we know that the storm cannot rend from it a shred, that the electric flash will but more clearly show to us the glorious words inscribed upon it, "Equality of Rights."

Document 2

Elizabeth Cady Stanton and Frederick Douglass, First Meeting, c. 1840; Douglass at Seneca Falls Convention, 1848

The lives of the two towering figures of Elizabeth Cady Stanton and Frederick Douglas were intertwined for almost a half-century. Sometimes on the same side of history, sometimes as opponents, they nonetheless respected each other's great intelligence and far-reaching vision. From the very first time she met him, Stanton was taken with Douglass as a man "with such self-respect, such love of liberty." These sentiments only deepened over time. She refracted what she imagined to be his experience through her own. "To be the equals yea the superiors of those who have the impudence to prescribe our spheres," she wrote to him in 1884 about both of their experiences, "is enough to exasperate a saint" (see Document 18).

Stanton and Douglass first met in the early 1840s in Boston. She was newly married and pregnant with her first child; he was recently escaped from slavery. Decades later, both recalled the impact that the other had made. Douglass recalled their meeting in 1885 on the occasion of Stanton's seventieth birthday.

Philip Foner, ed., *Frederick Douglass on Women's Rights* (Westport, CT: Greenwood Press 1978) p. 163

> ... I am no stranger to the life and work of that excellent lady, and am proud to be one of the great cloud of witnesses who will on her 70th birthday, bear ample testimony to her high character as a woman, and to her immeasurable services to the cause of woman, as an advocate. Five and forty years ago in Boston, before the snows of time had settled upon the locks of either of

us, and before the cause of woman had taken its place among the great reforms of the nineteenth century, Mrs. Stanton, then just returned from her wedding tour in Europe, sat by my side and taught me the new Gospel of woman's rights. I was then only a few years out Slavery, and I freshly remembered the lash and sting of bondage at the South, and the intense bitterness of the popular prejudice at the North, and was all the more ready to listen to, and learn of such a beautiful teacher. Perhaps, no man is more debtor for her noble work in the world, than myself. While she clothed woman in my mind with a dignity and grandeur which I had not before recognized, she gave me a higher estimate of my own worth by disregarding popular prejudice and taking pains to impart to me the great truth with which her mind was illuminated.... Honor to whom honor. Respectfully yours, Fredk Douglass

Ten years later, at the memorial at Douglass' death, Anthony urged Stanton, now disabled and housebound, to send a message recalling their first meeting. Anthony read it at the memorial.

Helen Pitts Douglas, *In Memoriam Frederick Douglass* (Philadelphia: John C. Vorster, & Co.., 1897), p. 44.

Trained in the severe school of slavery, I saw him first before a Boston audience, fresh from the land of bondage. He stood there like an African prince, conscious of his dignity and power, grand in his physical proportions, majestic in his wrath, as with keen wit, satire and indignation he portrayed the bitterness of slavery, the humiliation of subjection to those who in all human virtues and capacities were inferior to himself. His denunciation of our national crime, of the wide and guilty fantasy that men could hold property in man, poured like a torrent that fairly made his hearers tremble.

Thus as I first saw him, and wondered as I listened that any mortal man should have ever tried to subjugate a being with such marvelous powers, such self-respect, such love of liberty.

Around him sat the great anti-slavery orators of the day, watching his effect on that immense audience, completely magnetized with his eloquence, laughing and crying in turns with his rapid flights from pathos to humor. All other speakers seemed tame after Douglass.

In 1847, each moved to western New York, he to Rochester, she fifty miles east to Seneca Falls. The next year, Douglass attended the Seneca Falls Convention, the first public meeting on behalf of women's rights in the U.S. and "ably supported the cause of woman."[49] In 1878, at the Third Decade Celebration of that meeting, Stanton credited Douglass with the passage of the most contested resolution at the convention, which called for political rights for women.

Excerpted from Gordon, et al., *Selected Papers of Stanton and Anthony*, vol. 3, p. 389.

To you noble representative of a long oppressed race, who honors our platform to-day, words are inadequate to express our thanks for your steadfast, unwavering devotion to our cause. In advancing the same freedom for us as for yourselves, you have proved that to your minds liberty is the watchword not for color and class alone, but for all humanity. Your voice, Frederick Douglass, was heard in our first convention, and but for you, I fear the elective franchise for Woman, would not have been adopted, as many of our friends thought the demand premature. May your voice be the first to congratulate us when our success shall be secured.

In 1888, at the International Council of Women meeting in Washington, D.C., Douglass also recalled his contribution at Seneca Falls and at the subsequent meeting in Rochester. His characterization of women's rights as a newborn infant is highly gendered and bears the mark of time long past. Directly addressing Stanton, he reveals a deep understanding of the contrast between the subtle oppressions faced by free women and the gross abuse suffered by slaves. Like herself, he too seemed to be thinking of middle-class women, not of the African American women still working in the fields and white kitchens of the South.

National Woman Suffrage Association,
Report of the International Council of Women
(Washington, D.C.: Rufus M. Darby, Printer, 1888), pp. 327–29.

There was a time when, perhaps, we men could help a little. It was when this woman suffrage cause was in its cradle, when it was not big enough to go alone, when it had to be taken in the arms of its mother from Seneca Falls, N.Y., to Rochester for baptism. I then went along with it and offered my services to help it, for then it needed help; but now it can afford to dispense with me and all of my sex. Then its friends were few—now they are many. Then it was wrapped in obscurity—now it is lifted in sight of the whole civilized world, and people of all lands and languages give it their hearty support.

 I thought my eye of faith was tolerably clear when I attended those meetings in Seneca Falls and Rochester, but it was far too dim to see at the end of forty years a result so imposing as this International Council, and to see yourself and Miss Anthony alive and active in its proceedings....

 Ever since this Council has been in session, my thoughts have been reverting to the past. I have been thinking, more or less, of the scene presented forty years ago in the little Methodist Church at Seneca Falls, the manger in which this organized suffrage movement was born. It was a

Document 2. Stanton and Douglass, First Meeting

very small thing then. It was not then big enough to be abused or loud enough to make itself heard outside, and only a few of those who saw it had any notion that the little thing would live. I have been thinking, too, of the strong conviction, the noble courage, the sublime faith in God and man it required at that time to set this suffrage ball in motion.... War, intemperance and slavery are open, undisguised, palpable evils. The best feelings of human nature revolt at them.... But no such advantage was found in the beginning of the cause of suffrage for women. On the contrary, everything in her condition was supposed to be lovely, just as it should be. She had no rights denied, no wrongs to redress. She herself had no suspicion but that all was going well with her. She floated along on the tide of life as her mother and grandmother had done before her, as in a dream of Paradise. Her wrongs, if she had any, were too occult to be seen, and too light to be felt. It required a daring voice and a determined hand to wake her from this delightful dream, and call the nation to account for the rights and opportunities of which it was depriving her....

Then who were we, for I count myself in, who did this thing? We were few in numbers, moderate in resources, and very little known in the world. The most that we had to commend us was a firm faith that the right must prevail. But the case was well considered. Let no man imagine that the step was taken recklessly and thoughtlessly. Mrs. Stanton had dwelt upon it at least six years before she declared it in the Rochester convention.... She saw more clearly than most of us that the vital point to be made prominent, and the one that included all others, was the ballot, and she bravely said the word. It was not only necessary to break the silence of woman and make her voice heard, but she must have a clear, palpable and comprehensive measure set before her, one worthy of her highest ambition and her best exertions, and hence the ballot was brought to the front.

There are few facts in my humble history to which I look back with more satisfaction than to the fact, recorded in the history of the Woman Suffrage movement, that I was sufficiently enlightened at the early day, when only a few years from slavery, to support your resolution for woman suffrage. I have done very little in this world in which to glory, except this one act—and I certainly glory in that. When I ran away from slavery, it was for my people; but when I stood up for the rights of women, self was out of the question, and I found a little nobility in the act....

Document 3

"Immediate Causes of the Demand for Women's Political Rights" *History of Woman Suffrage, volume 1*, eds., Stanton, Anthony and Matilda Joslyn Gage, 1881

The project of recording the history of woman suffrage—even as the movement was happening—began in the immediate aftermath of the 1876 Centennial demonstration. Initially envisaged as a single, short volume, it ultimately became six, three of which are credited to Stanton, Anthony and Matilda Joslyn Gage, then president of the National Woman Suffrage Association (NWSA). They are listed as editors, because so many of the pages were cut and pasted from others' reminiscences, newspaper articles, etc. Nonetheless, a considerable amount of the *History* was written rather than edited. We know that Anthony did little writing, but managed the project while Stanton and Gage did the writing. There were no individual attributions except Gage's work on the final chapter.

Even as the editors diligently consulted many of their sister activists to ensure that their account of their movement's history was as comprehensive and accurate as possible, they had another purpose. Suffragists were still being treated as "a few unbalanced minds" and their efforts with "ridicule." Their purpose was to establish, if not for their contemporaries then for later generations, that their efforts were "the legitimate outgrowth of American ideals—a component part of the history of our republic."

Working in the aftermath of emancipation and Black suffrage, even as Reconstruction was shutting down, they emphasized the roots of their movement in the "double battle ... against the tyranny of sex and color at the same time."

Document 3. Demand for Women's Political Rights

Stanton, Anthony and Gage, eds., *History of Woman Suffrage*, vol. 1, pp. 51–53

And when in the progress of civilization the time had fully come for the recognition of the feminine element in humanity, women, in every civilized country unknown to each other, began simultaneously to demand a broader sphere of action. Thus the first public demand for political equality by a body of women in convention assembled, was a link in the chain of woman's development, binding the future with the past, as complete and necessary in itself, as the events of any other period of her history. The ridicule of facts does not change their character. Many who study the past with interest, and see the importance of seeming trifles in helping forward great events, often fail to understand some of the best pages of history made under their own eyes. Hence the woman suffrage movement has not yet been accepted as the legitimate outgrowth of American ideas—a component part of the history of our republic—but is falsely considered the willful outburst of a few unbalanced minds, whose ideas can never be realized under any form of government.

Among the immediate causes that led to the demand for the equal political rights of women, in this country, we may note three:

1. The discussion in several of the State Legislatures on the property rights of married women, which, heralded by the press with comments grave and gay, became the topic of general interest around many fashionable dinner-tables, and at many humble firesides. In this way all phases of the question were touched upon, involving the relations of the sexes, and gradually widening to all human interests—political, religious, civil, and social. The press and pulpit became suddenly vigilant in marking out woman's sphere, while woman herself seemed equally vigilant in her efforts to step outside the prescribed limits.

2. A great educational work was accomplished by the able lectures of Frances Wright, on political, religious, and social questions. Ernestine L. Rose, following in her wake, equally liberal in her religious opinions, and equally well informed on the science of government, helped to deepen and perpetuate the impression Frances Wright had made on the minds of unprejudiced hearers.

3. And above all other causes of the "Woman Suffrage Movement," was the Anti-Slavery struggle in this country. The ranks of the Abolitionists were composed of the most eloquent orators, the ablest logicians, men and women of the purest moral character and best minds in the nation. They were usually spoken of in the early days as "an illiterate, ill-mannered, poverty-stricken, crazy set of long-haired Abolitionists." While the fact is, some of the most splendid specimens of manhood and womanhood, in physical appearance, in culture, refinement, and knowledge of polite life, were found among the early Abolitionists....

Thus Sarah and Angelina Grimké and Abby Kelly, in advocating liberty for the black race, were early compelled to defend the right of free speech for themselves. They had the double battle to fight against the tyranny of sex and color at the same time, in which, however, they were well sustained by the able pens of Lydia Maria Child and Maria Weston Chapman. Their opponents were found not only in the ranks of the New England clergy, but among the most bigoted Abolitionists in Great Britain and the United States. Many a man who advocated equality most eloquently for a Southern plantation, could not tolerate it at his own fireside.

Document 4

Anthony, Letter on Temperance, August 26, 1852; Stanton, "Appeal for the Maine Law," January 21, 1853

Although a women's temperance movement, the Daughters of Temperance, had existed in New York for some time, Stanton and Anthony considered it too conservative and limited in scope for their feminist purposes, and formed their own organization, the New York State Women's Temperance Society, in April 1852. Anthony was one of the society's traveling agents, and in this letter to *The Lily*, she described the women's temperance activity around the state with great sympathy and enthusiasm. Like the women she met, Anthony was a "soul dissatisfied," frustrated by the "senseless, hopeless work that man points out for woman to do."

Stanton, who had just given birth to her fifth child, was unable to travel away from Seneca Falls, but presided over the organization by proxy. Her address to the New York State Assembly was read for her in January 1853, by Anthony. In it, she elaborated the women's rights program she wanted the women's temperance forces to adopt, the basic elements of which were woman suffrage and liberalized divorce laws. More generally, she criticized the central role of government in supporting both the liquor industry and the oppression of women. The temperance legislation which she advocated for New York was modeled on a Maine law which prohibited the production or sale of liquor within state boundaries.

The Lily, September, 1852, pp. 73–74

Rochester, August 26, 1852

Dear Mrs. Bloomer:

... I attended the great Temperance demonstration held at Albion, July

7th, and as I took a view from a different stand point, from any of those who have heretofore described that monster gathering, I will say a few words. Messrs. Barnum, Cary and Chapin, were the speakers for the day. They talked much of the importance of carrying the Temperance question into politics, but failed to present a *definite* plan, by which to combine the temperance votes and secure concert of action throughout the State and country....

According to long established custom, after serving strong meats to the "lords of creation," the lecturers dished up a course of what they doubtless called delicately flavored soup for the Ladies. Barnum said it was a fact, and might as well be owned up, that this nation is under *petticoat* government; that every married man would acknowledge it, and if there were any young men who would not now, it was only necessary for them to have one week's experience as a husband, to compel them to admit that such is indeed the fact;—all of which vulgarity could but have grated harshly upon the ears of every intelligent, right-minded woman present.

At the close of the Mass Meeting, the women, mostly Daughters of Temperance—were invited to meet at the Presbyterian Church, at 3 o'clock P.M., to listen to an address from Susan B. Anthony, of Rochester. The Church was filled, quite a large number of men, (possessed no doubt of their full share of Mother Eve's curiosity,) were in attendance. They were reminded, that they ought highly to appreciate the privilege which woman permitted them to enjoy,—that of remaining in the house and being silent lookers on.

It was really hopeful to see those hundreds of women, with thoughtful faces—faces that spoke of disquiet within,—of souls dissatisfied, unfed, notwithstanding the soft eloquence, which had been that A.M., so bounteously lavished upon *"angel woman."* I talked to them in my plain way,—told them that to merely relieve the suffering wives and children of drunkards, and vainly labor to reform the drunkard was no longer to be called *temperance* work, and showed them that woman's temperance sentiments were not truthfully represented by man at the Ballot Box. On the whole, I am of the opinion that those women went away no better satisfied with the part that man has ever assigned to woman in this great reform, than when they came.

In the evening, S. F. Cary, T. W. Brown, and Mr. Chapin, addressed a large audience in the Presbyterian Church. Most excellent addresses, all of them, if they had only omitted the closing paragraphs to the *Ladies.* Oh! I am sick and tired of the senseless, hopeless work that man points out for woman to do. Would that the women of our land would rise, *en masse,* and proclaim with one united voice, that they repudiate the popular doctrine that teaches them to follow in the wake of the sin and misery, degradation and woe, which man for the gratification of his cupidity, chooses to inflict upon the race, to minister to their wretched victims words of comfort, and kindly point out to them how they may again enjoy the blessings of a good conscience. Such work is vain, worse than vain;—if woman may do nothing toward removing the CAUSE of drunkenness, then is she indeed powerless—then may she well sit down, and with folded hands weep over the ills that be.

During the month of July, I spoke at Caryville, Alabama Centre, Richville, Ackron, Clarence and Williamsville. Found Unions of D. of T. in the first four villages; the one at Ackron numbers 40, and is in a very flourishing condition. The Caryville Union donated the sum of three dollars to the Treasury of the Women's State Temperance Society, and that of Ackron the liberal sum of five dollars....

At Buffalo, I called on Mrs. H. B. Williams, an active member of the "Ladies' Temperance Union." That society numbers fourteen hundred Women, and has done a great deal during the last twenty years, by way of ameliorating the condition of the wretched victims of Intemperance and its attendant vices. Mrs. W. read me a copy of a letter, which the Buffalo "Ladies' Temperance Union," sent to the Annual Meeting of the State Temperance Society, held at Syracuse in June last. It called the Temperance question home to the ballot box. The D. of T. of that City, also sent a letter to that memorable meeting, but both of those letters were, with woman's voice, suppressed by those Pharasaical Priests, who pretended to be the representatives of the State Temperance Society.

I hope you have told your readers ... of the first Women's Temperance Meeting, on the evening of the 6th [in Elmira]. Miss Clark spoke on the 7th and 9th. I again addressed the citizens of that village. The meetings were all fully attended and much interest was manifested. While stopping at the Depot, the A.M. of the 10th, a lady addressed me and said: "It is rude to thus speak to a stranger, but I want to say to you, that you have done one thing in Elmira." "And what is that?" "You have convinced me that it is proper for women to talk Temperance in public as well as in private. A gentleman told me that Miss Anthony was going to lecture on Temperance; said I, she had better be home washing dishes. He replied, 'perhaps she does not know how.' Well, said I, let her come to my house, & I will give her a few lessons."

The women of Elmira formed a woman's temperance society, auxiliary to the State society—obtained about one hundred members, and forthwith appropriated their funds to the purchase of Temperance tracts and newspapers for gratuitous circulation.... By the way, Mrs. Bloomer, the temperance newspapers are trying to work themselves and their leaders into the belief that the position which we, as a temperance society, take, "that Confirmed Drunkenness is a just ground of Divorce," is all wrong and calculated to produce much evil in society. Now I am a firm believer in the doctrine which man is continually preaching, that woman's influence over him is all powerful; hence I argue that for man to know, that his pure minded and virtuous wife, would, should he become a confirmed Drunkard, assuredly leave him, and take with her the property and the children, it would prove a powerful incentive to a correct, consistent life. As public sentiment and the laws now are, the vilest wretch of a husband knows that his wife will submit to live on in his companionship, rather than forsake him, and by so doing subject herself to the world's cold charity, and be robbed of her home and her children. Men may prate on, but we women are beginning to know that the life and happiness of a *woman* is of equal value with that of a *man;* and that for a woman to sacrifice her health, happiness and perchance her earthly existence in the hope of reclaiming a drunken, sensualized man, avails but little. In nine cases out of ten, if the man *ever* reforms, it is not until after the wife sinks into an untimely grave; or if not in her *grave,* is physically and mentally unnerved, and unfitted for any earthly enjoyment....

During last week I visited Palmyra, Marion, Walworth, Farmington and Victor.... Auxiliary Temperance Societies have been formed in very nearly all the towns I have visited and the women are beginning to feel that they have something to do in the Temperance Cause—that woman may speak and act in public as well as in the home circle—and now is the time to inscribe upon our banner, "NO UNION WITH DISTILLERS, RUM-SELLERS, AND RUMDRINKERS."

Yours for Temperance without Compromise,
S. B. ANTHONY.

The Lily, February 1, 1853, p. 4

Appeal for the Maine Law, Written by Mrs. Stanton and Read by Miss Anthony in the Assembly Chamber:

This is, I believe, the first time in the history of our State, that Woman has come before this Honorable Body to state the legal disabilities under which, as women, we have thus far lived and labored. Though our grievances are many, and our causes of complaint, if set forth, would be as numerous as those made by our forefathers against their King; yet, in behalf of the women of this State, I appeal to you at this time, for the redress of those only, growing out of the legalized traffic in ardent spirits.... [W]e come to propose to you to do for us one of two things—either so remodel your State constitution, that woman may vote on this great political and social evil, and thus relieve herself of the terrible injustice that now oppresses her, or, be in fact what, as men, you now claim to be, her faithful representatives, her legal protectors, her chivalrous knights.

If you wisely choose the first proposition, and thus relieve yourself of the burthen of all special legislation for one million and a half of disenfranchised subjects, giving us equal rights, as citizens, with all "white male citizens," then we have nothing to ask. Our course, under such circumstances, would be clear and simple. We should not long stand gaping into the heavens as our temperance saints now do, voting rum into high places, and then praying it to walk out. But if you still hug the delusion that you can legislate for us far better than we could for ourself, and still insist on looking after our best interests, and protecting us in our sacred rights, at least permit us from time to time, to tell you of our wants and needs....

1st. Then, as our "faithful representatives," we ask you to give us the Maine Law which has been so glorious in those States where it has been fairly tried. Now that we see a door of escape open, from the long line of calamities that intemperance has brought upon the head of woman, we would fain enter in and be at peace. We have long and impatiently waited for you to take some effective action on this abominable traffic, and now, feeling that the time has fully come, we pray you to act promptly and wisely.... But if you are not prepared to give us the Maine Law, and thus suppress this traffic altogether, then, as you love justice, remove from it all protection. Do not legalize it in any way. Let the trade be free and then let all contracts in which rum is involved be null and void. A man cannot come into court with his gambling debts, neither let him with his rum debts; for what better is rumselling than gambling, or the rumseller than the gamester? Then, do away with all license laws, and take no cognizance of the monster evil; for what a government licenses, it does not condemn. Now this traffic is either right or wrong. If right, let it be subject to the same laws as all other articles of commerce; if wrong, let those who carry it on be treated as criminals by the government, throwing on them the responsibility of all the pauperism and crime they directly or indirectly produce....

But above all, we conjure you not to let this session pass, without giving us a law making drunkenness a just cause of divorce. Such a law would be far greater in its permanent results than the Maine Law, even. Suppose we have the Maine Law today—you have then disposed of all intoxicating drinks; but you have still the animal natures,—the morbid appetite for stimulants and excitement entailed on generation after generation which will work themselves out in some direction. But back up the Maine Law by the more important one on Divorce and you make a permanent reform in so regulating your laws on marriage that the pure and noble of our sex may be sustained by the power of Government in dissolving all union with gross and vicious natures. It would create a strong public sentiment against drunkenness for you to declare, that, in your opinion, it is a crime so enormous, as to furnish just cause for the separation of man and wife....

2d. As our legal protectors, we ask you to release us from taxation.

Under the present system, the drunkard's wife is doubly taxed. As she has no right to what she has helped to earn, the rumseller can take all she has for her husband's debts, and leave her to-day, houseless, homeless, and penniless. Verily, "no just government can be formed but by the consent of the governed." ... You have in your hands the means of self-protection. Not so with us. The law gives to man the right to all he can get, and to what we get too. The new property law protects what we inherit, but not what we jointly earn; hence you see how hopeless is the condition of the drunkard's wife. Seeing that you would consider women voters a terrible scourge on the body politic,—if you would not have us press our claims to the exercise of our right to the elective franchise, see that we have justice at your hands. The women of this State are not satisfied with such representation and protection, as we have had thus far,—and unless our interests can be better looked after, unless you can give us more equable laws—we demand the right to legislate for ourselves.

3d. As our chivalrous knight, ... we only ask, that in your leisure hours, you will duly consider the unjust laws that now disgrace your statute books,—that you will unite with us against our national foe, Intemperance,—that you will lend us your influence to create a healthful public sentiment, that shall deny to drunkards the rights of husbands and fathers,—that shall give the drunkard's wife her property, without taxation, and her children, without fear of molestation. You would fain have women in the retirement of private life;—then protect her in her home. You love to look upon her as a sacred being;—then make her so in her holiest relations.... We, the women of the nineteenth century—your mothers, wives and sisters—ask you to throw around us a shield of defence against social tyranny and civil injustice—against a code of laws unworthy Nero himself, so grievous are they in their bearing upon the poor and helpless of our sex. Alas! that such laws should now bear the sanction of our husbands, sires and sons. Alas! for this proud Republic, if its women, the repository of all that is noble and virtuous in national character, can command no higher honors, no purer homage, no juster laws at your hands.

Elizabeth C. Stanton

DOCUMENT 5

Stanton and Anthony, Letters, 1852–1859

These fifteen letters run from 1852, less than a year after Stanton and Anthony first met, to 1859, when Anthony was a paid organizer for the American Anti-Slavery Society and Stanton had just given birth to her seventh and last child. The letters show Anthony struggling to learn self-confidence and the "a, b, c, of the reformer";[50] they reveal the degree to which Stanton was caught between her political ambitions and her domestic realities; and they tell us a good deal about the characters of both women—Anthony's intensity and anxiety, Stanton's wit and brilliance. Overall, the letters give the impression that, from the very beginning of their collaboration, both women took a long-range perspective on the tasks of challenging traditional ways of seeing women's position and of building a women's rights movement. When their effort to turn the women's temperance movement in a feminist direction failed, Stanton consoled Anthony by reminding her that they had "other and bigger fish to fry." These first three letters refer to: the organization of the New York State Women's Temperance Society in Rochester in April 1852; Stanton's address, as the society's president, to the New York legislature in January 1853, in which she called for the right of women to divorce drunkards; and the defeat six months later of the women's rights platform that she and Anthony had advocated for the organization (see Document 4).

[For the first two editions of the present work, letters were gathered from several sources: (1) the Elizabeth Cady Stanton manuscript collections at the Library of Congress and Vassar College; (2) Ida H. Harper, *The Life and Work of Susan B. Anthony* (Indianapolis: Bowen-Merrill Co., 1899); and (3) *Elizabeth Cady Stanton as Revealed in her Letters, Diary and Reminiscences,* eds. Theodore Stanton and Harriot Stanton Blatch (New York: Harper & Brothers, 1922). Since then, the Elizabeth Cady Stanton/Susan B. Anthony Papers Project has produced six scrupulously edited volumes of select documents, including several of the letters noted below, which corrections have been here included.]

Gordon, et al., *Selected Letters of Stanton and Anthony*, vol. 1, pp. 194–95.

Seneca Falls, March 1st 1852

Miss Susan B. Anthony Dear friend

   I do not know that the world is quite willing or ready to discuss the question of marriage. I feel in my innermost that the thoughts I sent your convention are true. It is in vain to look for the elevation of woman, so long as she is degraded in marriage. I say it is a sin, an outrage on our holiest feelings to pretend that anything but deep, fervent love & sympathy constitutes marriage. The right idea of marriage is at the foundation of all reforms. How strange it is, man will apply all the improvements in the arts & sciences to everything about him animate & inanimate, but himself. A child conceived in the midst of hate, sin, & discord, nurtured in abuse & injustice cannot do much to bless the world or himself. If we properly understood the science of life—it would be far easier to give to the world, harmonious, beautiful, noble, virtuous children, than it is to bring grown-up discord into harmony with the great divine soul of all. I ask for no laws on marriage I say ... remove law & a false public sentiment & woman will no more live as wife with a cruel, beastly drunkard, than a servant in this free country will stay with a pettish, unjust mistress. If law makers insist upon exercising their prerogative in some way on this question, let them forbid any woman to marry until she is twenty one. Let them fine a woman fifty dollars for every child she conceive by a Drunkard. Women have no right to saddle the state with idiots to be supported by the public. Only look at the statistics of the idiot asylums, nearly all the offspring of Drunkards. Woman must be made to feel that the transmitting of immortal life is a most solemn responsible act & never should be allowed, except when the parents are in the highest condition of mind & body. Man in his lust has regulated this whole question of sexual intercourse long enough; let the mother of mankind whose prerogative it is to set bounds to his indulgence rouse up and give this whole question a thorough fearless examination.... If by martyrdom I can advance my race one step I am ready for it. I feel this whole question of woman's rights turns on the point of the marriage relation, & sooner or later it will be the question for discussion. I would not hurry it on, neither would I avoid it....

Stanton Letters, pp. 38–41; supplemented from Harper, *Life of Susan B Anthony*, vol. 1, pp. 66–67

Document 5. Stanton and Anthony, Letters

Seneca Falls, April 2 1852

My dear friend (Susan B. Anthony),

I think you are doing up the temperance business just right. But do not let the conservative element control. For instance, you must take Mrs. Bloomer's suggestions with great caution, for she has not the spirit of the true reformer. At the first woman's rights convention, but four years ago, she stood aloof and laughed at us. It was only with great effort and patience that she has been brought up to her present position. In her paper, she will not speak against the fugitive slave law, nor in her work to put down intemperance will she criticize the equivocal position of the Church....

I will gladly do all in my power to help you. Come and stay with me and I will write the best lecture I can for you. I have no doubt a little practice will make you an admirable speaker. Dress loosely, take a great deal of exercise, be particular about your diet and sleep enough. The body has great influence upon the mind. In your meetings, if attacked, be cool and good-natured, for if you are simple and truth-loving, no sophistry can confound you. As for my own address, if I am to be president it ought perhaps to be sent out with the stamp of the convention, but as anything from my pen is necessarily radical no one may wish to share with me the odium of what I may choose to say. If so, I am ready to stand alone. I never write to please any one. If I do please I am happy, but to proclaim my highest convictions of truth is always my sole object....

I have been re-reading the report of the London convention of 1840. How thoroughly humiliating it was to us! ... Men and angels give me patience! I am at the boiling point! If I do not find some day the use of my tongue on this question, I shall die of an intellectual repression, a woman's rights convulsion! Oh, Susan! Susan! Susan! You must manage to spend a week with me before the Rochester convention, for I am afraid that I cannot attend it; I have so much with all these boys on my hands. But I will write a letter. How much I do long to be free from housekeeping and children, so as to have some time to read, and think, and write. But it may be well for me to understand all the trials of woman's lot, that I may more eloquently proclaim them when the time comes. Good night.

Stanton Letters, p. 50–52.

Seneca Falls, June 20, 1853

Dear Susan,

Say not one word to me about another convention. I forbid you to ask me to send one thought or one line to any convention, any paper, or any individual; for I swear by all the saints that whilst I am nursing this baby I will not be tormented with suffering humanity. I am determined to make no effort to do anything beyond my imperative home duties until I can bring about the following conditions: 1st, Relieve myself of housekeeping altogether; 2nd, Secure some capable teacher for my children; 3rd, See my present baby on her feet. My ceaseless cares begin to wear upon my spirit. I feel it in my innermost soul and am resolved to seek some relief. Therefore, I say adieu to the public for a time, for I must give all my moments and my thoughts to my children. But above all this I am so full of dreams of the true associative life that all the reforms of the day beside that seem to me superficial and fragmentary. You ask me if I am not plunged in grief at my defeat at the recent convention for the presidency of our society. Not at all. I am only too happy in the relief I feel from this additional care. I accomplished at Rochester all I desired by having the divorce question brought up and so eloquently supported by dear little Lucy Stone. How proud I felt of her that night! We have no woman who compares with her. Now, Susan, I do beg of you to let the past be past, and to waste no powder on the Woman's State Temperance Society. We have other and bigger fish to fry.

The following two letters concern Stanton's important women's rights speech to the New York legislature, delivered in February 1854 (see Document 6).

Excerpted from Gordon, et al., *Selected Letters*, vol. 1, pp. 237–38.

Seneca Falls, January 16, 1854

Dear Susan,

... Women have grievances without number, but I want the exact wording of the most atrocious laws. I can generalize and philosophize by myself, but I have not time to look up statistics. While I am about the house, surrounded by my children, washing dishes, baking, sewing, I can think up many points, but I cannot search books, for my hands as well as my brains, would be necessary for that work. If I can, I shall go to Rochester as soon as I have finished my Address and submit it ... to [Reverend William H.] Channing's criticism. But prepare yourself to be disappointed in its merits, for I seldom have one hour to sit down and write undisturbed. Men who can shut themselves up for days with their books and thoughts know little of what difficulties a woman must surmount.

Stanton Letters, pp. 55–56.

Seneca Falls, January 20, 1854

Dear Susan,

My Address is not nearly finished; but if I sit up nights, it shall be done in time. I fear, however, it may not suit the committee, for it does not suit me. But make no arrangements with reference to my coming to Rochester, for I cannot say when I can come, if even I may come at all. Yesterday one of the boys shot an arrow into my baby's eye. The eye is safe, but oh! my fright when I saw the blood come and the organ swell, and witnessed her suffering! What an escape! Imagine if I had been in Rochester when this happened! Then, to-day, my nurse has gone home with a felon on her finger. So you see how I am bound here. In haste.

The following three letters reveal, on the one hand, the pressures, responsibilities, and outright prejudice that held Stanton to domestic life so long; and, on the other hand, her love of politics and desire to become a public speaker and reformer. In 1855, Henry Stanton was helping to form the Republican party, and Elizabeth was filled with enthusiasm for this new political movement.

Stanton Letters, pp. 59–60.

Peterboro, September 10, 1855

Dear Susan,

    I wish that I were as free as you and I would stump the state in a twinkling. But I am not, and what is more, I passed through a terrible scourging when last at my father's. I cannot tell you how deep the iron entered my soul. I never felt more keenly the degradation of my sex. To think that all in me of which my father would have felt a proper pride had I been a man, is deeply mortifying to him because I am a woman. That thought has stung me to a fierce decision—to speak as soon as I can do myself credit. But the pressure on me just now is too great. Henry sides with my friends, who oppose me in all that is dearest to my heart. They are not willing that I should write even on the woman question. But I will both write and speak. I wish you to consider this letter strictly confidential. Sometimes, Susan, I struggle in deep waters.... I have sent six articles to the *Tribune*, and three have already appeared. I have promised to write for the *Una*. I read and write a good deal, as you see. But there are grievous interruptions. However, a good time is coming and my future is always bright and beautiful. Good night.

Stanton Letters, pp. 62–63.

Seneca Falls, November 4, 1855

Dear Susan,

    I am rejoiced to say that Henry is heart and soul in the Republican movement and is faithfully stumping the state once more. I have attended all the Republican meetings and have had Senator John P. Hale staying with us. The day he was expected I met a Republican editor in the street. "Well, I suppose we are to hear Hale to-night," I remarked. *"We,"* he replied, "we do not wish to spare any room for ladies; we mean to cram the hall with voters." "I have done my best to be a voter," was my response, "and it is no fault of mine if unavailable people occupy your seats. So I for one am determined to go and hear Hale." I went to the meeting with Mr. Hale and Henry, and we found a dozen women already there....

Excerpted from Gordon, et al., *Selected Letters*, vol. 1, p. 316.

Seneca Falls, Thursday Evening, January 24, 1856

Dear Susan,

What has been the fate of my letter. I corrected it & sent it straight back to you as directed ....

Where are you Susan & what are you doing. Your silence is truly appalling Are you dead or married Well I have got out the sixth edition of my admirable work, another female child is born into the world!

Last Sunday afternoon, Harriot Eaton Stanton, oh the little heretic, thus to desecrate that holy day, opened her soft blue eyes on this mundane sphere.

Maggie's joy over her little sister is unbounded. I am very ... happy, that the terrible ordeal is passed & that the result is another daughter.

Yours E. C. Stanton

In her interesting letter of May 1856, Anthony described the various reactions of conservative women, in particular the wife of the noted evangelical minister Charles G. Finney, and Catharine Beecher herself, to women's rights. The speech Anthony gave was the result of the report she had been charged to give to the New York State Teacher's Convention as a result of pressure from other women members. The anxiety it caused her was the subject of the subsequent three letters.

Excerpted from Gordon, et al., *Selected Letters*, vol. 1, pp. 319–321.

Rochester, May 26, 1856

Dear Mrs. Stanton,

Taking it for granted that you are at home more, I'll say a word to you by way of "exhortation and prayer"—I ought to be more pious than formerly, since I traveled all the way from Seneca Falls to Schenectady in company with President [of Oberlin] Finney & Lady—& heard [William

Lloyd] Garrison, [Theodore] Parker & all of us Woman's Rights actors duly trounced as *"Infidels"* I told him our cause *was Infidel* to the *popular Theology* and *popular interpretation* of the Bible—Mrs. Finney took me to another seat & with much earnestness enquired all about, what we were doing & the growth of our movement—Said she you have the sympathy of a large proportion of the educated women with you—In my circle I hear the movement much talked of & earnest hopes for its spread expressed—but these women dare not speak out their sympathy....

I attended the Anniversary of the "American Woman's Education Association" headed by Catharine E. Beecher.... Some parts of the Secretarys report were very fine—I said Mrs. W[ebster] I would rather see the weight of your influence exerted to open the doors of the existing colleges to woman ... far greater good would be done for woman by such work, than by the establishment of separate Colleges. Said she, that is my mind exactly—isn't it strange that such women as these ... are so stupid, Yes so *false* as to work for anything secondar—but any thing other than their *highest* conviction but those women are bound by the fashionable Church & dare not take sides with the unpopular....

I am now just done with house fixing & ready to commence operations on that Report [to the New York State Teacher's Convention]—Don't you think it would be a good plan to first state *what* we mean by educating the sexes together—then go in to show how the few institutions that profess to give *equal* education *fail* in the Physical, Moral & Intellectual departments & lastly that it is folly to talk of giving to the sexes, *equal advantages,* while you *withhold* from them *equal motive* to improve those advantages—Do you please mark out a plan & give me as soon as you can—Oh, that I had the requisite power to do credit to woman hood in this emergency—why is nature so *sparing* of her gifts—When will you come to Rochester to spend those days, I shall be most happy to see whenever it shall be—only let me know a few days before—that I may be as much at leisure as may be. Amelia [Stanton's housekeeper] & the two babies of course & as many more as convenient—With love.

Excerpted from Gordon, et al., *Selected Letters,* vol. 1, pp. 321–325.

Home-getting, along towards 12 o'clock
Thursday Evening, 5th, June 1856

Private

... And, Mrs. Stanton, not a *word written* on that Address for Teacher's Con.—*This* week was to be *leisure* to me & lo, our *girl, a wife,* had a *miscarriage, ...* & what is *worse,* as the *Lord knows full well,* is, if I *get all the time* the *world has,* I *can't get up* a *decent document,* so, for the love of me,

& for the saving of the *reputation* of *womanhood*, I beg you, with one baby on your knee & another at your feet & four boys whistling buzzing hallooing *Ma, Ma* set yourself about the work—it is of but small moment *who writes* the Address, but of *vast moment* that it be *well done*—I promise you to work hard, oh, how hard, & *pay you whatever you say* for your *time* & *brains*—but oh Mrs. Stanton *don't* say *no* nor *don't delay* it a moment, for I must have it all done and almost commit it to memory.... Now will *you load my gun*, leaving me only to pull the trigger & let fly the powder & ball.

Don't delay one mail to tell me what you *will do*—for I *must not* & *will not* allow these *school masters* to say, *see* these *women can't*, or *won't* do anything when we do give them a chance—*No*, they sha'n't say that, even if I have to get a *man* to write it—but no man can write from *my stand point*—nor no woman but *you*—for *all, all* would base their *strongest* argument on the *un*likeness of the *sexes*—Nette [Brown] wrote me that she should, were she to make the Address—& more than any other place does the *difference* of sex, if there is any, need to be *forgotten* in the school room—

... Now do, I pray you, give heed to my prayer—those of you who have the *talent* to do honor to poor oh! how poor womanhood, have all given yourself over to *baby* making, & left poor brainless *me* to battle alone—It is a shame—such a body as I might be *spared to rock cradles*, but it is a *crime* for *you* & *Lucy* & *Nette*—I have just engaged to attend a progressive meeting in Erie Co. the 1st of Sept. just because there is no other woman to be had, not because I feel in the least competent—oh, dear, dear If the *spirits* would only just make me a *trance medium* & put the *rights* into my mouth—You can't think how earnestly I have prayed to be made a speaking medium for a whole week—If they would only come to me thus, I'd give them a hearty welcome–

Now don't fail to write me—Is your sister with you—how I do wish I could step in to see you & make you feel all my infirmities—*mental I mean*

...*d*o get all on fire, & be as *cross* as you please, you remember Mr. Stanton told how cross you always get in a speech. Good By Susan B

Enclosure

Why the sexes should be Educated together
Because their life work is so nearly identical
   By such education they get true ideas of each other—the College Student associates with only two classes of women, the kitchen drudge & parlor doll—The Seminary girl has only stolen interviews, gets her idea of man mostly from works of fiction—
   Because the endowment of Educational Institutions by both public & private munificence is ever for those of the male sex—while all the Seminaries & Boarding Schools for Females are left to maintain themselves as best they may by means of their Tuition Fees—consequently cannot afford a faculty of 1st class Professors—

Because there are already colleges enough established for all of both sexes—*Economy* favors it

Not a school in the Country gives to the girl equal privileges with the boy—not Oberlin Lima McGrawville nor Antioch.[51] ... No school r*equires* & but a very few *allow* the *girls* to declaim & discuss side side with the boys—thus are they robbed of their right the *one half* of education—

The grand thing that is needed, is to give the sexes *like motives* for acquirement—Very rarely a person studies closely, without hope of making that knowledge useful—as means of support or house or something to them

That man may learn from his boyhood that woman is his *intellectual equal* & no longer look upon her as his inferior—oh, dear dear, there is so much to say & I am without *constructive power* to put in symmetrical order

Because separation & restraint stimulates the desires & passions

---

Excerpted from Gordon, et al., *Selected Letters*, vol. 1, pp. 325–36.

Seneca Falls, June 10, 1856

Dear Susan,

Your servant is not dead but liveth. Imagine me, day in and day out, watching, bathing, dressing, nursing, and promenading the precious contents of a little crib in the comer of the room. I pace up and down these two chambers of mine like a caged lioness, longing to bring nursing and housekeeping cares to a close. Is your speech to be exclusively on the point of educating the sexes together, or as to the best manner of educating women? Have you Horace Mann on that point? Come here and I will do what I can to help you with your address, if you will hold the baby and make the puddings. Love to Antoinette and Lucy when you write them. Womankind owes them a debt of gratitude for their faithful labors in the past. Let them rest in peace and quietness, thinking great thoughts. It is not well to be in the excitement of public life all the time, so do not keep stirring them up or mourning over their repose. You, too, must rest, Susan; let the world alone awhile. We can not bring about a moral revolution in a day or year. Now that I have two daughters, I feel fresh strength to work for women. It is not in vain that in myself I have experienced all the wearisome cares to which woman in her best estate is subject. Good night. Yours in love, E. C. Stanton

---

Excerpted from Gordon, et al., *Selected Letters*, vol. 1, pp. 351–352.

Seneca Falls, August 20? 1857

Dear Susan,

I did indeed see by the papers that you had once more stirred that part of intellectual stagnation the educational convention. What an infernal set of fools these school-*marms* must be!! Well if in order to please men they wish to live on air let them. The sooner the present generation of women die out the better, we have jackasses enough in the world without such women propagating any more.

The *Times* was really quite complimentary. Henry amused me very much, he brought ever notice he could see about you, well my dear he would say, another notice about Susan. "You stir up Susan & she stirs the world." I was glad you went to torment these devils. I guess they will begin to think their time has come. I glory in your perseverance. Oh! Susan I will do anything to help you on. If I do nothing else this fall I am bound to aid you to get up an antislavery address. ... you must come here for a week or two & we will do wonders. Courage Susan this is my last baby & she will be two years old in January. Two years more & & &, time will tell what.—You and I have a prospect of a good long life we shall not be in our prime before fifty & after that we shall be good for twenty years at least....

Write soon & often good night yours as ever E. Cady Stanton

In her letter of September 29, 1857, Anthony described for Stanton a debate she had with the spiritualist-reformer Andrew Jackson Davis over "the likeness and unlikeness of the sexes." Anthony argued that the differences between men and women were socially created, the products of dress and the deliberate intent to attract the opposite sex, an assertion which her opponents charged was "gross" and "animal."

Excerpted from Gordon, et al., *Selected Letters*, vol. 1, pp. 352–57. Ellipses indicate omission.

Collins Sept. 29, 1857

Dear Mrs. Stanton,

How I do long to be with you this very minute—to have one look into your very soul & one sound of your soul stirring voice—

... How are you, & how comes on the letter for the *National [Women's Rights] Convention*—It seems impossible to array our forces for effective action this Autumn—I, therefore, a few days since, wrote Lucy Stone, begging her to *Postpone* the Convention into *May next*.... That Convention has been a heavy burden to me, the last two months—nothing looked promising—nobody seemed to feel any personal responsibility and, *alone*, feeling utterly incompetent to go forward, unless sure of reliable & effective speakers to sustain the Con.; could but grope in the dark—but I now hope Lucy will say *amen* to any proposition.

... I can't Remember whether I have answered your last letter or not—be that as it may, I well remember how good a word it brought to me, and how it cheered me onward—Mrs. Stanton, I have *very weak* moments—& long to lay my weary head somewhere and nestle my full soul close to that of another in full sympathy—I sometimes fear that *I too* shall faint by the wayside—and drop out the ranks of the faithful few.

There is so much, mid all that is so hopeful, to discourage & dishearten—and I feel *alone* Still I know I am *not alone,* but that all the true & the good souls, both in & out of the body, keep me company, and that the Good Father more than all is ever a host in every good effort

But you will see that this is one of my *tired* moments—so no more—but to the Cause thereof

I left home the 1st of Sept., and commenced Anti-Slavery work at Binghamton ... had three weeks of cold hard labor among people not yet initiated into the first principles of true freedom—I returned home the 19th Sept—found *company* there—& company *came* & *came*—Our folks were in the midst of a heavy *Peach* harvest—my mother was very feeble—the *Hibernian* unskilled—my *ward robe* in need of repair, my brain and body in need of rest—For a week I was in such a home *whirl*—on Friday the 25th I left for the "Collins Progressive Friends" Meeting—arrived Saturday A.M. ...

... Mrs. D[avis]. from the Committee read a Paper on Womans Rights going back to Woman's position in marriage as the starting point—*Mr.* Davis spoke first—he set forth his idea of the nature of the sexes & their relation to each—spoke truthfully & nobly of re-production—of the *abuses* in marriage &c, &c.—but to his idea of the sexes—he said woman's inherent nature *is Love & Man's Wisdom—that* Love reaches out to Wisdom—man—and Wisdom reaches out to Love—woman—& the two meet & make a beautiful blending of the two principles....

My soul was on fire—this is but a *revamp* of the Worlds idea from the beginning—the very same doctrine that consigned woman from the beginning to the sphere of the affections, that subjugated her to man's wisdom ... the *question* was *called for—. I must out*—and said Mr. President—I must say a word—and I did say a word—I said *Women.* if you accept the theory given you by Davis, you may give up all talk of a change for woman—she is now where God & nature intended she should be—If it be a fact that the principle of Wisdom is indigenous in Man, & Love an exotic, then must Wisdom *prevail—&* so with woman, must *Love prevail.* Therefore woman must look to *man* for *Wisdom*—must ever feel it impossible for her to attain Wisdom equal to him—Such a doctrine makes my heart *sink* within me, said I—And did I accept it—I would return to my own Father's house, and never again raise my voice for Woman's right to the control of her own person, the ownership of her own earnings—the guardianship of her own children—For if this be true, she ought not to possess those rights—She ought to make final appeal to the wisdom of her husband, Father & brother—My word stirred the waters—and brought Davis to his feet again, but he failed to extricate himself from the conclusions to which his premises philosophically lead....

...all day yesterday, the likeness & unlikeness of the sexes has been the topic of discussion Phillip D. Moore of Newark N.J. took sides with me—says my note at Waterloo, last spring, was the *first* he ever heard sounded on that side, & there he came forthwith to me & expressed his sympathy. Well on the Love and Wisdom side, we had [Aaron M.] Powell, George Taylor, Dr. Mary Taylor of Buffalo, & a Mr. Lloyd of Pa.—the discussion has been loud & long—and have I wished that *you* could be here—I tell you, Mrs. Stanton after all, it is very *precious* to the soul of man, that *he shall reign supreme in intellect,* and it will take Centuries if not ages to dispossess him of the fancy that he is born to do so

... The Female Doctor urged as a Physiological fact that *girl babies* have from their births less physical vigor, than the boy baby—then she claimed that there is ever passing from the Woman out to Man a "*female [aura]*"—influence she meant—that thrills his soul—all unlike that of man to man &c.—Well then here is a fact, a girl dressed in boys clothes stands at a type case side by side with a young man for three years—and this "female [aura]" is never perceived, at least not sufficiently to cause the recipient to suspect the *sex* at his side other than his own.

Take that same being, array her in womans dress, & tomorrow morning place her at the same case while the tones of her voice, the move of her hand, the glance of her eye are all the same as yesterday—her presence causes the sensuous thrill to rush to his very fingers & toes ends—Now tell me the cause. Is the "[aura]" in the being, does it go out to that young man from the brain, the soul, the femininity of that young woman—or is it in the flowing robes and waving tresses, in the *knowledge* of the *difference* of *sex—the latter I say—at* least to a very great extent—but, say our opponents, such an admission is so gross, so animal—Well I can't help that *if it is fact*—there it is—to me it is not coarse or gross, it is simply the answering of the highest & holiest function of the physical organism that is that of *reproduction—to* be a *Mother* to be a *Father* is the last & highest wish of any human being—to *re-produce himself* or *herself the* accomplish[ment] of this purpose is only through the inciting of the sexes—And when we come into the presence of one of the opposite sex, who embodies what to us seems the true and & the noble, & the beautiful, our souls are stirred, and whether we realize it or not,—it is a thrill of joy that such qualities are re-producible—*&* that we may be the *agents* the *artists* in such re-production—

It is the *knowledge* that the two together may be the instruments, that shall execute a work so *God like—*

But I have wearied you already, I fear and surely have exhausted my moment of time—I must add that many women came to me & thanked me for the word I uttered in opposition to Davis said they—had you not spoken we should have gone home burdened in soul—

Oh Mrs Stanton how my soul longs to see you in the great Battle field—when will the time come you say in two or three years—God & the Angels keep you safe from all hindrances—and keep you from all mountain barriers—If you come not to the rescue, who shall? ....

Don't fail to write me it always does me so much good to get a letter from you—A Kiss for Maggie & Hattie & Sadie [another servant] and a kindly word for the boys.... With best Love Susan B. Anthony

In the following enthusiastic letter, Stanton's fantasy of a world's woman's convention draws on her experience with Mott eighteen years before at the World's Anti-Slavery Convention. The occasion was a letter from Wendell Phillips announcing an anonymous donation of $5000 for women's rights tracts, lectures and tours. "Our Napoleon" was Susan B. Anthony. Stanton was incapacitated by an unusually difficult first trimester of her last pregnancy.

Excerpted from Gordon, et al., *Selected Letters*, vol. 1, pp. 381–382.

Seneca Falls
Dec 1, 1858

Dear Susan

I can think of nothing better at the first blush that lectures & tracts. Emily Howland would get up a course in N.Y. at once could she feel sustained.[52] Antoinette [Brown Blackwell] is ready to work all winter, why not send her to every city in the union & to London at some future time, where you might hold a *world's* woman's *convention.* It would be a great thing for the women of England France & America to meet in London & have Lucretia preside there just where it was decided that she did not belong to the world. I should like to have Lucy Stone & Antoinette lecture in England I never felt so thankful in the days of my life as when I read Phillips letters. Now our Napoleon can do something Praise the Lord !! ... I say emphatically *no* to your question. I cannot go to R. I cannot even visit you. I am too unwell to travel. I was really thankful to get home....

Do come down and see me & mine The boys are doing well in Geneva.[53] they are contented & happy They would be glad to hear from you Henry goes to Washington to morrow morning . Come down, yours as ever

E. Cady Stanton

Stanton usually described most of her childbirth experiences as easy and not debilitating, but the birth of her seventh child left her weak and depressed. As she struggled to regain her strength, the conflict over slavery was reaching a climax. The raid on Harpers Ferry, Virginia, and the subsequent martyrdom of John Brown affected her as it affected all abolitionists; her cousin Gerrit Smith had supported Brown and nearly went mad in the following weeks.

Vassar College Library, Stanton Letters

April 2, (1859)

Dear Susan,

I have a great boy now three weeks old. He weighed at his birth without a particle of clothing 12 ¼ lb. My labour was long and very very severe. I never suffered so much before. I was sick all the time before he was born, and I have been very weak ever since. He seemed to take up every particle of my vitality soul and body. He is a great specimen so every body says. He looks like Gattie and Maggie. Think However! I am through the siege once more! ....

Excerpted from *Selected Letters of Stanton and Anthony*, vol. 1, 387.

April 10th (1859)

Dear Susan,

You need expect nothing from me for some time. I have no vitality of body or soul. All I had & was has gone with the development of that boy.[54] It is now four weeks since my confinement & I can scarcely walk across the room. You have no idea how weak I am & I have to keep my mind in the most quiet state in order to sleep. I have suffered so much from wakefulness

I am always glad to hear from you & hope to see you on your way to N.Y....

In haste your friend E. C. Stanton

Excerpted from Gordon, et al., *Selected*, vol. 1, p. 400.

Seneca Falls, c. December 15, 1859

Indeed it would do me such great good to see some reformers just now. The death of my father, the worse than death of my dear Cousin Gerrit, the martyrdom of that great and glorious John Brown, all conspire to make me regret more than ever my dwarfed and perverted womanhood.[55] In times like these every soul should do the work of a fullgrown man. When I pass the gate of the celestials and good Peter asks me where I wish to sit, I will say, "Anywhere so that I am neither a negro nor a woman. Confer on me, great angel, the glory of white manhood, so that henceforth I may feel unlimited freedom."

Document 6

Stanton, "Address to the Legislature of New York on Women's Rights," February 14, 1854

After their ouster from the women's temperance society, Stanton and Anthony began to work directly for women's legal rights in New York. In February 1854, they held a convention in Albany to demand a revision of the state's legal code, and Elizabeth Stanton made a rare trip from Seneca Falls to address the legislature herself. This is the speech which caused her father such distress that he threatened to disown her; he eventually retracted his threat and helped her with the legal details. Stanton's speech contains all the basic elements of the legal program of the early women's rights movement. In addition to the vote, the right to sit on juries, and other rights of citizenship, she also demanded changes in the laws regulating those familial institutions—marriage, parenthood, widowhood—which structure the relations between men and women.

History of Woman Suffrage, Vol. 1, eds. Stanton, Anthony, and Matilda J. Gage (Rochester: Susan B. Anthony, 1881), pp. 595–605

... Gentlemen, in republican America, in the nineteenth century, we, the daughters of the revolutionary heroes of '76, demand at your hands the redress of our grievances—a revision of your State Constitution—a new code of laws. Permit us then, as briefly as possible, to call your attention to the legal disabilities under which we labor.

1st. Look at the position of woman as woman. It is not enough for us that by your laws we are permitted to live and breathe, to claim the necessaries of life from our legal protectors—to pay the penalty of our crimes; we demand the full recognition of all our rights as citizens of the Empire

State. We are persons; native, free-born citizens; property-holders, tax-payers; yet are we denied the exercise of our right to the elective franchise. We support ourselves, and, in part, your schools, colleges, churches, your poor-houses, jails, prisons, the army, the navy, the whole machinery of government, and yet we have no voice in your councils. We have every qualification required by the Constitution, necessary to the legal voter, but the one of sex. We are moral, virtuous, and intelligent, and in all respects quite equal to the proud white man himself, and yet by your laws we are classed with idiots, lunatics, and negroes; and though we do not feel honored by the place assigned us, yet, in fact, our legal position is lower than that of either; for the negro can be raised to the dignity of a voter if he possess himself of $250; the lunatic can vote in his moments of sanity, and the idiot, too, if he be a male one, and not more than nine-tenths a fool; but we, who have guided great movements of charity, established missions, edited journals, published works on history, economy, and statistics; who have governed nations, led armies, filled the professor's chair, taught philosophy and mathematics to the savants of our age, discovered planets, piloted ships across the sea, are denied the most sacred rights of citizens, because, forsooth, we came not into this republic crowned with the dignity of manhood! ... Can it be that here, where we acknowledge no royal blood, no apostolic descent, that you, who have declared that all men were created equal—that governments derive their just powers from the consent of the governed, would willingly build up an aristocracy that places the ignorant and vulgar above the educated and refined—the alien and the ditch-digger above the authors and poets of the day—an aristocracy that would raise the sons above the mothers that bore them? Would that the men who can sanction a Constitution so opposed to the genius of this government, who can enact and execute laws so degrading to womankind, had sprung, Minerva-like, from the brains of their fathers, that the matrons of this republic need not blush to own their sons!

...we demand in criminal cases that most sacred of all rights, trial by a jury of our own peers. The establishment of trial by jury is of so early a date that its beginning is lost in antiquity; but the right of trial by a jury of one's own peers is a great progressive step of advanced civilization. No rank of men have ever been satisfied with being tried by jurors higher or lower in the civil or political scale than themselves; for jealousy on the one hand, and contempt on the other, has ever effectually blinded the eyes of justice. Hence, all along the pages of history, we find the king, the noble, the peasant, the cardinal, the priest, the layman, each in turn protesting against the authority of the tribunal before which they were summoned to appear.... And shall woman here consent to be tried by her liege lord, who has dubbed himself law-maker, judge, juror, and sheriff too?—whose power, though sanctioned by Church and State, has no foundation in justice and equity, and is a bold assumption of our inalienable rights.... Having seen that man fails to do justice to woman in her best estate, to the virtuous, the noble, the true of our sex, should we trust to his tender mercies the weak, the ignorant, the morally insane? It is not to be denied that the interests of man and woman in the present undeveloped state of the race, and under the existing social arrangements, are and must be antagonistic. The nobleman can not make just laws for the peasant; the slaveholder for the slave; neither can man make and execute just laws for woman, because in each case, the one in power fails to apply the immutable principles of right to any grade but his own.

Shall an erring woman be dragged before a bar of grim-visaged judges, lawyers, and jurors, there to be grossly questioned in public on subjects which women scarce breathe in secret to one another? Shall the most sacred relations of life be called up and rudely scanned by men who, by their own admission, are so coarse that women could not meet them even at the polls without contamination? and yet shall she find there no woman's face or voice to pity and defend? ... His peers made the law, and shall law-makers lay nets for those of their own rank? Shall laws which come from the logical brain of man take cognizance of violence done to the moral and affectional nature which predominates, as is said, in woman? ....

2d. Look at the position of woman as wife. Your laws relating to marriage—founded as they are on the old common law of England, a compound of barbarous usages, but partially modified by progressive civilization—are in open violation of our enlightened ideas of justice, and of the holiest feelings of our nature. If you take the highest view of marriage, as a Divine relation, which love alone can constitute and sanctify, then of course human legislation can only recognize it. Men can neither bind nor loose its ties, for that prerogative belongs to God alone, who makes man and woman, and the laws of attraction by which they are united. But if you regard marriage as a civil contract, then let it be subject to the same laws which control all other contracts. Do not make it a kind of half-human, half-divine institution, which you may build up, but can not regulate. Do not, by your special legislation for this one kind of contract, involve yourselves in the grossest absurdities and contradictions.

So long as by your laws no man can make a contract for a horse or piece of land until he is twenty-one years of age, and by which contract he is not bound if any deception has been practiced, or if the party contracting has not fulfilled his part of the agreement—so long as the parties in all mere civil contracts retain their identity and all the power and independence they had before contracting, with the full right to dissolve all partnerships and contracts for any reason, at the will and option of the parties themselves, upon what principle of civil jurisprudence do you permit the boy of fourteen and the girl of twelve, in violation of every natural law, to make a contract more momentous in importance than any other, and then hold them to it come what may, the whole of their natural lives, in spite of disappointment, deception, and misery? Then, too, the signing of this contract is instant civil death to one of the parties, The woman who but yesterday was sued on bended knee, who stood so high in the scale of being as to make an agreement on equal terms with a proud Saxon man, to-day has no civil existence, no social freedom. The wife who inherits no property holds about the same legal position that does the slave of the Southern plantation. She can own nothing, sell nothing. She has no right even to the wages she earns; her person, her time, her services are the property of another....

There is nothing that an unruly wife might do against which the husband has not sufficient protection in the law. But not so with the wife. If she have a worthless husband, a confirmed drunkard, a villain, or a vagrant, he has still all the rights of a man, a husband, and a father. Though the whole support of the family be thrown upon the wife, if the wages she earns be paid to her by her employer, the husband can receive them again....

But the wife who is so fortunate as to have inherited property, has, by the new law in this State, been redeemed from her lost condition. She is no longer a legal nonentity. This property law, if fairly construed, will overturn the whole code relating to woman and property. The right to property implies the right to buy and sell, to will and bequeath, and herein is the dawning of a civil existence for woman, for now the "femme covert" must have the right to make contracts.... The right to property will, of necessity, compel us in due time to the exercise of our right to the elective franchise, and then naturally follows the right to hold office.

3d. Look at the position of woman as widow. Whenever we attempt to point out the wrongs of the wife, those who would have us believe that the laws can not be improved, point us to the privileges, powers, and claims of the widow. Let us look into these a little.... Behold the magnanimity of the law in allowing the widow to retain a life interest in one-third the landed estate, and one-half the personal property of her husband, and taking the lion's share to itself! Had she died first, the house and land would all have been the husband's still. No one would have dared to intrude upon the privacy of his home, or to molest him in his sacred retreat of sorrow. How, I ask you, can that be called justice, which makes such a distinction as this between man and woman? ....

4th. Look at the position of woman as mother. There is no human love so strong and steadfast as that of the mother for her child; yet behold how ruthless are your laws touching this most sacred relation. Nature has clearly made the mother the guardian of the child; but man, in his inordinate love of power, does continually set nature and nature's laws at open defiance. The father may apprentice his child, bind him out to a trade, without the mother's consent—yea, in direct opposition to her most earnest entreaties, prayers and tears.

He may apprentice his son to a gamester or rum-seller, and thus cancel his debts of *honor*. By the abuse of this absolute power, he may bind his daughter to the owner of a brothel, and, by the degradation of his child, supply his daily wants: and such things, gentlemen, have been done in our very midst. Moreover, the father, about to die, may bind out all his children wherever and to whomsoever he may see fit, and thus, in fact, will away the guardianship of all his children from the mother. The Revised Statutes of New York provide that "every father, whether of full age or a minor, of a child to be born, or of any living child under the age of twenty-one years, and unmarried, may by his deed or last will, duly executed, dispose of the custody and tuition of such child during its minority, or for any less time, to any person or persons, in possession or remainder." ... Thus, by your laws, the child is the absolute property of the father, wholly at his disposal in life or at death....

Again, as the condition of the child always follows that of the mother, and as by the sanction of your laws the father may beat the mother, so may he the child. What mother can not bear me witness to untold sufferings which cruel, vindictive fathers have visited upon their helpless children? Who ever saw a human being that would not abuse unlimited power? Base and ignoble must that man be who, let the provocation be what it may, would strike a woman: but he who would lacerate a trembling child is unworthy the name of man. A mother's love can be no protection to a child; she can not appeal to you to save it from a father's cruelty, for the laws take no cognizance of the mother's most grievous wrongs. Neither at home nor abroad can a mother protect her son. Look at the temptations that surround the paths of our youth at every step; look at the gambling and drinking saloons, the club rooms, the dens of infamy and abomination that infest all our villages and cities—slowly but surely sapping the very foundations of all virtue and strength.

By your laws, all these abominable resorts are permitted. It is folly to talk of a mother moulding the character of her son, when all mankind, backed up by law and public sentiment, conspire to destroy her influence. But when woman's moral power shall speak through the ballot-box, then shall her influence be seen and felt....

Many times and oft it has been asked us, with unaffected seriousness, "What do you women want? What are you aiming at?" Many have manifested a laudable curiosity to know what the wives and daughters could complain of in republican America, where their sires and sons have so bravely fought for freedom and gloriously secured their independence, trampling all tyranny, bigotry, and caste in the dust, and declaring to a waiting world the divine truth that all men are created equal. What can woman want under such a government? Admit a radical difference in sex, and you demand different spheres—water for fish, and air for birds.

It is impossible to make the Southern planter believe that his slave feels and reasons just as he does—that injustice and subjection are as galling as to him—that the degradation of living by the will of another, the mere dependent on his caprice, at the mercy of his passions, is as keenly felt by him as his master. If you can force on his unwilling vision a vivid picture of the negro's wrongs, and for a moment touch his soul, his logic brings him instant consolation. He says, the slave does not feel this as I would. Here, gentlemen, is our difficulty: When we plead our cause before the law-makers and savants of the republic, they can not take in the idea that men and women are alike; and so long as the mass rest in this delusion, the public mind will not be so much startled by the revelations made of the injustice and degradation of woman's position as by the fact that she should at length wake up to a sense of it....

But if, gentlemen, you take the ground that the sexes are alike, and, therefore, you are our faithful representatives—then why all these special laws for woman? Would not one code answer for all of like needs and wants? Christ's golden rule is better than all the special legislation that the ingenuity of man can devise: "Do unto others as you would have others do unto you." This, men and brethren, is all we ask at your hands. We ask no better laws than those you have made for yourselves. We need no other protection than that which your present laws secure to you.

In conclusion, then, let us say, in behalf of the women of this State, we ask for all that you have asked for yourselves in the progress of your development, since the *Mayflower* cast anchor beside Plymouth rock; and simply on the ground that the rights of every human being are the same and identical. You may say that the mass of the women of this State do not make the demand; it comes from a few sour, disappointed old maids and childless women.

You are mistaken; the mass speak through us. A very large majority of the women of this State support themselves and their children, and many their husbands too. Go into any village you please, of three or four thousand inhabitants, and you will find as many as fifty men or more, whose only business is to discuss religion and politics, as they watch the trains come and go at the depot, or the passage of a canal boat through a lock; to laugh at the vagaries of some drunken brother, or the capers of a monkey dancing to the music of his master's organ. All these are supported by their mothers, wives, or sisters.

Now, do you candidly think these wives do not wish to control the wages they earn—to own the land they buy—the houses they build? to have at their disposal their own children, without being subject to the constant interference and tyranny of an idle, worthless profligate? Do you suppose that any woman is such a pattern of devotion and submission that she willingly stitches all day for the small sum of fifty cents, that she may enjoy the unspeakable privilege, in obedience to your laws, of paying for her husband's tobacco and rum? Think you the wife of the confirmed, beastly drunkard would consent to share with him her home and bed, if law and public sentiment would release her from such gross companionship? Verily, no! ... The drunkards' wives speak through us, and they number 50,000. Think you that the woman who has worked hard all her days in helping her husband to accumulate a large property, consents to the law that places this wholly at his disposal? Would not the mother whose only child is bound out for a term of years against her expressed wish, deprive the father of this absolute power if she could?

For all these, then, we speak. If to this long list you add the laboring women who are loudly demanding remuneration for their unending toil; those women who teach in our seminaries, academies, and public schools for a miserable pittance; the widows who are taxed without mercy; the unfortunate ones in our work-houses, poor-houses, and prisons; who are they that we do not now represent? But a small class of the fashionable butterflies, who, through the short summer days, seek the sunshine and the flowers; but the cool breezes of autumn and the hoary frosts of winter will soon chase all these away; then they too, will need and seek protection, and through other lips demand in their turn justice and equity at your hands.

DOCUMENT 7

Anthony, Diary of a Lecture Tour with Ernestine Rose to Washington, Baltimore, and Philadelphia, 1854

After the presentation of Stanton's memorial and the women's rights petitions to the New York legislature in Albany, Anthony joined Ernestine Rose, the well-known feminist and freethinker, in a four-week lecture tour of the slave border cities. Thus began Anthony's fifty-year career as a traveling organizer for women's rights. Although she had been earning her own living and participating in temperance and teachers' organizations for several years, the trip broadened her horizons considerably. The diary gives an excellent picture of the world of antebellum reform in which Anthony was moving—its uncompromising moralism, individualism, impatience with "expediency," and eagerness to challenge time-honored beliefs. Anthony provides a marvelous portrait of Ernestine Rose, a woman every bit as intense as herself, who was painfully isolated, even from other reformers, by her Jewish origins and atheism. The trip was Anthony's first direct encounter with slavery, and her observations of the effects of slavery on southern society, the slaves themselves, and her own feelings are keen and moving.

Susan B. Anthony Papers, Schlesinger Library, Harvard University; except for starred entries excerpted from Gordon, et al., *Selected Letters*, vol. 1, pp. 264–735.
Otherwise from Susan B. Anthony Papers, Schlesinger Library, Harvard University.

March 24, 1854. [Washington, D.C.] Directed tickets to Mrs. Rose Meeting on Political and Legal Rights of Woman this evening at Carusi's Saloon, to both Representatives and Senators, in all about 300 in number.

Asked the Speaker of the House for the use of the Capitol on Sunday A.M. He referred me to Mr. Milburn the Chaplain. Called on him. He could not allow her to speak there because she was not a member of some religious society. I remarked to him that ours was a country professing Religious as well as Civil Liberty and not to allow any and every faith to be declared in the Capitol of the nation, made the profession to religious freedom a perfect mockery. Though acknowledging the truthfulness of my position he could not allow a person who failed to recognize the Divine, to speak in his place....

March 25. Mrs. Davis called in evening. We went into the Parlor, and all hands, save me, joined in the dance. Tired and weary I slipped out at an early hour and laid my head upon my pillow.

March 26. Went to the Capitol and listened to Mr. Milburn on Home Life. He said many good things and many things that indicated gross ignorance, misrepresentation. Said "It is here in the home that *most* men and *all* women's chiefest duties lie."

... Called also at Gerrit Smith's and spent the evening, had a delightful conversation. Mrs. Smith is a most splendid woman, plays beautifully on the Piano and sings most sweetly....

Mr. Smith said he wished to share with us in the pecuniary loss of one meeting and insisted on my accepting a Bill which I afterward learned to be a $20 bank note. Expressed himself *very glad* that Mrs. R. had come to Washington....

March 29. Left Washington at ¼ to 9 o'clock for Mt. Vernon, where we arrived about 11 o'clock. The weather cold and windy, but more mild than the day before. The location of Washington's home is most beautiful and commanding, but oh the air of dilapidation and decay that every where meets the eye, the tottering out-buildings, the mark of slavery o'ershadows the whole. Oh, the thought that it was here, that he whose name is the pride of this nation was the *Slave Master.* The humorous, little buildings surrounding, or rather in rear of the great house plainly tell the tale—a Slave, Woman, the cook of the present owner, Grand Nephew of Gen. Washington, told me these buildings were the Servants' Quarters.

The tomb is humble indeed. It would seem that if the profession of reverence for the "Father of his Country" were *real,* that this home of Washington would be rescued from the curse of slave labor, and made to blossom in the sunshine of free labor....

(P.M.) This noon, I ate my dinner without once asking myself, are these human beings who minister to my wants *Slaves* to be bought and sold and hired out at the will of a master? And when the thought first entered my mind, I said, even I am getting *accustomed* to *Slavery,* so much so that I ceased continually to be made to feel its blighting, cursing influence, so much so that I can sit down and eat from the hand of the bondman [*sic*], without being once mindful of the fact that he is such. Oh Slavery, hateful thing that thou art, thus to blunt the keen edge of men's conscience, even while they strive to shun thy poisonous touch.

I learn to day that the present owner of Mt. Vernon is an *intemperate* man. This fact added to slave holding, accounts for the ruinous state of the Plantation.

A white woman here, a slave holder, says she frequently gets perfectly disgusted with Slavery, the *Licentiousness* between the White men and the Slave women is so universal and so revolting, *free* colored women will boast of rooming with a white man for a whole week. The Proprietor of this City Hotel hires slaves of their masters....

*March 31. Baltimore. Had a small meeting last night. The landlord agreed to see me started from Alexandria in time to connect with the 8 O'clock Train from Washington but he did not,—seemed to be perfectly indifferent to my request. There is no promptness no order, no anything about these southerners. I have had Pro Slavery People tell me just go South once, & see Slavery as it is, & then you will talk very differently. I can assure all such, that contact with Slavery has not a tendency to make me hate it *less, no,* the ruinous effect of the institution, upon the white man alone, causes me to hate it....

I came on to Baltimore on the 3 ½ P.M., ... went in search of a private boarding house, finally decided to take rooms at Mrs. Waters, 49 Hanover st. Every thing is plain but so far seems cleanly, learned from the Chambermaid Sarah, that she & four others of the Servants were Slaves.—It is perfectly astonishing to see what an array of Servants there is about every establishment, three northern girls, with the engineering of a northern boarding house keeper would do all the work of one Dozen of these men, women & children, whether Slaves or free. Such is the baneful effect of Slavery upon labor. The free blacks who receive wages, expect to do no more work than do the Slaves. Slave labor is the Standard—& it need but a glance at southern life, to enable an Abolitionist to understand, why it is that the northern man is a more exacting slave master than is a southern one—he requires of the Slave an amount of labor equal to that he has been accustomed to get from the well paid northern free laborer....

April 2. A little colored boy came into our room with Sarah, the Chambermaid. Said Mrs. R. whose boy is that Sarah? He *belongs* to Mrs. Waters, Miss. Where is his mother? She is Cook in the kitchen Miss. Where is his Father? On the Eastern Shore, Miss. Is he a Slave? Yes, Miss. Does he come to see his wife? No, Miss, not since my mistress moved to the City. Has the Cook any more children? Yes, Miss, two more little boys younger than this. Oh, how did my blood run chill.

Before this I said to Sarah, are you *free* Sarah? No, Miss! Do you belong to Mrs. Waters? No Miss, she hires me of my Master for $8 per month. And don't you get any portion of it? No Miss, only my Master gives me my clothes. Does he keep you well clothed? Sometimes, Miss, and sometimes

I gets short. And don't you have any pocket money of your own? Yes, Miss, what the ladies gives me. Sarah is a bright girl, fine expression of face. Oh how I long to probe her soul in search of that Divine spark that scorns to be a slave. But then would it be right for me by so doing to add to the burden of her wretched life?

April 4. Mrs. Rose meeting small. Sold only about 54 tickets. Some 60 free tickets present. The people are so *afraid* that some thing will be said on Slavery that they will not countenance the meeting, and more than that there is at the bottom a sad want of intelligence. Science and literature have no charms for them any more than the Reforms....

*April 6. I lectured this evening by invitation from the Marion Temperance Society of Baltimore, had a full house. The meeting was called to order by the President of the Society & opened by prayer by an old Methodist man who made the stereotype prayer of Stephen S. Foster's Slave holder—"O Lord we thank thee, that our lives have been cast in places & that we live in a land where every man can sit under his own vine & fig tree, and none dare to molest or make him afraid." Oh, how did my blood boil within me & then to go on with my lecture & not protest against a mans telling the Lord such terrible falsehoods....

*April 9. ... Mrs. R. & myself were talking of the *"Know Nothing"* organization, when she criticized Lucy Stone & Wendell Philips [sic] with regard to their feelings toward foreigners. Said she had heard them both express themselves in terms of prejudice against granting to foreigners the rights of Citizenship. I expressed disbelief as to either of them having that narrow, mean prejudice in their souls. She then said I was blinded & could see nor hear nothing wrong in that clique of Abolitionists. She thought she being connected with no Society or association, either in religion or reforms could judge all impartially.—I then ventured to say that Kossuths non committal course while in this country, it seemed to me, she did not criticise as she would an American.—She thought she did, & could see reasons why he pursued the course he did. Yes said I you excuse him, because you can see the causes why he acted & spoke thus, while you will not allow me to bring forward the probable causes of Lucy's seeming fault—It seemed to *me* that *she* could not ascribe *pure motives* to any of our Reformers, & while to her it seemed, that I was blindly bound to see no fault, however glaring—At length in the anguish of my soul, I said Mrs. Rose, "there is not *one* in the Reform ranks, whom you think true, not one but whom panders to the popular feeling"—She answered I can't help it, I take them by the words of their own mouths. I trust all until their words or acts declare them false to truth & right, & continued she, no one can tell the hours of anguish I have suffered, as one after another I have seen those whom I had trusted, betray falsity of motive, as I have been compelled to place one after another on the list of panderers to public favor—Said I, do you know Mrs. Rose, that I can but feel that you place *me too* on that list. Said she, I will tell you when I see you untrue—A silence ensued, while I copied the verse from the hymn sung in Church this A.M., &, subscribed it Susan B. Anthony, for her dear friend Ernestine L. Rose, as I handed it to her, I observed tears in her eyes. Said I Mrs. Rose, have I been wicked, & hurt your feelings. She answered, No, but I expect never to be understood while I live—her anguish was extreme I too wept, for it filled my soul anguish to see one so noble, so true (even though I felt I could not comprehend her) so bowed down, so overcome with deep swelling emotions—At length she said, no one knows how I have suffered from not being understood—I know you must suffer & heaven forbid that I should add a feathers weight to your burdens—

Mrs. Rose is not appreciated, nor cannot be by this age—She is too much in advance of the extreme ultraists even, to be understood by them.

Almost every reformer, feels that the odium of his own Ultraisms is as much as he is able to bear & therefore shrinks from being identified with one in whose view their ultraism is sheer Conservatism—this fact has been most plainly brought home to me—Every [one] says, "I am *ultra enough*, the mercy knows. I don't want to seem to be any more so by identifying myself with one whose every sentiment is so shocking to the public mind...."

April 13. I went to the [Philadelphia] Female Anti Slavery Society. In attendance was a young lady, Virginia _____, of Maryland. She and her sister had left them by their Father, *three* slaves worth $1000 each of whom they set at liberty. Beside these three, their Father left 13 slaves, all of whom save one they have been instrumental in freeing. This one is a Cooper, and belongs to their only brother, who is ill and not expected to live long. He has an offer of $800 for the slave but tells the girls, if they can give him $400 he will take it and thus set the last of the 16 at liberty. Virginia has raised over $200 and I hope she may succeed in getting the remaining $200. In consequence of their Slaves, she and her sister have been compelled to resort to day labor. She has a fine expressive face. It is indeed noble to see two such young girls make "such a sacrifice of their all"....

*April 14. Dined at James Motts.... We had a very chat—Spiritualism as usual being the principle topic, Mrs. Rose & Mr. [Thomas] Curtis believing the spirit inseparable from the body, of course, were on the unbelieving side while Sarah Grimpke [sic] was all enthusiasm in the faith. Eliab Capron doesn't *believe*, he *knows* there is a reality in spirits disembodied, communicating with the living. The rest of the company, with myself, seemed not to know whether or not there is any truth in these modern manifestations. Mrs. R returned ... immediately after dinner to rest for the evening meeting to be held at Samson's Street Hall—I remained & with Lucretia Sarah Grimpke & myself on one side & Thomas Curtis on the other, had an argument as to the probable future existence of the mind or soul or spirit of man—Not an argument could one of us bring, other than an intuitive feeling that we were not to cease to exist when the body dies. while Mr. Curtis reasoned, (as has Mrs. Rose often done with me) that all things in nature die, or rather that the elements of all things are separated & assume new forms, that if the soul, the vital spark of man lives eternally so must the essence of the tree, the animal, the fern & the flower. There certainly is no argument to be brought against such reasonings—But if it be true that we die like the flower, leaving behind, only the fragrance or the contrary while the elements that compose us go to form new bodies, what a delusion has the race ever been in—what a dream is the life of man....

Document 8

Stanton, "Speech to the Anniversary of the American Anti-Slavery Society," 1860

Stanton was invited to deliver this speech before the May 1860, annual meeting of the American Anti-Slavery Society, six months after John Brown's raid on Harpers Ferry. While the speech is an attack on slavery and praises abolitionists, it also offers a series of connections between antislavery and women's rights. First, abolitionism's "universal" principles of truth and freedom had undermined the superstition and bigotry fostered by religious orthodoxy. In addition, women were treated as equals in the antislavery movement and abolitionist men defended their rights. Stanton also spoke of the "subjective" link between white women and slaves, both of whom knew oppression from the inside. Most powerfully, she described the condition of women under chattel slavery, emphasizing their sexual abuse and mental crippling in such a way that some of her audience could not tell if she was speaking of Black women or white. Undoubtedly, this ambiguity was intentional.

The Liberator, May 18, 1860, pp. 78.

This is generally known as the platform of one idea—that is negro slavery. In a certain sense this may be true, but the most casual observation of this whole anti-slavery movement, of your lives, conventions, public speeches and journals, show this one idea to be a great humanitarian one. The motto of your leading organ, "The world is my country and all mankind my countrymen," proclaims the magnitude and universality of this one idea, which takes in the whole human family, irrespective of nation, color, caste, or sex, with all their interests, temporal and spiritual—a question of religion, philanthropy, political economy, commerce, education and social life on which depends the very existence of this republic, of the state, of the family, the sacredness of the lives and property of Northern freemen, the holiness of the marriage relation, and the perpetuity of the Christian religion. Such are the various phases of the question you are wont to debate in your conventions. They all grow out of and legitimately belong to that *so-called* petty, insignificant, annoying subject, which thrusts up its head everywhere in Church and State—"the eternal nigger." But in settling the question of the negro's rights, we find out the exact limits of our own, for rights never clash or interfere; and where no individual in a community is denied his rights, the mass are the more perfectly protected in theirs; for whenever any class is subject to fraud or injustice, it shows that the spirit of tyranny is at work, and no one can tell where or how or when the infection will spread....

It was thought a small matter to kidnap a black man in Africa, and set him to work in the rice swamps of Georgia; but when we look at the panorama of horrors that followed that event, at all the statute laws that were enacted to make that act legal, at the perversion of man's moral sense and innate love of justice in being compelled to defend such laws; when we consider the long, hard tussle we have witnessed here for near a century between the spirit of Liberty and Slavery, we may, in some measure, appreciate the magnitude of the wrong done to that one, lone, friendless negro, who, under the cover of darkness and the star-spangled banner, was stolen from his African hut and lodged in the hold of the American slaver. That one act has, in its consequences, convulsed this Union. It has corrupted our churches, our politics, our press; laid violent hands on Northern freemen at their own firesides; it has gagged our statesmen, and stricken our Northern Senators dumb in their seats; yes, beneath the flag of freedom, Liberty has crouched in fear.

That grand declaration of rights made by WILLIAM LLOYD GARRISON, while yet a printer's boy, was on a higher plane than that of '76. His was uttered with the Christian's view of the dignity of man, the value of the immortal being; the other but from the self-respect of one proud race. But, in spite of noble words, deeds of thirty years of protest, prayers and preaching, slavery still lives, the negro toils on in his weary bondage, his chains have not yet melted in the intense heat of the sun of righteousness; but in the discussion of this question, in grappling with its foes, how many of us have worked out our salvation; what mountains of superstition have been rolled off the human soul! I have always regarded Garrison as the great missionary of the gospel of Jesus to this guilty nation, for he has waged an uncompromising warfare with the deadly sins of both Church and State. My own experience is, no doubt, that of many others. In the darkness and gloom of a false theology, I was slowly sawing off the chains of my spiritual bondage, when, for the first time, I met

Garrison in London. A few bold strokes from the hammer of his truth, I was free! Only those who have lived all their lives under the dark clouds of vague, undefined fears can appreciate the joy of a doubting soul suddenly born into the kingdom of reason and free thought. Is the bondage of the priest-ridden less galling than that of the slave, because we do not see the chains, the indelible scars, the festering wounds, the deep degradation of all the powers of the God-like mind? ....

I do not believe that all history affords another such example as the so-called "Garrisonian Conspiracy"—a body of educated men of decided talent, wealth, rank and position, standing for a quarter of a century battling a whole nation, Church and State, law and public sentiment, without the shadow of ever wavering, turning or faltering, as if chained to the great Gibraltar—truth of human freedom and equality. This unheard-of steadfastness can only be accounted for in the fact that woman too is represented in this "conspiracy." Yes, the Marys and the Marthas have gathered round the prophets of our day. With noble words and deeds, and holy sympathy, they have cheered these exiles from the love and honor of their own false countrymen. At their family altars they have been remembered, and unseen spirits of the brave and good have hovered over them, and rejoiced in these true sons of earth.

Yes, this is the only organization on God's footstool where the humanity of woman is recognized, and these are the only men who have ever echoed back her cries for justice and equality. I shall never forget our champions in the World's Anti-Slavery Convention; how nobly [Wendell] Phillips did speak, and how still more nobly Garrison would not speak, because woman was there denied her rights. Think of a World's Convention and one half the world left out! Shame on the women of this nation who help to swell the cry of "INFIDEL" against men like these! All time would not be long enough to pay the debt of gratitude we owe these noble men, who spoke for us when we were dumb, who roused us to a sense of our own rights, to the dignity of our high calling.

No the mission of this Radical Anti-Slavery Movement is not to the African slave alone, but to the slaves of custom, creed and sex, as well; and most faithfully has it done its work. As we rejoice this day in our deliverance from the sad train of fears and errors that have so long crippled and dwarfed the greatest minds of earth, let us seek a new and holier baptism for the work that lies for each of us in the future.

The last fear from which man may hope deliverance is the fear of man. To this glorious freedom did the immortal John Brown arrive. He feared neither man nor God; he was made perfect in love, the future was bright and beautiful to him! ... Noble John Brown! thou wert true to thyself and thy race, and loyal to thy God. I ask no higher honor in the gift of this nation for any sons of mine than a gallows and a grave like thine! As these sons now gather round me, and ask questions about different nations, governments and laws, think you it is with pride I read to them our constitutions, statute laws, and late judicial decisions on great questions of human rights? Ah, no! ...it is with the deepest sorrow that I check the budding patriotism in their young hearts—that I unveil to them our falsehood and hypocrisy, in the face of those grand and glorious declarations of freedom and equality which, when first proclaimed at the mouth of the cannon, raised us head and shoulders above the nations of the earth. It is all-important, in a republican government, that our laws be always on the side of justice. Here where we have neither Pope nor King, no royal family, crown or sceptre, no nobility, rank or class, nothing outward to cultivate or command our veneration, Law, the immutable principles of right, are all and everything to us.

See to it, you have the best interests of our Republic in your care, that your laws keep pace with public sentiment. If you would have us teach our sons a sacred reverence for law, so frame your constitutions and your codes that, in yielding obedience to their requirements, they are not false to the holy claims of humanity—that they degrade not the mothers who gave them life. No one can be more awake than I am to all the blessings of a republican form of government, nor, as a mother, more apprehensive lest her sons should confound liberty with license. Here, where individual responsibilities are so great, and the influence of one so all-powerful, I fain would have them lovers of law and order, and meekly to suffer wrong themselves, if need be, to preserve it; but when the panting fugitive throws himself on our generosity and hospitality, I dare not check the noble, God-given impulses of their natures to place the man above all law. Yes, I must ever teach them that man alone is divine; his words and works are fallible; his institutions, however venerable with age and authority, his constitutions, laws and interpretations of Holy Writ, may all prove false. That alone is sacred that can fully meet the wants of the immortal soul—that can stand the test of time and eternity....

Eloquently and earnestly as noble men have denounced slavery on this platform, they have been able to take only an objective view. They can describe the general features of that infernal system—the horrors of the African slave trade, the agonizing sufferings of the middle-passage, the auction-block, the slave-pen and coffle, the diabolism of the internal traffic, the cruel severing of family ties, the hopeless degradation of woman; all that is outward they can see; but a privileged class can never conceive the feelings of those who are born to contempt, to inferiority, to degradation. Herein is woman more fully identified with the slave than man can possibly be, for she can take the subjective view. She early learns the misfortune of being born an heir to the crown of thorns, to martyrdom, to womanhood. For while the man is born to do whatever he can, for the woman and the negro there is no such privilege. There is a Procrustean bedstead ever ready for them, body and soul, and all mankind stand on the alert to restrain their impulses, check their aspirations, fetter their limbs, lest, in their freedom and strength, in their full development, they should take an even platform with proud man himself. To you, white man, the world throws wide her gates; the way is clear to wealth, to fame, to glory, to renown; the high places of independence and honor and trust are yours; all your efforts are praised and encouraged; all your successes are welcomed with loud hurrahs and cheers; but the black man and the woman are born to shame. The badge of degradation is the skin and sex—the "scarlet letter" so sadly worn upon the breast. Children, even, can define the sphere of the black man, and the most ignorant Irishman hiss him into it, while striplings, mere swaddlings of law and divinity, can talk quite glibly of woman's sphere, and pedant priests at the altar discourse most lovingly of her holy mission to cook him meat, and bear him children, and minister to his sickly lust.

In conversation with a reverend gentleman, not long ago, I chanced to speak of the injustice done to woman. Ah! said he, so far from complaining, your heart should go out in thankfulness that you are an American woman, for in no country in the world does woman hold so high a position as here. Why, sir, said I, you must be very ignorant, or very false. Is my political position as high as that of Victoria, Queen of the mightiest nation on the globe? Are not nearly two millions of native-born American women, at this very hour, doomed to the foulest slavery that angels ever wept to witness? Are they not doubly damned as immortal beasts of burden in the field, and sad mothers of a most accursed race? Are not they raised for the express purposes of lust? Are they not chained and driven in the slave-coffle at the crack of the whip of an unfeeling driver? Are they not sold on the auction-block? Are they not exposed naked to the coarse jests and voluptuous eyes of brutal men? Are they not trained up in ignorance of all laws, both human and divine, and denied the right to read the Bible? For them there is no Sabbath, no Jesus, no Heaven, no hope, no holy mission of wife and mother, no privacy of home, nothing sacred to look for, but an eternal sleep in dust and the grave. And these are the daughters and sisters of the first men in the Southern states: think of fathers and brothers selling their own flesh on the auction-block, exposing beautiful women of refinement and education in a New Orleans market, and selling them, body and soul, to the highest bidder! And this is the condition of woman in republican, Christian America, and you dare not look me in the face, and tell me that, for blessings such as these, my heart should go out in thankfulness! No, proud priest, you may cover your soul in holy robes, and hide your manhood in a pulpit, and, like the Pharisee of old, turn your face away from the sufferings of your race; but I am a Christian—a follower of Jesus—and "whatever is done unto one of the *least* of these my sisters is done also unto me." Though, in the person of the poor trembling slave mother, you have bound me with heavy burthens most grievous to bear, though you have done all you could to quench the spark of immortality, which, from the throne of God, brought me into being ... yet can I still speak to him I have asked the everlasting hills, that in their upward yearnings seem to touch the heavens if I, an immortal being, though clothed in womanhood, was made for the vile purposes to which proud Southern man has doomed me, and in solemn chorus they all chanted, NO! I have turned my eyes within, I have asked this bleeding heart, so full of love to God and man, so generous and self-sacrificing, ever longing for the pure, the holy, the divine, if this graceful form, this soft and tender flesh was made to crawl and shiver in the cold, foul embrace of Southern tyrants; and in stifled sobs, it answered, NO! Think you, oh Christian priests, meekly I will take your insults, taunts and sneers? To you my gratitude is due for all the *peculiar blessings* of slavery, for you have had the morals of this nation in your keeping. Behold the depths into which you have plunged me—the bottomless pit of human misery! But perchance your head grows dizzy to look down so far, and your heart faint to see what torture I can bear! It is enough. But I rejoice that it has been given to woman to drink the very dregs of human wretchedness and woe. For now, by an eternal law of matter and of mind, when the reaction comes, upward and upward, and still upward, she shall rise. Behold how far above your priestly robes, your bloody altars, your foul incense, your steepled synagogues she shall stand secure on holy mounts, mid clouds of dazzling radiance, to which, in your gross vision, you shall not dare even to lift your eyes! (Applause.)

Part Two

1863–1878

Introduction

The issue which dominated reform politics after the Civil War was Black suffrage. The abolition of slavery left southern Black people in an unsettled position, neither slave nor free. They were extremely vulnerable to attacks by their former masters—"legal" attacks like the postwar Black codes, and violent, illegal ones, like the terrorism of the Ku Klux Klan. Friends of the freedmen contended that the very meaning of emancipation would be eroded if they did not have the political power to protect themselves against the re-establishment of virtual slavery in another form. Former abolitionists, fresh from the victory of emancipation, joined with their allies in the Republican party, known as "Radicals," to make the cause of Black suffrage their foremost postwar goal.

The emergence of Black suffrage as the central issue in Reconstruction politics very much influenced the struggle for woman suffrage. That the debate on the ex-slaves' legal status focused on the franchise helped to destroy whatever doubts remained that suffrage was the key to the legal position of women as well. Women like Mary Livermore and Julia Ward Howe, who supported women's rights in the 1850s but had been hesitant about asking for the vote, became active proponents of woman suffrage soon after the war. Indeed, almost without anyone noticing the change, "women's rights" was replaced by "woman suffrage" as the designation of the movement for equality for women.

Stanton and Anthony began their efforts to bring women into the political debates created by the fate of slavery even as the Civil War continued to rage. In May 1863 they joined with other veteran female abolitionists—Lucy Stone, the Grimké sisters, Ernestine Rose and later Harriet Jacob—to create a women's "Loyal League." Their organization was patterned after men's Loyal Leagues established to counter Democratic Party proposals to end the war while leaving southern slavery untouched. The Women's Loyal League had another purpose, in Stanton's words, to understand "what is women's legitimate work" during the nation's crisis (Document 9). Over its two-year existence, the organization collected over one hundred thousand petitions calling for the constitutional abolition of slavery, making it the first mass movement organized on behalf of an amendment to the U.S. Constitution.

Prior to Reconstruction, the demand for woman suffrage was addressed to the state legislatures. Now it began to move to the U.S. Congress, where postwar debates on Black suffrage were taking place. Suffragists were part of a whole generation of reformers who lost their prewar suspicion of the federal government for its role in harboring slavery in their postwar admiration for the power of a constitutional amendment to abolish slavery. They now believed that the federal government could become a major force for increasing democratization and radical social reform. Indeed, a strong national state seemed the best protection for individual rights and universal equality.[1] In 1865, Anthony and Stanton petitioned Congress for woman suffrage for the first time.

Universal Suffrage

In cooperation with Lucy Stone, Lucretia Mott and others, Stanton and Anthony reorganized the women's rights movement in 1866 to bring it more into conjunction with the drive for Black suffrage. They formed the American Equal Rights Association (AERA), the object of which was to combine the demands for Black and woman suffrage into a single campaign for universal citizenship suffrage. The AERA's basic task was to convince former abolitionists and Radical Republicans to advocate woman suffrage along with Black suffrage as the basis of Reconstruction (see Document 10). "Has not the time come to bury the Black man and the woman in the citizen?"[2] Stanton proclaimed at the founding convention.

AERA worked both at the state and federal level. Its most important and hard fought battle for voters' support was conducted in 1867 in Kansas, site of a mini-war in the 1850s over national slavery policy. There AERA campaigned for separate Black and woman suffrage state constitutional amendments, but was overcome by local politicians who set the two measures against each other (see Document 10). The resulting defeats weakened AERA's unity around universal suffrage.

These lingering conflicts flared up over the framing of the Fourteenth and Fifteenth amendments to the U.S. Constitution. The Fourteenth Amendment was designed to offer minimal protection for the male freedmen's political rights by requiring that, as a condition for readmission, the former Confederate states enfranchise their male ex-slaves or have their congressional delegations cut proportionately.

The first section of the amendment defined, for the first time, the rights and privileges of national citizens and did so in an expansive way, reaching out to include "all persons born or naturalized in the United States." This later became the basis for a revival of the universal suffrage framework for women's enfranchisement (see Document 13).

Initially however it was the second section of the Fourteenth Amendment which caused woman suffragists distress by specifying "male" citizens as the basis for calculating congressional representation. The AERA petitioned Congress and protested to former abolitionists and Radical Republicans, but the Fourteenth Amendment was ratified as written. Of "that word 'male,'" Stanton predicted "it will take us a century at least to get it out."[3]

It was becoming increasingly clear that the universal suffrage formula for reconciling Black suffrage and woman suffrage no longer had a "fighting chance."[4] Radicals and former abolitionists refused to "trammel" their demand for Black suffrage with women's enfranchisement. Woman suffragists either had to defer their own demand or oppose the enfranchisement of Black men. This conflict culminated at the 1869 AERA meeting over whether to support or oppose a Fifteenth Amendment, which explicitly prohibited disfranchisement "on the grounds of race, color or previous condition" but not "sex" (Documents 11 and 12). With Stanton serving as the meeting's chair, Anthony and Frederick Douglass angrily debated the group's priorities. No compromise between Black and universal suffrage was possible and the AERA did not survive.

Anthony and particularly Stanton reacted to the conflict between Black and woman suffrage in a racist fashion. Political forces beyond their control had made it impossible to unite the demands of women and the freedmen, but Stanton and Anthony took the further step of openly opposing them. Stanton repeatedly argued that those white women who were educated and virtuous were more deserving of the vote than the ex-slaves. At times, Stanton even fueled white women's sexual fears of Black men to rouse them against Black suffrage and for their own enfranchisement (see Document 11). After the amendment's ratification, her outright racism subsided, but the habit of seeing women's grievances from the viewpoint of white women had been established within the suffrage movement.

Reconstruction Era Feminist Militancy

With the collapse of the AERA, woman suffragists split into two camps, a division which was only repaired after two decades (see

Document 19). The American Woman Suffrage Association, under the leadership of Lucy Stone and husband Henry Blackwell, accepted the priority of Black suffrage over woman suffrage, as well as Republicans' promises—never met—that they would eventually work for women's enfranchisement. NWSA, led by Stanton and Anthony, was determined to agitate for woman suffrage without any expectation of Republican party support.

Although the process by which Stanton and Anthony broke with Black suffrage and some woman suffrage supporters was difficult, at times disturbing, and often emotionally grueling, the dominant mood with which they confronted their political prospects in the later years of Reconstruction was hopeful. "Woman must lead the way to her own enfranchisement and work out her own salvation with a hopeful courage and determination that knows no fear nor trembling," they declared.[5]

In 1868, with support from their controversial ally in Kansas, George Francis Train, Stanton and Anthony established a bold radical feminist newspaper, *The Revolution.* "While we would not refuse man an occasional word in our columns," the editors wrote, "yet as masculine ideas have ruled the race for six thousand years, we especially desire that THE REVOLUTION shall be the mouth piece for women."[6] In the pages of *The Revolution*, and then after in NWSA, Stanton investigated the sexual exploitation of women, the nature of marriage, and the need for divorce reform. Anthony's concerns were in the economic realm—the low wages, lack of mobility, and general powerlessness of wage-earning women. Between them, they began to produce a bold and comprehensive portrait of the exploitation of women. Perhaps nothing else so characterized their activity in late Reconstruction as the expansion of the demand for woman suffrage into a radical and multifaceted feminism.

Sex and Work

In many ways, Stanton's contribution to the call for women's sexual and reproductive autonomy was as important as her pioneering role in demanding woman suffrage. She was by no means the first nineteenth-century woman to speak out on these matters, but she approached them with unusual forthrightness and clarity. She had first spoken on questions of marriage and sexuality in the 1850s, in connection with temperance, and then in 1860, with respect to divorce law liberalization.

After the war, Stanton returned enthusiastically to her investigations of women's sexual and marital discontent. In 1868, she and Anthony organized a mass meeting of women to protest the murder sentence of Hester Vaughn, an immigrant domestic servant who had been raped by her employer, become pregnant and given birth, and then was found guilty of infanticide. In 1870, they organized a similar meeting in conjunction with the notorious McFarland-Richardson affair, in which an abusive husband who had fatally shot his ex-wife's lover was found innocent of murder on the grounds of insanity and then awarded custody of their child (see Document 14). A third such meeting was held to protest efforts to bring prostitution under state regulation in New York.[7]

Stanton also spoke to small private groups of women on sex and marriage during this period. Everywhere she lectured on suffrage in the evenings, she held parlor meetings of women only on "marriage and maternity" in the afternoons.[8] Her central point was that women ought to be able to control their own bodies, a right which she called "self sovereignty." She struggled against the stifling euphemisms of the nineteenth century to mount a feminist attack against the laws and customs which institutionalized marital rape by granting men the right of sexual access to their wives whenever they wanted. "The fundamental falsehood on which the decision of the court, the defense of the prisoner, and his bloody deed are based," Stanton declared at the McFarland-Richardson protest meeting, "[is] the husband's right of property in the wife" (see Document 14).

Stanton's ideas on sex and marriage reflected the material conditions of nineteenth-century women's lives, including her own, namely the realities of many children and long years of motherhood. She was critical of the fact that "the subject of marriage is usually discussed as if the interests of the children were everything and those of grown persons nothing," but she focused more on the question of how and when women would conceive than on their sexual pleasure as such.[9] She was one of the pioneers of the nineteenth-century approach to women's sexual rights known as "voluntary motherhood," which asserted a woman's right to refuse her husband intercourse except when she wanted to have a baby. This was an argument which her daughter, Harriot Stanton Blatch, more fully elaborated in the 1890s.[10]

Philosophically, Stanton believed that the principles of individual rights were as applicable to sex and marriage as to government and economics. She argued that the values of equality, independence, and enlightened self-interest could be extended from the public sphere, where they were the standards for civil life, to domestic relations, which were still shaped by feudal standards of hierarchy and obedience to higher authority. "The same law of equality that has revolutionized the state and the church is now knocking at the door of our homes," she declared, "and sooner or later there too it must do its work" (see Document 16).

Stanton especially advocated for the reform of divorce laws and the liberalization of public opinion to make it easier for women to leave loveless marriages and to remarry if they chose. She wanted marriage to become just like any other contractual relation, which either party had equal freedom to dissolve. She thought that marriage as a sacrament, a holy and indissoluble relation, was a fiction designed to reconcile women to something that men had never considered permanent and which they had abandoned at will.

At first, Stanton's insistence that feminists declare for individual freedom and equality in marriage as well as in politics was not well received. The notion that a woman should have what she called her "sovereignty" over her sexuality and reproduction, that her own wishes should take precedence over her husband's or that of any other external authority, seemed even to some feminists to spell the end of marriage and the family. Many even resisted the idea of liberalizing divorce laws for fear that it would be men who would take advantage. According to her daughter, Lucy Stone believed that although Mrs. Stanton was "sincere in her antagonism to inequitable laws as between men and women," she mistakenly sought an "equal license accorded to both, instead of equal restraint imposed on both."[11] There was "a good deal of fear about saying 'sole and absolute right over her own person,'" Anthony wrote in her diary after a debate on marital equality at a NWSA meeting in 1870.[12]

By the mid–1870s, however, sexual topics were frequently discussed among suffragists, and there was much more boldness in speaking about prostitution, marital abuse, and involuntary pregnancy. "To [Stanton's] lectures ... is due a healthier tone of public sentiment on the marriage question," Paulina Wright Davis wrote. "It is slowly beginning to be felt that in that relation, there is a vast amount of legalized prostitution, bearing the semblance of virtue, which is rotten below the fair exterior."[13]

Stanton's arguments in favor of liberalized divorce were closely connected to the question of self-support for women, an issue that particularly concerned Anthony. Stanton connected the rise of divorce in her day to women's growing economic independence, and Anthony pointed to the increasing number of wage-earning women. During the Civil War years, the numbers and militancy of working women had increased significantly, and the labor movement was forced to begin to recognize women. Anthony was affected by and tried to contribute to this development. In 1868 she helped to form a short-lived but pioneering organization of working women that tried to integrate feminist and trade union goals.[14] From then on, she maintained a strong sympathy and identification with wage-earning women. At a time when most middle-class women still disapproved of labor organizations and feared strikes, Anthony's sympathies were quite unusual. Like Stanton's concerns with women's sexual and marital emancipation, Anthony's interest in the woman wage-earner helped to broaden the scope of nineteenth-century feminism.

What Anthony wanted for working women was what working men had been demanding for themselves since the first factories were established—an "honorable independence," a wage adequate to support a respectable life, and work that led to dignity and self-respect (see Document 15). However, much like the impact of extending the demand for the vote from men to women, economic freedom had different implications for women than for men, and women faced different obstacles. In Anthony's hands, the ideology and vision of "free labor" became a feminist idea, as that of political democracy had become. The labor movement was responding to men's experiences of seeing their work degraded and their artisan's independence eroded when it demanded an honorable independence for them. Women, however, came to the factories from dependent positions within their families. They were not trying to recover something they had lost, but were demanding something they had never before enjoyed.

The independence Anthony demanded on their behalf was not only from low wages and sweated labor but from the authority of husbands and fathers over their economically dependent wives and daughters. This was the spirit behind her speech, "Homes of Single Women," in which she described a new generation of self-supporting women who had achieved economic and therefore personal independence (see Document 17). "As young women become educated in the industries of the world, thereby learning the sweetness of independent bread," she wrote with great optimism, "it will be more and more impossible for them to accept the Blackstone marriage limitation that 'husband and wife are one, and that one the husband.'"

The strength of Anthony's approach was that she linked her militant feminism to workingmen's political traditions through her attack on "dependence." In the face of the strong anti-woman sentiment of the labor movement, this was an important and difficult bond to forge. When she first gave her speech in San Francisco in 1871, she told the story of a brutal father who had prohibited his wife and daughter from coming to hear her. "I appeal to you men," she said to her audience, "If you were under such control of another man, would you not consider it an absolute-slavery?" (see Document 15). In a strong union town like San Francisco, such pleas must have appealed to men, who may have harbored similar thoughts against their employers.

Anthony had a deep faith in wage labor, a belief she shared with the great majority of mid-nineteenth-century male labor leaders.[15] She saw the economy as a free enterprise and free labor system, participation in which meant economic independence and personal freedom. She believed that poverty could be eliminated and the excesses of the system controlled to ensure that hard-working individuals would rise to positions of relative security. Yet just as Anthony was developing the feminist case for equality for women in industrial society, this free labor ideology was beginning to show its inadequacies. The spread of factories, the erosion of skilled labor, and the deepening economic pressures on workers were eating away at the possibility for independence, especially among women and other unskilled factory laborers. Anthony did not fully understand these developments.

Stanton and Anthony discovered that grievances about sex and work were more deeply felt among women than disfranchisement. When they talked about the terribly depressed conditions of working women or sexual abuse in and out of marriage, they spoke directly to the experiences which enraged women and forged their aspirations for freedom. "Women respond to my divorce speech as they never did to suffrage," Stanton wrote to Anthony. "Oh! How they flock to me with their sorrows."[16] "I had a splendid audience of ladies in St. Paul to hear my lecture on 'Marriage and Maternity,'" she wrote in *The Revolution*. "That subject seems to touch a deeper chord in the feminine soul than Suffrage, as few perceive how much the social status is affected by political equality."[17]

Yet they continued to insist on the primacy of the demand for woman suffrage and the importance of a political perspective on the emancipation of women. Anthony strenuously argued against the opinion that all working women needed was "bread, not the ballot." "While we would yield to none in the earnestness of our advocacy of these claims [to sexual and economic emancipation]," they wrote in *The Revolution*, "we make a broader demand for the enfranchisement of women, as the only way in which all her just rights can be permanently secured."[18] What seems like a contradiction in their analysis—whether politics, or sex and work, were at the root of women's oppression—dissolves when we examine what they meant by enfranchisement. They were living through a period of intense mass political activity, among the freed people, working people, and in and around the Republican party, and they were demanding the right of women to engage in politics too. They assumed that in fighting for the vote, they were fighting not merely for individual political rights, but for the possibility of collective political action among women. Thus, when Stanton spoke on women's position within marriage, she proceeded from an evocation of the sexual abuses individual women suffered to proposals for changes in marriage and divorce law. And when Anthony insisted that the vote would enable working women to raise their wages and win their strikes, she was only arguing for their right to combine politically to protect their interests as working men were doing.

Victoria Woodhull and Militant Suffragism

The militant spirit of late Reconstruction feminism soon spread to agitation for the vote itself, which had been stalled ever since it had become clear that the Republican party would not include woman suffrage in the Fourteenth or Fifteenth amendments. The most notorious advocate of militant suffragism in the last years of Reconstruction was Victoria Woodhull. She was both the first woman stockbroker and a leader of the American wing of Karl Marx's International Workingmen's Association.

In January 1871, Woodhull appeared at a hearing of a congressional committee with a new and radical approach to woman suffrage. Woodhull's argument was that women were already enfranchised by the Constitution, the Fourteenth and Fifteenth amendments having declared all persons born or naturalized in the United States to be national citizens, and all citizens to be protected by the Constitution in their rights. As women were people, and assuming that suffrage was a right of national citizenship, women must therefore be entitled to vote. Woodhull's argument suggested a much simpler strategy for woman suffrage than getting another constitutional amendment. A congressional act or judicial decision would be sufficient to substantiate the argument and declare women enfranchised.

Woodhull's dramatic appearance before Congress, the first ever by a woman on behalf of woman suffrage, took suffragists by surprise, but by all accounts they found her lucid and charismatic. "She is very charming," Anthony wrote in her diary, "utterly forgetful of difference of sex in her approach to *men*."[19] The Woodhull constitutional argument was immediately adopted by the NWSA, and Woodhull was welcomed into suffragism's inner circle.

Two years before Woodhull made her arguments before a congressional committee, Missouri suffragist Virginia Minor had made a very similar case to the NWSA. Minor was eventually the one who carried these constitutional issues to the U.S. Supreme Court. However, Woodhull was able to draw much greater attention to the argument that women were already enfranchised, and to encourage the NWSA to look in new strategic directions.

This constitutional argument, designated the New Departure, provided an activist approach to woman suffrage, asserting as it did that women did not need to ask for the vote but rather must find a way to take what was already theirs. Hopes for social change were so strong during Reconstruction and yet women's demands were so repeatedly and universally ignored, that many women had grown angry and impatient to have their political rights recognized. As Anthony explained before a group of congressmen, "Such tantalization endured by yourselves or any class of men would have wrought rebellion.... It is only the friendly relations that exist between the sexes that has prevented any such result from this injustice to women."[20] Privately Stanton said the same thing with less care and more passion. "[It] is enough to rouse one's blood to the white heat of rebellion against every 'white male' on the Continent. When I think of all the wrongs that have been heaped upon womankind, I am ashamed that I am not forever in a condition of chronic wrath, stark mad, skin and bone, my eyes a fountain of tears, my lips overflowing with curses, and my hand raised against every man and brother!"[21]

After it adopted the New Departure, the NWSA advised women to go to the polls, submit their ballots, and dare election officials to refuse them. "Women should attempt to qualify and attempt to vote...," NWSA leaders announced. "This action not only serves the purpose of agitation of the question of suffrage, but it puts upon men, our brothers, the onus of refusing votes of their fellow citizens, and compels them to show just cause for such proceedings."[22] The notion that women should take the lead in their own enfranchisement corresponded to the mood of many women, and in the elections of 1871 and 1872, hundreds of women all over the country tried to vote.[23]

In 1872 Anthony assembled a group of women, including her sisters and many of her friends, to try to vote in her home town of Rochester, New York. She had expected their votes to be refused and intended to sue the election officials on constitutional grounds. Instead, the poll officials accepted her vote. The experience of voting literally thrilled her and she rushed home to write Stanton about it. Two weeks later, a United States marshal came to her house and, citing a law passed to keep former Confederates from voting in federal elections, declared her under arrest for "illegal voting." Anthony's arrest on federal charges represented an extraordinary response on the part of the Grant government and suggests that suffragists' constitutional arguments were perceived in high places as a threat.

Placed in the spotlight by government persecution for her suffrage convictions, Anthony was at her best. After her arrest, she spoke in every district of the county in which she was to be tried, on the legal and constitutional issues involved in her case (see Document 13). The speech she gave focused primarily on questions of constitutional law but within this framework she was able to communicate some sense of the political struggle of which her arrest was a part. On one side, she saw those who defended the principle, established by the Thirteenth, Fourteenth and Fifteenth amendments, that the only legitimate object of a strong federal government was the extension and protection of equal rights to all citizens. On the other side was what she called the "political exigency of the Republican party," the efforts of its leaders to limit the democratic implications of the postwar amendments and to turn back the popular movements set loose by emancipation and Black suffrage. The U.S. District Attorney ruled that since Anthony's speaking would prejudice the jury, the venue of her trial must be changed to another county. In less than three weeks, she covered the second county so well that when the trial began the judge would not permit the jury to decide the case but directed it to find a verdict of guilty.[24] Because of a technicality firmly insisted on by the presiding judge, Anthony was unable to appeal the decision and was immensely frustrated.

Victoria Woodhull's own interest in the election of 1872 was less in the act of voting than in organizing a radical political alternative to the Republican party. Stanton became enthusiastic at the prospect. She believed that woman suffrage should be raised, not as an isolated issue, but as the center of a comprehensive program for the revolution of women's position and radical change throughout the society. She supported Woodhull's indictment of the Republican party for "building up a commercial feudalism dangerous to the liberty of the people," but added her own feminist note. "As the women of the country are to take part for the first time in political action," it declared, "we propose that the initiative steps in the Convention shall be taken by them."[25]

The Woodhull convention exposed a conflict slowly emerging between Stanton and Anthony.[26] The AERA experience had affected both of them profoundly, but in different ways. Stanton responded to the separation from Black suffrage by searching for another political framework in which to situate woman suffrage and feminism. Anthony on the other hand had concluded that woman suffrage should never again be united in coalition with other reforms. She began to fear that the connection with Woodhull would undercut the independence and dilute the feminism of suffragists. She distrusted Woodhull because suffrage was not her only goal and because many of her political comrades were men. "Mrs. Woodhull ... persistently means to run our craft into her port and none other," Anthony insisted.[27] She tried but was unable to stall off Woodhull's convention. "I never was so *hurt with folly of Stanton,*" Anthony wrote in her diary the day after the fiasco.

After the convention, Woodhull began to be the object of severe harassment. In response, Woodhull revealed a scandal that had been gossip in reform circles for some time: the adulterous affair of America's most famous liberal minister, Henry Ward Beecher, with Elizabeth Tilton, wife of the prominent reform editor Theodore Tilton.[28] Woodhull's goal in publicizing the scandal was to challenge the moral canon of "Respectability" which reformers like Beecher supported and advanced, and sexual radicals and utopian socialists like Woodhull and her friends repudiated.[29] The scandal intensified the suffrage fractionalization as Beecher was president of the American Woman Suffrage Association, while Tilton was friend and political adviser to Stanton and Anthony. Woodhull had publicized her claims in her newspaper, *Woodhull and Claflin's Weekly,* which led to a federal warrant being issued under the Comstock law, a new federal statute intended to increase the government's power to police public morality. On election eve 1872, Woodhull became the first person ever arrested under this statute. Woodhull thought that Republican authorities were threatened by her political radicalism. "I fear they intend ... to establish a precedent for the suppression of recalcitrant journals," she wrote to Anthony, and suggested a connection between her own indictment and Anthony's arrest and trial.[30]

In a surprising turn of events, once Woodhull had left the political scene Stanton and Anthony ended up supporting the Republican party in the election of 1872. Anxious to bring rebel reformers back into the fold, it offered suffragists a small political plank—Stanton called it a "splinter"—promising "respectful consideration" for women's demands for "additional rights."[31]

The Republican victory in 1872 solidified the party's political control, and, in a very basic way, began the end of this era of reform. After the election, the party showed no further interest in courting woman suffragists, and the "splinter" was never redeemed. In 1875, the U.S. Supreme Court ruled against the suffragists' New Departure argument. In the case of (Virginia) *Minor* vs. *Happersett,* the Court asserted that suffrage was not a right of national citizenship, but a privilege which each state granted to those whom it deemed fit. The decision was not an attack on militant woman suffragism solely, but a reaction against the expansion of political rights signaled by the Fifteenth Amendment as well. Anthony recognized this, predicting that the defeat of the New Departure would be followed "by no ends to the petty freaks and cunning devices that will be resorted to, to exclude one and another class of citizens from the right of suffrage."[32]

Reconstruction suffragism had one last burst of militancy. On July 4, 1876, Anthony led a small group of suffragists to take the stage at the Centennial Celebration in Philadelphia—to which they had not been invited—to present a Declaration of the Rights of Women, written by Stanton and Matilda Joslyn Gage. Even as the nation was celebrating its survival and promising future, they declared, "We cannot forget ... that while all men of every race, and clime, and condition, have been invested with the full rights of citizenship, ... all women still suffer the degradation of disfranchisement."[33]

Radical Reconstruction was definitively ended in 1877, when all federal troops were withdrawn from the South, depriving the freedmen of the last vestiges of federal protection. In the same year, the U.S. Army was used for the first time against workers in an industrial labor dispute, a fitting indication that the political issues of the future would not be racial equality but class conflict. The Republican Party was increasingly committed to protecting big business and established power rather than individual rights and political democracy. In 1886, the Supreme Court ruled that corporations could be considered "persons" before the law, and enjoyed the privileges of the Fourteenth Amendment and other Constitutional protections.

The formation of a new, important women's organization in 1873, the Woman's Christian Temperance Union (WCTU), signaled a new era in suffrage and feminism. Under the leadership of Frances Willard, the WCTU, originally formed to combat men's alcohol abuse, became a leading supporter of woman suffrage under the banner of "home protection."[34] It did not emphasize liberal individual rights arguments but stressed instead the special needs and distinctive nature of women. Stanton's individualism, her opposition to organized religion and other coercive systems and her support for liberalized divorce laws were not acceptable to this new sort of women's movement. This, and Anthony's quite different response to the growth and transformation of the late nineteenth-century women's movement, are the subjects of the next section.

Document 9

The Woman's National Loyal League, May 1863

The Woman's National Loyal League (WNLL) was organized in the spring of 1863 primarily by Stanton and Anthony. It was a bold initiative that sought to bring together women's ambitions to play a political role in the Union cause with determination to pressure the Lincoln administration to pursue a truly comprehensive abolitionist campaign. The northern "treason" to which Stanton referred was the growing threat of the Democratic party to secure a rapid end to the war, leaving untouched the fate of southern slavery. Stanton contrasted the threat mounted by these "Copperhead" Democrats to the American republic, to its historic commitment to liberty. She used her unmatched literary and rhetorical powers to conjure the terrors of slavery, especially the sale of human beings and the wresting of children from their mothers. This was clearly a speech directed at women but one with an explicitly political intention.

Nonetheless, a more specific plan for the WNLL lay ahead. The president had issued his Emancipation Proclamation two months earlier but it only declared the emancipation of slaves not under his government's control. At the WNLL's first meeting it committed itself to a mass petitioning effort on behalf of legislation (later a constitutional amendment) on behalf of universal emancipation. Petitioning was the way that women, lacking the franchise, had long addressed their government, but the project of winning woman suffrage lay close to the surface of the organization. One of the WNLL's first resolutions referred to the injustice of denying political representation to "all citizens of African descent and all women."

Document 9. The Women's National Loyal League

Proceedings of the Meeting of the Loyal Women of the Republic Held in New York, May 14, 1863, New York: Phair & C., Printers, 1863, pp. i–iv, 3–4.

Address of Elizabeth Cady Stanton to the Women of the Republic, March 30, 1863

When our leading journals, orators, and brave men from the battlefield, complain that Northern women feel no enthusiasm in the war, the time has come for us to pledge ourselves loyal to freedom and our country.

Thus far, there has been no united expression from the women of the North as to the policy of the war. Here and there one has spoken and written nobly. Many have vied with each other in acts of generosity and self-sacrifice for the sick and wounded in camp and hospital. But we have, as yet, no means of judging where the majority of Northern women stand.

If it be true that at this hour the women of the South are more devoted to their cause than we are to ours, the fact lies here. They see and feel the horrors of the war; the foe is at their firesides; while we, in peace and plenty, live as heretofore. There is an inspiration, too, in a definite purpose, be it good or bad. The women of the South know what their sons are fighting for. The women of the North do not. They appreciate the blessings of slavery; we not the blessings of liberty. We have never yet realized the glory of those institutions in whose defence it is the privilege of our sons to bleed and die. They are aristocrats, with a lower class, servile and obsequious, intrenched in feudal homes. We are aristocrats under protest, who must go abroad to indulge our tastes, and enjoy in foreign despotisms the customs which the genius of a Republic condemns.

But, from the beginning of the Government, there have been women among us who, with the mother of the immortal John Quincy Adams, have lamented the inconsistencies of our theory and practice, and demanded for all the people the exercise of those rights that belong to every citizen of a republic.

The women of a nation mold its morals, religion, and politics. The Northern treason, now threatening to betray us to our foes, is hatched at our own firesides, where traitor snobs, returned from Europe and the South, out of time and tune with independence and equality, infuse into their sons the love of caste and class, of fame and family, of wealth and ease, and baptize it all in the name of Republicanism and Christianity.

Let every woman understand that this war involves the same principles that have convulsed the nations of the earth from Pharaoh to Lincoln—liberty or slavery—democracy or aristocracy—equality or caste—and choose, this day, whether our republican institutions shall be placed on an enduring basis, and an eternal peace secured to our children, or whether we shall leap back through generations of light and experience, and meekly bow again to chains and slavery.

Shall Northern freemen yet stand silent lookers-on when through Topeka, St. Paul, Chicago, Cleveland, Boston, and New York, men and women, little boys and girls, chained in gangs, shall march to their own sad music, beneath a tyrant's lash? On our sacred soil shall we behold the auction-block—babies sold by the pound, and beautiful women for the vilest purposes of lust; where parents and children, husbands and wives, brothers and sisters, shall be torn from each other, and sent East and West, North and South? Shall our free presses and free schools, our palace homes, colleges, churches, and stately capitols all be leveled to the dust? Our household gods be desecrated, and our proud lips, ever taught to sing paeans to liberty, made to swear allegiance to the god of slavery? Such degradation shall yet be ours, if we gird not up our giant freemen now to crush this rebellion, and root out forever the hateful principle of caste and class. Men who, in the light of the nineteenth century, believed that God made one race all booted and spurred, and another to be ridden; who would build up a government with slavery for its corner-stone, can not live on the same continent with a pure democracy.

To counsel grim-visaged war seems hard to come from women's lips; but better far that the bones of our sires and sons whiten every Southern plain, that we do their rough work at home, than that liberty, struck dumb in the capital of our Republic, should plead no more for man. Every woman who appreciates the grand problem of national life must say war, pestilence, famine, anything but an ignoble peace. ....

And here we are, the grandest nation on the globe. By right no privileged caste or class. Education free to all. The humblest digger in the ditch has all the civil, social, and religious rights with the highest in the land. The poorest woman at the wash-tub may be the mother of a future President. Here all are heirs-apparent to the throne. The genius of our institutions bids every man to rise, and use all the powers that God has given him.

It cannot be, that for blessings such as these, the women of the North do not stand ready for any sacrifice.

A sister of Kossuth, with him an exile to this country, in conversation one day, called my attention to an iron bracelet, the only ornament she wore. "In the darkest days of Hungary," said she, "our noble women threw their wealth and jewels into the public treasury, and clasping iron bands around their wrists, pledged themselves that these should be the only jewels they would wear till Hungary was free." If darker hours than these should come to us, the women of the North will count no sacrifice too great. What are wealth and jewels, home and ease, sires and sons, to the birthright of freedom, secured to us by the heroes of the Revolution? Shall a priceless heritage like this be wrested now from us by Southern tyrants, and Northern women look on unmoved, or basely bid our freemen sue for peace? No! No! The vacant places at our firesides, the void in every heart says No!! Such sacrifices must not be in vain!! The cloud that hangs o'er all our Northern homes is gilded with the hope that through these present sufferings the nation shall be redeemed.

Call for a Meeting of the Loyal Women of the Nation

In this crisis of our country's destiny, it is the duty of every citizen to consider the peculiar blessings of a republican form of government, and decide what sacrifices of wealth and life are demanded for its defense and preservation.

The policy of the war, our whole future life, depends on a clearly-defined idea of the end proposed, and the immense advantages to be secured to ourselves and all mankind, by its accomplishment.

No mere party or sectional cry, no technicalities of Constitution or military law, no mottoes of craft or policy are big enough to touch the great heart of a nation in the midst of revolution. A grand idea, such as freedom or justice, is needful to kindle and sustain the fires of a high enthusiasm.

At this hour, the best word and work of every man and woman are imperatively demanded. To man, by common consent, is assigned the forum, camp, and field. What is woman's legitimate work, and how she may best accomplish it, is worthy our earnest counsel one with another.

We have heard many complaints of the lack of enthusiasm among Northern women; but, when a mother lays her son on the altar of her country, she asks an object equal to the sacrifice. In nursing the sick and wounded, knitting socks, scraping lint, and making jellies, the bravest and best may weary if the thoughts mount not in faith to something beyond and above it all. Work is worship only when a noble purpose fills the soul.

Woman is equally interested and responsible with man in the final settlement of this problem of self-government; therefore let none stand idle spectators now. When every hour is big with destiny, and each delay but complicates our difficulties, it is high time for the daughters of the revolution, in solemn council, to unseal the last will and testament of the Fathers—lay hold of their birthright of freedom, and keep it a sacred trust for all coming generations.

To this end we ask the Loyal Women of the Nation to meet in the church of the Puritans (Dr. Cheever's), New York, on Thursday, the 14th of May next.

Let the women of every State be largely represented both in person and by letter. ....

On behalf of the Woman's Central Committee,
Elizabeth Cady Stanton

Document 10

Stanton, "Speech at Lawrence, Kansas," 1867

Stanton and Anthony were among the half-dozen representatives of the American Equal Rights Association who went into Kansas in 1867 to campaign on behalf of two amendments to the state constitution—one on Black suffrage and the other on woman suffrage. Anthony stayed in Lawrence to give some much-needed organization to the teams of speakers canvassing the state, while Stanton went from town to town—the first extended political touring of her life—speaking on behalf of both referenda. The core of her speech was "the gospel of equality, that good time coming when all men and women, black and white, shall stand equal before the law," which she proclaimed with almost religious fervor. At the same time, Stanton recognized the limitation of natural rights as a reform ideology, that it was "selfish" and "slow," and she began to anticipate the kind of feminism which would emphasize women's special moral sensibility and eventually supersede natural rights arguments. Although local Republicans supported Black suffrage and opposed woman suffrage, neither referendum passed.

Elizabeth Cady Stanton Papers, Library of Congress

The battles of the past, says Mazzini, have been fought for rights and on that selfish principle progress ever has been and must be slow. But when the most fortunate shall have to think of the multitude below them sunk in ignorance, poverty and vice, then will a divine power inspire those who would move the world. And this hour has come, and we see this divine power in this nineteenth century moving over the whole surface of society.... Look in our country how many men of wealth and family, high in the shining walks of life, have with a holy zeal given up luxury, ease, name and fame, and devoted themselves to the lifting up of the fallen and forsaken, to be mouths for the dumb, eyes for the blind and ears for those who could not hear.

And all these men have been led to the consideration of these moral questions by the women at their side. John Stuart Mill tells us in one of his works that his own wife first drew his attention to the importance of the enfranchisement of women and opened to him a new world of thought. Now while such men as Herbert Spencer, Garth Wilhelm Mazzini, Gasperin La Bridge are all writing up Republican institutions [and] the dignity of man, and all alike pointing to woman as the new element of the higher civilization, shall not woman in this republic clothe herself with new dignity and strength and take that lofty position that by right belongs to the mother of the race?

There is an old German proverb that says, "that every woman comes into the world with a stone on her head" and that is as true now as the day it was said. Your creeds, your codes, your conventionalisms have indeed fallen with crushing power on woman in all eyes. But nature is mightier than laws and customs, and in spite of the stone on her head, already behold woman close on your heels in the whole world of thought, art, science, literature and government.... [These] are so many protests against the degraded political condition of woman and so many proofs that she is destined everywhere to stand the peer of man.... What have all these old creeds and codes and customs amounted to? Have not true women stood up under all these crushing weights and walked forward as easily as did Sampson with the gates of the city? And now if you will only take the stone off her head she will be able to scale diviner heights—commune with the Gods and draw man up to her level, to lift him from the dust into which he is too prone to grovel. As in the degradation of woman, man has tasted sorrow, shame and death, so in her exaltation shall his moral and spiritual power gather new strength and hold the animal beneath his feet....

Since meeting you citizens of Lawrence three weeks ago, I have addressed audiences of the people of Kansas every day. I have looked in their earnest faces, felt the deep beatings of the great popular heart, in your cities and villages, in your pastures and on the highways. I have carefully noted the utterances of your pulpit and press and your leading men and women, and I feel assured that the people of Kansas are all right on both [Black and woman suffrage]. Here and there I have found some good republicans sitting anxious and distracted on the fence not knowing exactly which way to jump, and I have told these gentlemen if they would only take out their opera glasses and survey the opposing armies they would not be long in coming to a decision.

On the one side behold the ... forces divided into three distinct regiments with their banners waving in the breeze bearing the inscriptions anti-sabbath, anti–Temperance, anti-suffrage, waging a hopeless war against all those principles most sacred in republican institutions, against the liberal opinions of the nineteenth century. On the other side behold the heroic women of Kansas who for the last twenty years have stood sentinels at your doors in the darkest hour of danger.... Behold the leaders of your press and pulpit, your ablest editors and clergy, statesmen and the soul of old John Brown all teaching, preaching, and singing the gospel of equality, that good time coming when all men and women, Black and white, shall stand equal before the law, that triumphant day in November when your cannon shall startle the civilized world with the news that a genuine republic is at last realized in the very heart of this western continent....

Your Legislature in submitting to you last winter the two propositions to strike the words white, male from your Constitution struck the key note of reconstruction. In the consideration of these propositions you are not legitimately called on to make any special arguments for women and negroes as if they were anomalous beings outside all law. The same arguments made by you for the last century for the extension of the suffrage to all white men, the same made by John Bright in England, the same made in Russia for the newly emancipated serfs are all the arguments we have to make for women and negroes. You are simply called to consider the rights of citizens of the republic. When you make negroes and women amenable to law, compel them to defend and support the state by war and taxation, you acknowledge their citizenship and are in justice bound to grant their rights parallel with their duties. We therefore appeal to the people of this state to vote thoughtfully and religiously on these two propositions.

The political wire-pullers of both parties endorse but one proposition.... Yet the fact that the most influential men of both parties as individuals favor both propositions is the most encouraging sign of the times showing that universal suffrage, which is the ultimatum of these propositions, is already accepted by the people and must form the basis of the liberal party of the not distant future. Just as freedom in the war was a "military necessity" and negro suffrage in peace a "political necessity," so in reconstruction is universal suffrage the moral necessity of the hour. As in our late political struggle the loyal element of the negro was needed to restore the balance of power, so in our legislation on all moral questions is the feminine element needed to secure success.

As the physical and moral necessities of the being ensure individual growth and development, so the commercial and political necessities of a nation compel each onward step of progress. When the great plough share of war roused this nation to the sin of slavery, few were ready for its death blow, so intertwined and incorporated was it with every branch of our government. But when defeat after defeat followed our armies and statesmanship stood at a deadlock, when dark clouds hung over the republic, in the depths of despair we learned the immutable law of justice. Then the nation rose in its majesty, emancipation was proclaimed, and man rejoiced in new found liberty. Then above the din of arms, the cannons' roar, the wail of mothers for their first born, rose soft and clear that divine symphony uttered on the cross and echoed round the world, "All men are created equal."

Then nerved for grand deeds, the people were ready for any onward step, but wily politicians who always have an eye to their personal aggrandizement, procrastinated ... , and instead of grand measures based on principle, they have been professing partial measures based on policy, and the result is the problem of reconstruction is no nearer its solution to day than it was at the end of the war; and now the moral necessities of this hour press upon us and it is with these necessities we urge the people of this state to grapple to day. Your education, your judgment on the great principles of government are vital at this hour, as to you in Providence is given the opportunity to make the first experiment of a genuine republic. Remember the civilized world awaits your action to see if the principles of our Fathers are possible in government.

A witty Frenchman pictured the first conservative as one going about at the dawn of creation exclaiming with eyes and hands uplifted, "My God, my God, conserve the chaos." To the philosopher, who seeing the discord and disorder of our political, religious and social world, proposes some measures for establishing order and harmony, the objections of those about everything new, to every onward step, are not more absurd than the anxiety of this first conservative, lest in disturbing chaos something worse should come of it.... The philosophers and far seeing statesmen of our day, viewing the moral chaos that surrounds, say, "Let there be light. Let us have free discussion of everything that concerns the deepest, broadest and holiest interests of mankind." But the narrow conservative, in view of all the selfishness and corruption of our politics, the bigotry and dissensions in our church, the jealousies and "heart burnings of" our homes, in view of all this, lifts up his hands and eyes with horror at every step....

Document 11

Stanton, "Manhood Suffrage," *The Revolution*, December 24, 1868

Enraged that former Republican and abolitionist male allies had deserted universal suffrage in amending the Constitution, Stanton turned all her considerable rhetorical powers against what she called "manhood suffrage." She published her argument in *The Revolution*, the new weekly she and Anthony had secured with funding by George Francis Train, the questionable ally they had gained in the 1867 Kansas campaign.

In her attacks on the pending Fifteenth Amendment, Stanton took a radical feminist position, indicting "the male element" for its violence and selfishness. Following the new "social science" of the time, she was beginning to move from a belief in the common humanity of men and women to an emphasis on the difference of the sexes.

She went further, expressing this argument in a disturbingly racist and nativist manner. She attacked immigrant and African American men, who she referred to contemptuously as "Patrick and Sambo and Hans and Yung Tung," contrasting them to "our Anglo Saxon men ... the best orders of manhood."

"Manhood Suffrage" is the article in the *Revolution* to which Frederick Douglass referred in his angry comments six months later at the May 1869 AERA meeting (see Document 12).

Excerpted in Gordon, et al. in *Selected Papers of Stanton and Anthony*, v. 2, pp. 194–96.

We object to the proposed amendment of the Constitution of the United States securing "Manhood Suffrage," for several reasons.[35]

1st, Because a government based on the caste and class principle, in the inequality of its citizens, cannot stand.... Of all kinds of aristocracy, that of sex is the most odious and unnatural, invading as it does our homes, desecrating our family altars, dividing those whom God has joined together, exalting the son above the mother who bore him, and subjugating everywhere moral power to brute force. A government like this would not be worth all the blood and treasure this nation so freely poured out in the last Revolution.

2d. We object to a "man's government" because the male element, already too much in the ascendant, is a destructive force; stern, selfish, aggrandizing; loving war, violence, conquest, acquisition; breeding discord, disorder, disease and death.

See what a record of blood and cruelty the pages of history reveal, through what slavery, slaughter and sacrifice, through what inquisitions and imprisonments, pains and persecutions, black codes and gloomy creeds, the soul of humanity has struggled for the centuries, while mercy has veiled her face, and all hearts have been dead alike to love and hope. Thus has the masculine element overpowered the feminine, crushing out all.

... What can we gain as a nation by "Manhood Suffrage," having too much of the man power in government already? ... To ignore the influence of woman in the legislation of the country, and blindly insist upon the recognition of every type of brutalized, degraded manhood, must prove suicidal to any government on the footstool, hence we protest against the extension of suffrage to another man, until enough women are first admitted to the polls to outweigh the dangerous excess of the male element already there.

So long as there is a disfranchised class in this country, and that class the women of the nation, "a man's government" is worse than "a white man's government," because in proportion as you multiply the tyrants, you make the condition of the subjects more hopeless and degraded. John Stuart Mill, in his work on Liberty, shows clearly that the condition of one disfranchised man in a nation is worse than that of a whole nation under one man, because in the latter case, if the one man is despotic, the nation can easily throw him off, but what can the one man do with a nation of tyrants over him.

Just so if woman find it hard to bear the oppressive laws of a few Saxon Fathers, of the best orders of manhood, what may she not be called to endure when all the lower orders, native and foreigners, Dutch, Irish, Chinese and African, legislate for her and her daughters?

This "Manhood Suffrage" is an appalling question, and it would be well for thinking women, who seem to consider it so magnanimous to hold their claims in abeyance until all men are crowned with citizenship, to remember, that the lowest classes of men are invariably the most hostile to the elevation of woman as they have known her only in ignorance and degradation and ever regarded her in light of a slave.

3rd. We object to the proposed amendment because it is an open, deliberate insult to the women of the nation. Now, when the attention of the whole world is turned to this question, when the women of France, England, Switzerland and even Russia are holding their conventions, and demanding enfranchisement, and their rulers everywhere giving them a respectful hearing, shall the women of "the freest government on the earth" be set aside in this way without notice or apology! While poets and philosophers, statesmen and men of science are all alike pointing to woman as the new hope for the redemption of the world, shall American Senators, claiming to be liberal, laugh at and suppress our petitions, and boast in our conventions of their courage to vote Woman's Suffrage down in the Capitol,[36] and thus degrade their own mothers, wives and daughters, in their political status, below unwashed and unlettered ditch-diggers, boot-blacks, hostlers, butchers and barbers.

Think of Patrick and Sambo and Hans and Yung Tung who do not know the difference between a Monarchy and a Republic, who never read the Declaration of Independence or Webster's spelling book, making laws for Lydia Maria Child, Lucretia Mott, or Fanny Kemble. Think of jurors drawing from these ranks to try young girls for the crime of infanticide.

Would these gentlemen who, on all sides, are telling us "to wait until the negro is safe" be willing to stand aside and trust all *their* interests in hands like these?

The educated women of this nation feel as much interest in republican institutions, in the preservation of the country and the god of mankind as Senators Wilson and Sumner, and are as sure that the highest good of all alike demands the elevation and enfranchisement of woman, as the Honorable gentlemen are that everything is safe in *their* hands.

4th We object to the proposed amendment because the history of American Statesmanship, for the last century, does not inspire us with confidence in man's capacity to govern a nation with equity, and we came to this conclusion from what wise men themselves say of our rulers, and of the condition in which the country is today.

The most casual observer can see the same causes at work here that have already impoverished the masses in the old world. With legislation practically in the hands of a few Capitalists who have the power to buy up all the votes they need for any measure, who regulate the banks, national debt, taxes, rates of interest, who own the railroads and dispose of the public lands, holding every position of profit and honor, the rich will perpetuate their own power and protect their own interests, while the many will be reduced to squalid poverty and utter dependence. All kinds of property are rapidly accumulating in the hands of the few, and already we see bloated wealth and gaunt poverty stalking side by side in New York as well as in London.

We do not regard politics as a succession of tricks; and government as a skillful piece of legerdemain, but as a fixed science, controlled by laws as immutable as those that govern the planetary world.... We simply rest in the knowledge that those who are managing the ship of state do not understand their business; but as the people are fast learning the ropes, and how to use the chart and compass, they will man the ship themselves in good time, and do their own reckoning. Then shall we have laws that will secure equal rights to all.

5th, We object to "manhood suffrage" because it is opposed to all recent revelations of science. All late writers on the science of government recognize that in woman the great humanizing element of the new era we are entering, in which moral power is to govern brute force. It is only through the infusion of the mother soul into our legislation, that life will be held sacred, the interests of the many guarded, capital reconciled to labor, the criminal treated like a moral patient, education made practical and attractive, and labor profitable and honorable to all.... We ask this influence be now directed towards the humanizing of our legislation.

6th, We object to the proposed amendment because it raises a more deadly opposition to the negro that any he has yet encountered. It creates an antagonism between him and woman, the very element most needed to be propitiated in his behalf. Suffrage for all could easily be carried in every state; but when you lift the negro above the woman, and make him her Ruler, Legislator, Judge and Juror, if even northern women rebel, what can you expect from the south? The "negro element" at the south, of which we hear so much, may make voters for the republican party, but it does not give us what we need in government. The people are concerned about deeper principles than such as serve the shifting purposes of politicians.

We hear much high-sounding talk about "saving the country," but what is country to the women who have no voice in the laws that govern them? What is a country to the suffering masses; the denizens of garrets and cellars, and mud cabins on the lonely prairies, so long as the fruits of their industry is stolen by their rulers.

Document 12

Anthony and Frederick Douglass Debate the Fifteenth Amendment at the May 1869 American Equal Rights Association

Douglass, Anthony and Stanton collaborated in the early years of the Civil War, as he supported the campaign that they conducted to petition Congress for the full abolition of slavery. Then, after the Thirteenth Amendment had been ratified and Congress moved on to address the citizenship and political rights of the ex-slaves, these decades of cooperation came to a dramatic halt. The Fifteenth Amendment, which extended suffrage protections to African American men, became the major issue of contention between them.

Anthony and even more Stanton reacted to the conflict between Black and woman suffrage in a racist fashion, despite their abolitionist backgrounds. Political forces beyond their control had made it impossible to unite the demands of women and the freedmen, but Stanton and Anthony took the further step of opposing the two. On the one hand, they argued that educated and virtuous white women were more deserving of the vote than the ex-slaves. On the other hand, they attempted to build feminism on the basis of white women's racism. At times, Stanton even fueled white women's sexual fears of Black men to rouse them against Black suffrage and for their own enfranchisement. (See "Manhood Suffrage," Document 11.)

The controversy peaked during the May 1869 meeting of the American Equal Rights Association. Founded to fight for universal suffrage, it now was mired in a debate over the Fifteenth Amendment, which only enfranchised Black men. Many Black suffrage activists and some woman suffragists came forward to condemn Stanton's words in her "Manhood Suffrage" article in the *Revolution*. But it was Frederick Douglass's response, and his rage at the brutal violence being suffered at just that moment in Memphis and elsewhere by recently emancipated slaves which went down in history.

History of Woman Suffrage, eds. Elizabeth Cady Stanton, Susan B. Anthony and Matilda Joslyn Gage (Susan B. Anthony, Rochester, 1887), v. 2, p. 382.

There is no name greater than that of Elizabeth Cady Stanton in the matter of women's rights and equal rights, but my sentiments are tinged a little against *The Revolution*. There was in the address to which I allude the employment of certain names, such as 'Sambo,' and the gardener and the bootblack, and the daughters of Jefferson and Washington, and all the rest that I can not coincide with. I have asked what difference there is between the daughters of Jefferson and Washington and other daughters. (laughter) I must say that I do not see how any one can pretend that there is the same urgency in giving the ballot to woman as to the negro. With us the matter is a question of life and death, at least, in fifteen States of the Union. When women, because they are women, are hunted down through the cities of New York and New Orleans; when they are dragged from their houses and hung upon lamp-posts, when their children are torn from their arms, and their brains dashed out upon the pavement; when they are the objects of insult and outrage at every turn when they are in danger of having their homes burnt down over their heads, when their children are not allowed to enter schools, then they will have an urgency to obtain the ballot equal to our own. (Great applause)

Stanton, chairing the meeting, did not respond, but Anthony did. Accused by her colleagues Wendell Phillips and Theodore Tilton and with resentment unusual to her, she explained that what "ailed Susan. It was the downright insolence of these two men ... among the most advanced & glorious men of the nation, that they should dare to look me in the face & speak of the great earnest purpose of mine as an 'intellectual theory' but not to be practiced, or for us to hope to attain." In defending her position, she linked suffrage with women's economic independence:

"Remarks by Anthony to the American Equal Rights Association in New York, May 12, 1869," excerpted in Gordon, et al., *Selected Papers of Stanton and Anthony*, vol. 2, pp. 238–41.

The question of precedence has no place on an equal right platform. The only reason why it ever found a place here was that there were some who insisted that woman must stand back & wait until another class should be enfranchised. In answer to that, my friend Mrs. Stanton & others of us have said, If you will not give the whole loaf of justice to the entire people, if you are determined to give it, piece by piece, then give it first to women, to the most intelligent & capable portion of the women at least, because in the present state of government it is intelligence, it is morality which is needed. We have never brought the question upon the platform, whether women should be enfranchised first or last....

If Mr. Douglass had noticed who clapped him when he said "black men first, & white women afterwards," he would have seen that they were all men. The women did not clap him. The fact is that the men cannot understand us women. They think of us as some of the slaveholders used to think of their slaves, all love & compassion, with no malice in their hearts, but they thought "The negro is a poor lovable creature, kind, docile, unable to take care of himself, & dependent on our compassion to keep them," & so they consented to do it for the good of the slaves. Men feel the same today. ...

When Mr. Douglass tells us today that the case of the black man is so perilous, I tell him that wronged & outraged as they are by this hateful & mean prejudice against color, he would not today exchange his sex & color, wronged as he is, with Elizabeth Cady Stanton.

MR. DOUGLASS. Will you allow me a question?

MISS ANTHONY. Yes; anything for a fight today.

MR. DOUGLASS. I want to inquire whether granting to woman the right of suffrage will change anything in respect to the nature of our sexes.

MISS ANTHONY. It will change the nature of one thing very much, that is the pecuniary position of woman. It will place her in a position in which she can earn her own bread, so that she can go out into the world an equal competitor in the struggle for life.... Men say that all women are to be married & supported by men, & the laws and customs & public sentiment are all based on that assumption. Wherever there is a woman loose—for we have sometimes women loose, as they had negroes loose, in slavery, & we have fugitive wives as they had fugitive slaves—...she is an interloper, & she is paid but one half or one third the price the men receive. When a woman therefore is thrown upon her own resources, she has to choose one of two things, marriage or prostitution.... What we demand is that woman shall have the ballot, for she will never get her other rights until she demands them with the ballot in her hand. It is not a question of precedent between women & black men. Neither has a claim to precedence upon an Equal Rights platform. But the business of this association is to demand for every man black or white, & for every woman, black or white, that they shall be this instant enfranchised & admitted into the body politic with equal rights & privileges.

Document 13

Anthony, "Constitutional Argument," 1873

In November 1872, Anthony was arrested in Rochester for "illegal voting." For the next few months, in preparation for her trial on these charges, she traveled around Monroe County, New York, lecturing on the principles by which she claimed the right to vote. Anthony's argument, the outlines of which had been established in 1869 by Virginia Minor and in 1871 by Victoria Woodhull, was based on the Fourteenth Amendment. It argued that suffrage was a right of national citizenship and that all persons, including women, were citizens; thus women's disfranchisement was merely a matter of "precedent and prejudice" and not constitutional law. Inalienable individual rights, irrespective of sex, was Anthony's major theme. However, she made other arguments as well: that the disfranchisement of women created "an aristocracy of sex" (a phrase used by Stanton) which was more pernicious than other inequalities, and that marriage constituted "involuntary servitude" for women, which was forbidden by the Thirteenth Amendment.

Ida. H. Harper, *Life and Work of Susan B. Anthony*, vol. 2, pp. 977–92.

Friends and Fellow-Citizens:—I stand before you under indictment for the alleged crime of having voted at the last presidential election, without having a lawful right to vote. It shall be my work this evening to prove to you that in thus doing, I not only committed no crime, but instead simply exercised my citizen's right, guaranteed to me and all United States citizens by the National Constitution beyond the power of any State to deny.

Our democratic-republican government is based on the idea of the natural right of every individual member thereof to a voice and a vote in making and executing the laws. We assert the province of government to be to secure the people in the enjoyment of their inalienable rights.

We throw to the winds the old dogma that government can give rights. No one denies that before governments were organized each individual possessed the right to protect his own life, liberty and property. When 100 to 1,000,000 people enter into a free government, they do not barter away their natural rights; they simply pledge themselves to protect each other in the enjoyment of them through prescribed judicial and legislative tribunals. They agree to abandon the methods of brute force in the adjustment of their differences and adopt those of civilization.... The Declaration of Independence, the United States Constitution, the constitutions of the several States and the organic laws of the Territories, all alike propose to *protect* the people in the exercise of their God-given rights. Not one of them pretends to bestow rights.

All men are created equal, and endowed by their Creator with certain inalienable rights. Among these are life, liberty and the pursuit of happiness. To secure these, governments are instituted among men, deriving their just powers from the consent of the governed.

Here is no shadow of government authority over rights, or exclusion of any class from their full and equal enjoyment. Here is pronounced the right of all men, and "consequently," as the Quaker preacher said, "of all women," to a voice in the government. And here, in this first paragraph of the Declaration, is the assertion of the natural right of all to the ballot; for how can "the consent of the governed" be given, if the right to vote be denied? ... The women, dissatisfied as they are with this form of government, that enforces taxation without representation. that compels them to obey laws to which they never have given their consent—that imprisons and hangs them without a trial by a jury of their peers—that robs them, in marriage, of the custody of their own persons, wages and children—are this half of the people who are left wholly at the mercy of the other half, in direct violation of the spirit and letter of the declarations of the framers of this government, every one of which was based on the immutable principle of equal rights to all. By these declarations, kings, popes, priests, aristocrats, all were alike dethroned and placed on a common level, politically, with the lowliest born subject or serf. By them, too, men, as such, were deprived of their divine right to rule and placed on a political level with women. By the practice of these declarations all class and caste distinctions would be abolished, and slave, serf, plebeian, wife, woman, all alike rise from their subject position to the broader platform of equality.

The preamble of the Federal Constitution says:

> We, the people of the United States, in order to form a more perfect union, establish justice, insure domestic tranquility, provide for the common defence, promote the general welfare and secure the blessings of liberty to ourselves and our posterity, do ordain and establish this Constitution for the United States of America.

It was we, the people, not we, the white male citizens, nor we, the male citizens; but we, the whole people, who formed this Union. We formed it not to give the blessings of liberty but to secure them; not to the half of ourselves and the half of our posterity, but to the whole people—women as well as men. It is downright mockery to talk to women of their enjoyment of the blessings of liberty while they are denied the only means of securing them provided by this democratic-republican government—the ballot.

The early journals of Congress show that, when the committee reported to that body the original articles of confederation, the very first one which became the subject of discussion was that respecting equality of suffrage....

James Madison said: Under every view of the subject, it seems indispensable that the mass of the citizens should not be without a voice in making the laws which they are to obey, and in choosing the magistrates who are to administer them.... Let it be remembered, finally, that it has ever been the pride and the boast of America that the rights for which she contended were the rights of human nature.

These assertions by the framers of the United States Constitution of the equal and natural right of all the people to a voice in the government, have been affirmed and reaffirmed by the leading statesmen of the nation throughout the entire history of our government. Thaddeus Stevens, of Pennsylvania, said in 1866: "I have made up my mind that the elective franchise is one of the inalienable rights meant to be secured by the Declaration of Independence." ....

Charles Sumner, in his brave protests against the Fourteenth and Fifteenth Amendments, insisted that so soon as by the Thirteenth Amendment the slaves became free men, the original powers of the United States Constitution guaranteed to them equal rights—the right to vote and to be voted for....

The preamble of the constitution of the State of New York declares the same purpose. It says: "We, the people of the State of New York, grateful to Almighty God for our freedom, in order to secure its blessings, do establish this constitution." Here is not the slightest intimation either of receiving freedom from the United States Constitution, or of the State's conferring the blessings of liberty upon the people; and the same is true of every other State constitution. Each and all declare rights God-given, and that to secure the people in the enjoyment of their inalienable rights is their one and only object in ordaining and establishing government. All of the State constitutions are equally emphatic in their recognition of the ballot as the means of securing the people in the enjoyment of these rights....

I submit that in view of the explicit assertions of the equal right of the whole people, both in the preamble and previous article of the constitution, this omission of the adjective "female" should not be construed into a denial; but instead should be considered as of no effect.... No barriers whatever stand today between women and the exercise of their right to vote save those of precedent and prejudice, which refuse to expunge the word "male" from the constitution.

... When, in 1871, I asked that senator to declare the power of the United States Constitution to protect women in their right to vote—as he had done for black men—he handed me a copy of all his speeches during that reconstruction period, and said:

> Put "sex" where I have "race" or "color," and you have here the best and strongest argument I can make for woman. There is not a doubt but women have the constitutional right to vote, and I will never vote for a Sixteenth Amendment to guarantee it to them. I voted for both the Fourteenth and Fifteenth under protest; would never have done it but for the pressing emergency of that hour; would have insisted that the power of the original Constitution to protect all citizens in the equal enjoyment of their rights should have been vindicated through the courts. But the newly-made freedmen had neither the intelligence, wealth nor time to await that slow process. Women do possess all these in an eminent degree, and I insist that they shall appeal to the courts, and through them establish the powers of our American magna charta to protect every citizen of the republic.

But, friends, when in accordance with Senator Sumner's counsel I went to the ballot-box, last November, and exercised my citizen's right to vote, the courts did not wait for me to appeal to them—they appealed to me, and indicted me on the charge of having voted illegally. Putting sex where he did color, Senator Sumner would have said:

Qualifications can be in their nature permanent or insurmountable. Sex cannot be a qualification any more than size, race, color or previous condition of servitude. A permanent or insurmountable qualification is equivalent to a deprivation of the suffrage. In other words, it is the tyranny of taxation without representation, against which our Revolutionary mothers, as well as fathers, rebelled.

For any State to make sex a qualification, which must ever result in the disfranchisement of one entire half of the people, is to pass a bill of attainder, an ex post facto law, and is therefore a violation of the supreme law of the land. By it the blessings of liberty are forever withheld from women and their female posterity. For them, this government has no just powers derived from the consent of the governed. For them this government is not a democracy; it is not a republic. It is the most odious aristocracy ever established on the face of the globe. An oligarchy of wealth, where the rich govern the poor; an oligarchy of learning, where the educated govern the ignorant; or even an oligarchy of race, where the Saxon rules the African, might be endured; but this oligarchy of sex which makes father, brothers, husband, sons, the oligarchs over the mother and sisters, the wife and daughters of every household; which ordains all men sovereigns, all women subjects—carries discord and rebellion into every home of the nation. This most odious aristocracy exists, too, in the face of Section 4, Article IV, which says: "The United States shall guarantee to every State in the Union a republican form of government." ...

It is urged that the use of the masculine pronouns *he*, *his* and *him* in all the constitutions and laws, is proof that only men were meant to be included in their provisions. If you insist on this version of the letter of the law, we shall insist that you be consistent and accept the other horn of the dilemma, which would compel you to exempt women from taxation for the support of the government and from penalties for the violation of laws. There is no *she* or *her* or *hers* in the tax laws, and this is equally true of all the criminal laws.

Take for example the civil rights law which I am charged with having violated; not only are all the pronouns in it masculine, but everybody knows that it was intended expressly to hinder the rebel men from voting. It reads, "If any person shall knowingly vote without *his* having a lawful right." I insist if government officials may thus manipulate the pronouns to tax, fine, imprison and hang women, it is their duty to thus change them in order to protect us in our right to vote....

Though the words persons, people, inhabitants, electors, citizens, are all used indiscriminately in the national and State constitutions, there was always a conflict of opinion, prior to the war, as to whether they were synonymous terms, but whatever room there was for doubt, under the old regime, the adoption of the Fourteenth Amendment settled that question forever in its first sentence:

All persons born or naturalized in the United States, and subject to the jurisdiction thereof, are citizens of the United States, and of the State wherein they reside.

The second settles the equal status of all citizens:

No State shall make or enforce any law which shall abridge the privileges or immunities of citizens of the United States; nor shall any State deprive any person of life, liberty or property without due process of law, or deny to any person within its jurisdiction the equal protection of the laws.

The only question left to be settled now is: Are women persons? I scarcely believe any of our opponents will have the hardihood to say they are not. Being persons, then, women are citizens, and no State has a right to make any new law, or to enforce any old law, which shall abridge their privileges or immunities. Hence, every discrimination against women in the constitutions and laws of the several States is today null and void, precisely as is every one against negroes,

Is the right to vote one of the privileges or immunities of citizens? I think the disfranchised ex-rebels and ex-State prisoners all will agree that it is not only one of them, but the one without which all the others are nothing. Seek first the kingdom of the ballot and all things else shall be added, is the political injunction....

I am proud to mention the names of the two United States judges who have given opinions honorable to our republican idea, and honorable to themselves—Judge Howe, of Wyoming Territory, and Judge Underwood, of Virginia. The former gave it as his opinion a year ago, when the legislature seemed likely to revoke the law enfranchising the women of that Territory that, in case they succeeded, the women would still possess the right to vote under the Fourteenth Amendment. The latter, in noticing the recent decision of Judge Cartter, of the Supreme Court of the District of Columbia, denying to women the right to vote under the Fourteenth and Fifteenth Amendments, says:

If the people of the United States, by amendment of their Constitution, could expunge, without any explanatory or assisting legislation, an adjective of five letters from all State and local constitutions, and thereby raise millions of our most ignorant fellow-citizens to all of the rights and privileges of electors, why should not the same people, by the same amendment, expunge an adjective of four letters from the same State and local constitutions, and thereby raise other millions of more educated and better informed citizens to equal rights and privileges, without explanatory or assisting legislation?

If the Fourteenth Amendment does not secure to all citizens the right to vote, for what purpose was that grand old charter of the fathers lumbered with its unwieldy proportions? The Republican party, and Judges Howard and Bingham, who drafted the document, pretended it was to do something for black men; and if that something were not to secure them in their right to vote and hold office, what could it have been? For by the Thirteenth Amendment black men had become people, and hence were entitled to all the privileges and immunities of the government, precisely as were the women of the country and foreign men not naturalized. According to Associate-Justice Washington, they already had:

> Protection of the government, the enjoyment of life and liberty, with the right to acquire and possess property of every kind, and to pursue and obtain happiness and safety, subject to such restraints as the government may justly prescribe for the general welfare of the whole; the right of a citizen of one state to pass through or to reside in any other State for the purpose of trade, agriculture, professional pursuit, or otherwise; to claim the benefit of the writ of habeas corpus, to institute and maintain actions of any kind in the courts of the State; to take, hold, and dispose of property, either real or personal, and an exemption from higher taxes or impositions than are paid by the other citizens of the State.

Thus, you see, those newly-freed men were in possession of every possible right, privilege and immunity of the government, except that of suffrage, and hence needed no constitutional amendment for any other purpose. What right in this country has the Irishman the day after he receives his naturalization papers that he did not possess the day before, save the right to vote and hold office? The Chinamen now crowding our Pacific coast are in precisely the same position. What privilege or immunity has California or Oregon the right to deny them, save that of the ballot? Clearly, then, if the Fourteenth Amendment was not to secure to black men their right to vote it did nothing for them, since they possessed everything else before. But if it was intended to prohibit the States from denying or abridging their right to vote, then it did the same for all persons, white women included, born or naturalized in the United States; for the amendment does not say that all male persons of African descent, but that all persons are citizens.

The second section is simply a threat to punish the States by reducing their representation on the floor of Congress, should they disfranchise any of their male citizens, and can not be construed into a sanction to disfranchise female citizens, nor does it in any wise weaken or invalidate the universal guarantee of the first section.

However much the doctors of the law may disagree as to whether people and citizens, in the original Constitution, were one and the same, or whether the privileges and immunities in the Fourteenth Amendment include the right of suffrage, the question of the citizen's right to vote is forever settled by the Fifteenth Amendment. "The right of citizens of the United States to vote shall not be denied or abridged by the United States, or by any State, on account of race, color or previous condition of servitude." How can the State deny or abridge the right of the citizen, if the citizen does not possess it? There is no escape from the conclusion that to vote is the citizen's right, and the specifications of race, color or previous condition of servitude can in no way impair the force of that emphatic assertion that the citizen's right to vote shall not be denied or abridged....

If once we establish the false principle that United States citizenship does not carry with it the right to vote in every State in this Union, there is no end to the petty tricks and cunning devices which will be attempted to exclude one and another class of citizens from the right of suffrage. It will not always be the men combining to disfranchise all women; native born men combining to abridge the rights of all naturalized citizens, as in Rhode Island. It will not always be the rich and educated who may combine to cut off the poor and ignorant; but we may live to see the hard-working, uncultivated day laborers, foreign and native born, learning the power of the ballot and their vast majority of numbers, combine and amend State constitutions so as to disfranchise the Vanderbilts, the Stewarts, the Conklings and the Fentons. It is a poor rule that won't work more ways than one. Establish this precedent, admit the State's right to deny suffrage, and there is no limit to the confusion, discord and disruption that may await us. There is and can be but one safe principle of government—equal rights to all. Discrimination against any class on account of color, race, nativity, sex, property, culture, can but embitter and disaffect that class, and thereby endanger the safety of the whole people. Clearly, then, the national government not only must define the rights of citizens, but must stretch out its powerful hand and protect them in every State in this Union.

If, however, you will insist that the Fifteenth Amendment's emphatic interdiction against robbing United States citizens of their suffrage "on account of race, color or previous condition of servitude," is a recognition of the right of either the United States or any State to deprive them of the ballot for any or all other reasons, I will prove to you that the class of citizens for whom I now plead are, by all the principles of our government and many of the laws of the States, included under the term "previous conditions of servitude."

Consider first married women and their legal status. What is servitude? "The condition of a slave." What is a slave? "A person who is robbed of the proceeds of his labor; a person who is subject to the will of another." By the laws of Georgia, South Carolina and all the States of the South, the negro had no right to the custody and control of his person. He belonged to his master. If he were disobedient, the master had the right to use correction. If the negro did not like the correction and ran away, the master had the right to use coercion to bring him back. By the laws of almost every State in this Union today, North as well as South, the married woman has no right to the custody and control of her person. The wife belongs to the husband; and if she refuse obedience he may use moderate correction, and if she do not like his moderate correction and leave his "bed and board," the husband may use moderate coercion to bring her back. The little word "moderate," you see, is the saving clause for the wife, and would doubtless be overstepped should her offended husband administer his correction with the "cat-o'-ninetails," or accomplish his coercion with blood-hounds.

Again the slave had no right to the earnings of his hands, they belonged to his master; no right to the custody of his children, they belonged to his master; no right to sue or be sued, or to testify in the courts. If he committed a crime, it was the master who must sue or be sued. In many of the States there has been special legislation, giving married women the right to property inherited or received by bequest, or earned by the pursuit of any avocation outside the home; also giving them the right to sue and be sued in matters pertaining to such separate property; but not a single State of this Union has ever secured the wife in the enjoyment of her right to equal ownership of the joint earnings of the marriage copartnership. And since, in the nature of things, the vast majority of married women never earn a dollar by work outside their families, or inherit a dollar from their fathers, it follows that from the day of their marriage to the day of the death of their husbands not one of them ever has a dollar, except it shall please her husband to let her have it....

A good farmer's wife in Illinois, who had all the rights she wanted, had made for herself a full set of false teeth. The dentist pronounced them an admirable fit, and the wife declared it gave her fits to wear them. The dentist sued the husband for his bill; his counsel brought the wife as witness; the judge ruled her off the stand, saying, "A married woman can not be a witness in matters of joint interest between herself and her husband." Think of it, ye good wives, the false teeth in your mouths are a joint interest with your husbands, about which you are legally incompetent to speak! If a married woman is injured by accident, in nearly all of the States it is her husband who must sue, and it is to him that the damages will be awarded.... Isn't such a position humiliating enough to be called "servitude?" That husband sued and obtained damages for the loss of the services of his wife, precisely as he would have done had it been his ox, cow or horse; and exactly as the master, under the old regime, would have recovered for the services of his slave.

I submit the question, if the deprivation by law of the ownership of one's own person, wages, property, children, the denial of the right as an individual to sue and be sued and testify in the courts, is not a condition of servitude most bitter and absolute, even though under the sacred name of marriage? ... The facts also prove that, by all the great fundamental principles of our free government, not only married women but the entire womanhood of the nation are in a "condition of servitude" as surely as were our Revolutionary fathers when they rebelled against King George. Women are taxed without representation, governed without their consent, tried, convicted and punished without a jury of their peers. Is all this tyranny any less humiliating and degrading to women under our democratic-republican government today than it was to men under their aristocratic, monarchial government one hundred years ago? ....

Is anything further needed to prove woman's condition of servitude sufficient to entitle her to the guarantees of the Fifteenth Amendment? Is there a man who will not agree with me that to talk of freedom without the ballot is mockery to the women of this republic, precisely as New England's orator, Wendell Phillips, at the close of the late war declared it to be to the newly emancipated black man? I admit that, prior to the rebellion, by common consent, the right to enslave, as well as to disfranchise both native and foreign born persons, was conceded to the States. But the one grand principle settled by the war and the reconstruction legislation, is the supremacy of the national government to protect the citizens of the United States in their right to freedom and the elective franchise, against any and every interference on the part of the several States; and again and again have the American people asserted the triumph of this principle by their overwhelming majorities for Lincoln and Grant.

The one issue of the last two presidential elections was whether the Fourteenth and Fifteenth Amendments should be considered the irrevocable will of the people; and the decision was that they should be, and that it is not only the right, but the duty of the national government to protect all United States citizens in the full enjoyment and free exercise of their privileges and immunities against the attempt of any State to deny or abridge. In this conclusion Republicans and Democrats alike agree. Senator Frelinghuysen said: "The heresy of State rights has been completely buried in these amendments, and as amended, the Constitution confers not only National but State citizenship upon all persons born or naturalized within our limits." ....

Benjamin F. Butler, in a recent letter to me, said: "I do not believe anybody in Congress doubts that the Constitution authorizes the right of women to vote, precisely as it authorizes trial by jury and many other like rights guaranteed to citizens." It is upon this just interpretation of the United States Constitution that our National Woman Suffrage Association, which celebrates the twenty-fifth anniversary of the woman's rights movement next May in New York City, has based all its arguments and action since the passage of these amendments. We no longer petition legislature or Congress to give us the right to vote, but appeal to women everywhere to exercise their too long neglected "citizen's right." We appeal to the inspectors of election to receive the votes of all United States citizens, as it is their duty to do. We appeal to United States commissioners and marshals to arrest, as is their duty, the inspectors who reject the votes of United States citizens, and leave alone those who perform their duties and accept these votes. We ask the juries to return verdicts of "not guilty" in the cases of law-abiding United States citizens who cast their votes, and inspectors of election who receive and count them.

We ask the judges to render unprejudiced opinions of the law, and wherever there is room for doubt to give the benefit to the side of liberty and equal rights for women, remembering that, as Sumner says, "The true rule of interpretation under our National Constitution, especially since its amendments, is that anything *for* human rights is constitutional, everything *against* human rights unconstitutional." It is on this line that we propose to fight our battle for the ballot—peaceably but nevertheless persistently—until we achieve complete triumph and all United States citizens, men and women alike, are recognized as equals in the government.

Document 14

Stanton, "Speech to the McFarland-Richardson Protest Meeting," May 1870

In 1869, Daniel McFarland was tried for the shooting of Albert Richardson, who was planning to marry McFarland's former wife, Abby Sage McFarland. A New York court found McFarland innocent by reason of insanity, and then granted him custody of the couple's twelve-year-old son. Richardson eventually died of his wounds, after a dramatic deathbed marriage to Mrs. McFarland. Stanton and Anthony organized a mass meeting of women in New York to protest the decision and took the opportunity to make a feminist analysis of contemporary marriage. Stanton believed that "the husband's right of property in his wife," his legal right to coerce her sexually, was the central problem in marriage. This analysis was considerably more acceptable to the majority of women than the solution Stanton proposed: liberalized divorce.

Elizabeth Cady Stanton Papers, Library of Congress

The deep interest of the entire nation in the McFarland trial for the last month is due not to any particular regard for the man, or abhorrence of the legal punishment for such crime, but to the fact that the trial indirectly involves the solution of the momentous questions of marriage and divorce, questions that underlie our whole social, religious and political life.

As I have never seen the faces of either Daniel McFarland or Abby Sage Richardson I have no personal prejudices or preferences to bias my judgment in this matter. I will not admit now what I confess I did feel in earlier life, a prejudice always in favor of my own sex, for with sons and daughters alike growing up my mother's heart has taught me to balance all questions with equal reference to both sexes. Nevertheless I have felt during the past month, as Boston abolitionists felt when Anthony Burns, the black man, the runaway slave, was condemned in their courts and marched through their streets, the sad helpless victim of a false American public sentiment, who having just tasted the sweets of liberty, was remanded by Massachusetts law to southern slavery.

As I sat alone late one night and read the simple truthful story of Abby Sage Richardson, the fugitive wife, I tried to weigh the mountain of sorrow that had rolled over that poor woman's soul, through these long years of hopeless agony, through the fiery ordeal of a public trial in our courts, the merciless hounding of the press, the garbled testimony and unjust decision setting a madman free to keep that poor broken hearted woman in fear for her life as long as he lives. As I pondered all these things in the midnight hour, and recalled the hideous insults through the person of Abby S. Richardson on the entire womanhood of the nation, I resolved that as I had devoted my life heretofore to the enfranchisement of woman, my future work should be to teach woman her duties to herself in the home.

In declaring [McFarland] "not guilty" our courts virtually declare that Mrs. Richardson, although she has married another man whom she loves, is still the wife of the criminal whom for years she has loathed. McFarland should have been pronounced "guilty" ... but as neither women or slaves can testify against their supposed masters, the effort was made to prove her divorce illegal and thus by declaring her still the wife of the defendant they excluded her evidence in the case. But in the face of this decision there is sympathy enough to day with Mrs. Richardson to redeem the mighty multitude of wretched wives she represents from the most degraded type of slavery the world knows, that of wife to a bloated drunkard or diseased libertine! But sympathy as a civil agent is vague and powerless until caught and chained in logical ... propositions, and coined into state law.

Let us then waste no energy or time in tears over the sufferings of any one woman or in anger at the cruel injustice of the courts and the press in this particular case, but learn what we can do to day towards an entire revision of the laws of New York on marriage and divorce; from the pleas, testimony, verdict and decision in the late trial, see what all women need for their protection and where to strike the right blow.

To begin then with the ugly present fact and go back step by step to the foundation question, how comes it that a man who by our courts has been declared so insane that he may commit murder without being morally responsible to the state is let loose on society to repeat such depradations while the helpless victim of his hate and lust still lives and is liable at any moment to be sacrificed by his hand? ... Although by the revised statutes of this state the mother is the equal guardian of her child to day, yet in the late trial we have the anomaly of a criminal acquitted on the ground of insanity, walking out of court with his child by his hand, its natural protector, while the mother of sound mind capable of supporting it, is denied the custody of its person. We have too a murderer with the crown and sceptre of American citizenship fully restored to him, though adjudged incapable of bearing the moral responsibilities of a man....

The fundamental falsehood on which the opinions of the press, the decision of the court, the defense of the prisoner and his bloody deed are based [is] "the Husband's right of property in the wife." The old common law of the barbarous ages reflected in our statutes controls the public sentiment of the nineteenth century, though the real character and position of woman has entirely changed, from the thoughtless ignorant toy or drudge of the past, to the enlightened, dignified moral being of to day. These one sided degrading statutes on marriage and divorce which at this hour our sons are reading in their law schools are daily educating them into low, gross ideas of their mothers, sisters, future wives; preparing them to contemplate with stolid indifference the hideous features of our present marriage institution; and to call that sacred that every pure woman feels to be unnatural and infamous.

Another demand that the women of this state should make of our Legislature is an entire revision of our laws on marriage and divorce making man and woman in all respects equal partners, and when by the cold indifferent or base conduct of either party the contract is practically annulled the state should declare it so....

[I hope] that my appeals may strengthen the bond of sisterhood between us, showing that while some have suffered, some prayed and others talked, we have all alike been working to the same end. While the stricken heart broken woman, to day a target for the nation's scorn, has through struggle and humiliation given us a glowing but painful picture of the depths of degradation a wife may be called to endure and thus touched a new chord of sympathy of the multitudes she represents, others of us not crushed or perplexed with domestic discord and tyranny, or cumbered with thoughts of our daily bread, have been solving the problem of woman's wrongs and revising for her benefit the statute laws of many of the states.

Though we are still in deep waters be not discouraged. The evils we are suffering today must needs be in this transition period of woman from slavery to freedom. Not one tear has been shed, one prayer uttered, one word spoken in vain. Even these protracted divorce trials, with all their sickening details, are giving women new courage to sunder the ties they loathe and abhor and slowly but surely educating public sentiment to a true marriage relation. Thus far we have had the man idea of marriage. Now the time has come for woman to give the world the other side of this question.

When the calendars of our courts are crowded with divorce cases and such details of private life are continually paraded before the public in all our daily journals, when there are 1600 divorce cases in Massachusetts in one year and as many in proportion in Illinois, Indiana and Connecticut, we who have sons and daughters growing up to be happy or miserable in their relations have a deep interest in finding the cause of all this social confusion and suggesting some remedy.... I bring you today what I think; it is but the opinion of one woman and as in every soul there is bound up some truth and some error, may you have the wisdom to accept the truth I utter and throw the error like chaff to the winds.

I think divorce at the will of the parties is not only right but that it is a sin against nature, the family, the state for a man or woman to live together in the marriage relation in continual antagonism, indifference, disgust. A physical union should in all cases be the outgrowth of a spiritual and intellectual sympathy and anything short of this is lust and not love.... Charlotte Bronte said ... "Though the only road to freedom be through the gates of death those gates must be passed for freedom is indispensable." John Stuart Mill says, "The subject of marriage is usually discussed as if the interests of children were everything, those of grown persons nothing." ... Mrs. McFarland's married life from her own confession of loathing and abhorrence was nothing more or less than legalized prostitution, as Richter said, "no better than a work of adultery," and every pure woman must feel that when she sundered that tie she took the first step towards virtue and self respect....

As every divorce helps to educate other wives similarly situated into higher ideas of purity, virtue, self respect, the more publicity given to the success of each case, the better. As the highest happiness of society and the individual always lie in the same direction, a woman with a ready pen and tongue should not fear criticism, opposition, or persecution or accept personal freedom except through a fair debate of the higher position she intends to take, that thus she may help to mould public sentiment in harmony with her opinions and enable society to sanction her action. Another good effect of trying to take the world with us is that we shall move with greater deliberation. This is my idea of true freedom, not to coquette with unjust law, thrust it to one side or try to get beyond its reach, but to fight it where it is, and fight it to the death. Let the women of this state rise in mass and say they will no longer tolerate statutes that hold pure virtuous women indissolubly bound to gross vicious men, whom they loathe and abhor, and we shall soon have a complete codification of our laws.

The Protestant world has never regarded marriage as an indissoluble tie. Therefore it is no great stretch of the civil or religious conscience of our rulers to multiply the causes for divorce with advancing civilization.

Document 15

Anthony, "Suffrage and the Working Woman," 1871

In this speech, different versions of which she delivered from the late 1860s through the 1890s, Anthony demanded that women be granted the twin rewards of American republicanism: equal opportunity to compete for wealth and advancement; and the ballot to protect them against injustice. The experience of recently emancipated and enfranchised Black men seemed to substantiate Anthony's case that the vote and "free labor" could bring honor and respect to previously despised classes. Anthony's relation to the wage-earning women for whom she spoke was ambiguous. On the one hand, she was clearly familiar with and sympathetic to their struggles and knew a good deal about the trade unions they had formed and the strikes they had waged. On the other hand, she understood them from the perspective of a middle-class woman, for whom work meant independence. She did not really understand the miserable and ill-paid work that many of them faced, and could only understand their aversion to wage-labor as "feminine" prejudice.

San Francisco Daily Evening Bulletin, July 23, 1871

I come to night ... as a representative of the working women. I lay down my doctrine that the first step for the alleviation of their oppression is to secure to them pecuniary independence.

Alexander Hamilton said 100 years ago "take my right over my subsistence and you possess absolute power over my moral being." That is applicable to the working women of the present day. Others possess the right over their subsistence. What is the cause of this? I will tell you. It is because of a false theory having been in the minds of the human family for ages that woman is born to be supported by man and to accept such circumstances as he chooses to accord to her. She not like him is not allowed to control her own circumstances. The pride of every man is that he is free to carve out his own destiny. A woman has no such pride.

A little circumstance happened at this hall last night which illustrates this. A mother and daughter came to the ticket office to purchase tickets, when they were confronted by a man who exclaimed, "Didn't I forbid you to come here to-night?" He had a heavy cane in his hand which he flourished over them, and finally drove them away from the hall.

I appeal to you men. If you were under such control of another man would you not consider it an absolute slavery? But you say that man was a brute. Suppose he is a brute, he is no more of a brute than the law permits him to be.

But to go back. Is it true that women are supported by men? If I was to go home with you all to-night, I should find ample proof of falsity. I should find among your homes many who support themselves. Then if I should go into your manufactories.... I should find hundreds and thousands who support themselves by the industry of their own hands. In Boston there are 10,000 women engaged in shoemaking. You say these are extreme cases. So they are, but it is in these large cities that the hardship and wrong is most apparent....

If you will take the stand with me on the main thoroughfares of New York, on the Bowery, at the ferries, you will see troops and troops of women going to their daily work. There are not quite so many as there are men, but the men think it is not disreputable to work. Not so with woman. If she makes an effort to support herself, she always makes an effort to conceal it. The young girl has her satchel as though going to the depot, or has her books as though going to school.

Some years ago we had a Woman's Benevolent Society in New York and appointed a committee to visit all over the city among the poor. The committee visited among others a family of rag pickers.... In one little garret was a mother and five little children. The committee appealed to the mother to allow them to put her in a way to support her children and send them to school. They pleaded with her for some time without avail and finally she straightened herself up and exclaimed, "No indeed, ladies. I'll have you to understand my husband is a gintleman and no gintleman allows his wife to go out to work." [Laughter]

That society is wrong which looks on labor as being any more degrading to woman than to man.

It was no more ridiculous for the rag picker's wife to scout the idea of going to work out than it is for the daughter of a well-to-do farmer to scout the idea of supporting herself....

I am proud of San Francisco that she is an exception to the rule, and that she has raised a woman to the position of Principal of one of the cosmopolitan schools with a full salary of $1,200 a year. But if to-morrow, the same model girl, whom I have just referred to, were to marry a banker and live a life of idleness, with horses, carriages, and house finely furnished, able to take her trip to Europe and with all the advantages wealth could purchase, though her husband were a drunkard, a libertine and a vile and depraved wretch, the woman would never again receive pity. Now we want this rule changed.

The first result of this false theory is this: no woman is even educated to work. Sons are educated while daughters are allowed to grow up mere adornments, and when the hour of necessity comes, then comes cruelty in the extreme. The woman has to skill her hands for labor, and has to compete with men who have been skilled from boyhood; and not only this but when she has attained ability to compete with them and to do just as well in every respect she is placed at work, if at all, on half pay. Society dooms her always to a subordinate position, as an inferior....

Nowhere can woman hold head offices and the reason is this, politicians can't afford to give an office to one who can't pay back in votes. If in New York the women could decide the fate of elections, don't you think they could afford to make women County Clerks or Surrogate Clerks or even Surrogate Judges? Said a Surrogate Judge to me, "Miss Anthony, I was almost converted by your lecture last night. I have one son and one daughter. The son is at college." I asked him, "Is your son possessed of the requisite ability to place him in your position?" "No," he replied; "he will spend his days in a garret daubing paints on a canvass. But my daughter has a splendid legal mind, and understands already much of my duties. What a pity she was not a boy!" Only think, a brain wasted because it happens to be a woman's. For this reason one half the brain in the world remain undeveloped. How will we remedy this? Give woman an equal chance to compete with men, educate her and surround her with the same legal advantages. Every one knows that the great stimulus for activity is to be paid for in having that activity recognized by promotion.

How will the ballot cure the evil? You tell me the ballot is not going to alleviate this. I will tell you how it is going to alleviate it. Never have the disfranchised classes had equal chances with the enfranchised. What is the difference between the working classes of the United States and Europe? Simply that, here the workman has the ballot and there he has not. Here, if he has the brains or energy, his chances are quite equal with the son of the millionaire. That is American Republicanism—the ballot in the hand of every man. [Applause] ... See how it works. Take the St. Crispins for example.... Well these three hundred St. Crispins strike against a reduction of wages, and not only they, but twenty other St. Crispin Societies, and not only they but other workmen. Now, suppose the New York *World* denounced those men, and the Democratic party manifested prejudice, not only those 300 men would vote against the party but all the other societies, the hod carriers, brick layers, the masons, the carpenters and the tailors would vote solidly against the party which opposed them, and that party would go to the wall. No political party can hope for success and oppose the interests of the working class. You can all see that neither of the great parties dared to put a plank in the platform directly opposed. Both wrote a paragraph on finance, but nobody knew what it meant. They did this not because of a desire to do justice to the workingmen, but simply because of the power of the workingmen to do them harm....

Now what do women want? Simply the same ballot. In this city, they, the women hat and cap makers, 2,000 of them, made a strike and held out three weeks, but finally they were forced to yield.

Their employers said "Take that or nothing," and although "that" was *almost* "nothing" they had to take it or starve. Until two weeks ago I never heard of a successful strike among women. I'll tell you why this was successful. The employers of the Daughters of St. Crispin at Baltimore undertook to cut their wages down, and the Daughters struck. They were about to be defeated when the men St. Crispins came to the rescue and said to the employers, "If you don't accede we will strike," and they carried their point. How happened the workmen to do this? Because they are beginning to see that as long as women work, the capitalists are able to use them to undermine the workmen....

In '68 the collar laundry women organized into a trades union. Their wages had once been but from $6 to $8 per week, but they gradually got them raised to $11 to $21 per week. You may all say that this is very good wages and so it was, compared with what they had been getting, but they thought they were poorly paid in proportion to the profits of their employers, and struck for an advance. Their employers said they must put a stop to this. Give women an inch and they will take an ell. The women called the men trades unions into counsel. The men said "Now is your time to make a strike; you are organized and your employers will come to terms." So one May morning in '69 the 1,000 women threw down their work. For three long months these women held out. They exhausted all their money. From all over the United States trade unions sent money to help them to carry the day. But their employers laughed at them; not a single paper advocated their cause, and they had to yield.

Not long ago I met the President of the organization and I asked her "If you were men you would have won?" "O yes," she said, "the men always win when they strike." "What was the cause of your defeat?" She said: "I guess it was the newspapers. They said if the women were not satisfied, they had better get married." [Laughter] "What made the newspapers oppose you?" "I guess our employers paid them money." "How much?" "I think $10,000." I asked her if the five hundred collar workers had had votes, would the newspapers dared to have opposed them? She said they would not. When the men strike, the employers try to bribe the newspapers in just the same way, but the newspapers dare not sell. The political editor of a party paper puts the votes in one scale and the cash in the other, and the cash knocks the beam every time. [Laughter] Simply because those five hundred women were helpless and powerless and represented the whole half of a country who were helpless and powerless, they failed....

Now let me give you an example for teachers. In a certain city in the East, the women teachers petitioned for an advance of salary. The School Board finding it necessary to retrench, instead of advancing their salaries deducted from the salaries of the women intermediate teachers $25 a month. They did not dare to reduce the salaries of the male teachers because they had votes.

I have a sister somewhat younger than I who has been in those schools for twenty years. [Laughter] Suppose six or seven women were members of the Board, do you believe the Board would have failed to receive that petition? ....

A few years ago in this house a colored woman would not have been allowed a seat. Now the negro is enfranchised and what is the result? We see the black man walk the streets as proud as any man, simply because he has the ballot. Now black men are mayors of cities, legislators and office holders. Nobody dares to vent his spleen on negroes to-day.

We always invite the mayor and governor to our conventions, but they always have important business which keeps them from attending. The negro invites them and they come. Two years ago they did not. To-day the conservative Republicans bid the negro good morning, and even the Democrats look wistfully at him.

I visited last year the Legislature of Tennessee. I inquired, "Who is that negro member?" I was answered that it was the honorable gentleman of Lynchburg, and that is the honorable gentleman of Hampton County, and that is the honorable gentleman of somewhere else. There were 20 of them. They did not occupy the black man's corner. They were seated with the white members. One black member was sitting on the same cushion on which sat his master three or four years ago.

I thought it would be nice to ask this Legislative body to attend my lecture; and when I extended my invitation, a gentleman asked that the courtesy of the Legislature be extended to me, and that I be allowed the use of the Legislative Hall. This called forth derisive laughter. The question was put on a suspension of the rules and was lost by a vote of 18 to 38. For the benefit of the Democracy, I will state that the negroes voted in favor of the suspension. A man stood near, who, from his appearance, might have been a slave-driver, and he launched out in a tirade of oaths and ended with, "If that had been a damned nigger who wanted the House, he could have had it." [Laughter] And so he could.... I believe that women have now the legal right to vote, and I believe that they should go to the polls and deposit their ballot, and if refused carry the officers and inspectors before the Supreme Court.

When we get the ballot those men who now think we are angels just before election will actually see our wings cropping out. [Laughter]

You say the women and the negro are not parallel cases. The negro was a down trodden race, but for the women there is no such necessity for they are lovely and beloved, and the men will guard them from evil. I suppose they will guard their own wives and daughters and mothers and sisters, but is every man as careful to guard another man's wife, daughter, mother and sister? It is not a question of safety to women in general. It is simply "Is she *my* property?" ... You women who have kind brothers and husband and sons, I ask you to join with us in this movement so that woman can protect herself.

DOCUMENT 16

Stanton, "Home Life," c. 1875

This speech on marriage and divorce, which Stanton gave on lecture tours around the country throughout the 1870s, was a probing and analytical account of the link between indissoluble marriage and the subjugation of women. She was especially interested in the role of religion in protecting "male headship," a theme which became very important in her later writings and which proved at least as disturbing to other feminists as her defense of liberalized divorce. In the McFarland-Richardson speech (Document 14), written at the height of Reconstruction political radicalism, Stanton emphasized laws and legal change. By contrast, morality, motherhood, and the shaping of children's characters, themes which became increasingly important in the post–Reconstruction women's movement, were her concerns in this speech, even down to its title—"Home Life."

Elizabeth Cady Stanton Papers, Library of Congress

The political phase of the woman's rights movement has been so thoroughly discussed in England and this country, and has already realized so many practical results, that it looks as if the suffrage battle were nearly fought and won. Hence those who feel a deeper interest in the more vital questions of this reform—the social problems—should now give their earnest thought and speech in such directions.

We are in the midst of a social revolution, greater than any political or religious revolution, that the world has ever seen, because it goes deep down to the very foundations of society.

A question of magnitude presses on our consideration, whether man and woman are equal, joint heirs to all the richness and joy of earth and Heaven, or whether they were eternally ordained, one to be sovereign, the other slave. Here is a question with half the human family, and that the stronger half, on one side, who are in possession of the citadel, hold the key to the treasury and make the laws and public sentiment to suit their own purposes. Can all this be made to change base without prolonged discussion, upheavings, heartburnings, violence and war? Will man yield what he considers to be his legitimate authority over woman with less struggle than have Popes and Kings their supposed rights over their subjects, or slaveholders over their slaves? No, no. John Stuart Mill says the generality of the male sex cannot yet tolerate the idea of living with an equal at the fireside; and here is the secret of the opposition to woman's equality in the state and the church—men are not ready to recognize it in the home. This is the real danger apprehended in giving woman the ballot, for as long as man makes, interprets, and executes the laws for himself, he holds the power under any system. Hence when he expresses the fear that liberty for woman would upset the family relation, he acknowledges that her present condition of subjection is not of her own choosing, and that if she had the power the whole relation would be essentially changed. And this is just what is coming to pass, the kernel of the struggle we witness to day.

This is woman's transition period from slavery to freedom and all these social upheavings, before which the wisest and bravest stand appalled, are but necessary incidents in her progress to equality. Conservatism cries out we are going to destroy the family. Timid reformers answer, the political equality of woman will not change it. They are both wrong. It will entirely revolutionize it. When woman is man's equal the marriage relation cannot stand on the basis it is to day. But this change will not destroy it; as state constitutions and statute laws did not create conjugal and maternal love, they cannot annul them.... We shall have the family, that great conservator of national strength and morals, after the present idea of man's headship is repudiated and woman set free. To establish a republican form of government [and] the right of individual judgment in the family must of necessity involve discussion, dissension, division, but the purer, higher, holier marriage will be evolved by the very evils we now see and deplore. This same law of equality that has revolutionized the state and the church is now knocking at the door of our homes and sooner or later there too it must do its work. Let us one and all wisely bring ourselves into line with this great law for man will gain as much as woman by an equal companionship in the nearest and holiest relations of life.... So long as people marry from considerations of policy, from every possible motive but the true one, discord and division must be the result. So long as the State provides no education for youth on the questions and throws no safeguards around the formation of marriage ties, it is in honor bound to open wide the door of escape. From a woman's standpoint, I see that marriage as an indissoluble tie is slavery for woman, because law, religion and public sentiment all combine under this idea to hold her true to this relation, whatever it may be and there is no other human slavery that knows such depths of degradations as a wife chained to a man whom she neither loves nor respects, no other slavery so disastrous in its consequences on the race, or to individual respect, growth and development.

The question to day with the Protestant world is not whether marriage is an indissoluble tie, a holy sacrament of the church, but as a civil contract for how many and what reasons it may be dissolved. In the beginning sacred and profane history alike show that this relation had not even the dignity of contract. The whole matter rested in the hand of the individual man, who took or put away his wife at pleasure. [There] it remained for centuries ... until by a Papal act of encroachment, the power and arbitrament of divorce were wrested from the master of the family, and marriage became a sacrament of the church.

Let us see how [marriage] is viewed by Protestants in our own country judging from their codes and canons. A new feature in the constitution of marriage in our day is the growing recognition of woman as a party to the contract, having an equal right with man to take and put away. Gov. Jewett of Connecticut told me ... that there were a third as many divorces as marriages in one year in that state and that a majority of the applications were made by women. It is this new element that embitters the discussion for what is considered a legitimate love of freedom in man, is rank rebellion in woman; and yet the tendency in church and state is to secure her greater latitude than she ever enjoyed before....

By the laws of several states in this republic made by Christian representatives of the people divorces are granted to day for ... seventeen reasons.... By this kind of legislation in the several states we have practically decided two important points: 1st That marriage is a dissoluble tie that may be sundered by a decree of the courts. 2nd That it is a civil contract and not a sacrament of the church, and the one involves the other....

A legal contract for a section of land requires that the parties be of age, of sound mind, [and] that there be no flaw in the title.... But a legal marriage in many states in the Union may be contracted between a boy of fourteen and a girl of twelve without the consent of parents or guardians, without publication of bans.... Now what person of common sense, or conscience, can endorse laws as wise or prudent that sanction acts such as these. Let the state be logical: if marriage is a civil contract, it should be subject to the laws of all other contracts, carefully made, the parties of age, and all agreements faithfully observed....

Let us now glance at a few of the popular objections to liberal divorce laws. It is said that to make divorce respectable by law, gospel and public sentiment is to break up all family relations. Which is to say that human affections are the result and not the foundation of the canons of the church and statutes of the state.... To open the doors of escape to those who dwell in continual antagonism, to the unhappy wives of drunkards, libertines, knaves, lunatics and tyrants, need not necessarily embitter the relations of those who *are* contented and happy, but on the contrary the very fact of freedom strengthens and purifies the bond of union. When husbands and wives do not own each other as property, but are bound together only by affection, marriage will be a life long friendship and not a heavy yoke, from which both may sometimes long for deliverance. The freer the relations are between human beings, the happier....

It is said that the 10,000 libertines, lechers and egotists would take a new wife every Christmas if they could legally and reputably rid themselves in season of the old one.... [This] objection is based on the idea that woman will always remain the penniless, helpless, resistless victim of every man she meets, that she is to-day. But in the new regime, when she holds her place in the world of work, educated to self-support, with land under her feet and a shelter over her head, the results of her own toil, the social, civil and political equal of the man by her side, she will not clutch at every offer of marriage, like the drowning man at the floating straw. Though men should remain just what they are, the entire revolution in woman's position now inaugurated forces a new moral code in social life....

People say though it may be better for unhappy husbands and wives to part for their own happiness, yet the best interests of the children require an indissoluble union. The best interests of the children, the parents, the state all require that such ties should be religiously dissolved. It is a great thing to be well born, and no amount of love, care or education can ever compensate a child for the moral and physical weaknesses and deformities, the unhappy morbid conditions that result in its organization from coldness, indifference, aversion or disgust in the parents for one another.... It is sometimes the case that two people equally well organized desire divorce who like oil and water never move in the same currents. If such separate who shall have the children? In such cases a pleasant friendship would or might ensue where conjugal love was impossible and they could agree themselves on some satisfactory disposition of their children....

It is objected that men and women would not exercise the deliberation and discrimination they now do if to marry were not considered a crime and the parties not doomed to suffer a life long penalty! As I have already shown, nothing could be more reckless than our present system, when merely to be seen walking together may be taken as evidence of intent to marry, and going through the ceremony in jest may seal the contract....

It is objected that the Bible is opposed to divorce.... I do not propose to go into the Bible argument.... On this as on every subject, the Bible can be quoted on both sides.... All this talk about the "indissoluble tie," and the sacredness of marriage irrespective of the character and habits of the husband, is for its effect on women. She never could have been held the pliant tool she is to day but for the subjugation of her religious nature to the idea that in whatever condition she found herself as man's subject, that condition was ordained by Heaven....

Women would not live as they now do in this enlightened age, in violation of every law of their being, giving the very hey-day of their existence to the exercise of one animal function, if subordination to man had not been made through the ages the cardinal point of their religious faith and daily life. It requires but little thought to see that the indissoluble tie was one of the necessary steps in this subjugation.... The indissoluble tie was found to be necessary in order to establish man's authority over woman. The argument runs thus: ...in the case of parent and child, husband and wife, as these relations cannot be dissolved, there must be some ultimate authority to decide all matters in which they cannot agree, hence man's headship....

Man waits today for woman's soul to meet him on the heights of science, philosophy, poetry and art where he has so long dwelt alone.... His isolation in the soul and intellect is the sad wail in nature that cannot be satisfied with simply a union of the flesh. The great and good in all ages have felt these yearnings for the higher truer marriage. Men have philosophised and poetized about it, legislated on it, but never touched the kernel of the question, because it is a relation that concerns man and woman equally and its corner stone must be laid in the freedom and equality of both parties. Many noble men and women who have suffered in their marriage relation have called aloud for its dissolution.... But suppose the tie dissolved, what then? Nothing but to form others equally unsatisfactory; for so long as woman remains man's subject, ever in the valley of humiliation, while he enjoys the purer atmosphere on the mountain tops and in hours of ease comes down to her, they meet only in their grosser natures. He is bereft of half his power, and she sad and dissatisfied because she knows she is cheated of her birthright to rise to the same sublime heights....

What a record of heartlessness and indifference some of our greatest men have left of their domestic life. Dr. Franklin, that old utilitarian kite-flyer, went to Europe leaving his wife behind him and never saw her face for eleven years. She had shared his poverty, practiced his poor Richard maxims, bred children and nursed them while Benjamin enjoyed the splendors of a court, velvet coaches, good dinners and choice society. Of course, when he came back the poor drudge was no match for the philosopher.... That her heart rebelled in her solitude and neglect is manifest in the headstrong acts of her children. He quarreled with his sons and disinherited one of them: thus were the mother's wrongs revenged. A just retribution for every injustice to woman is sure to come in the vice and crime of her children to the third and fourth generation. The less said of Franklin's private character the better. William Franklin, Governor of New Jersey, was his natural son and how many more of the same sort he had probably Franklin himself never knew.... Undazzled by the glories of Franklin stoves and lightning rods, one sees much to disapprove in the life of the great philosopher!! ....

Instead of leaving every thing in the home to chance as now, we should apply science and philosophy to our daily life. I should feel that I had not lived in vain if faith of mine could roll off the soul of woman that dark cloud, that nightmare, that false belief that all her weaknesses and disabilities are natural, that her sufferings in maternity are a punishment for the sins of Adam and Eve and teach her that higher gospel that by obedience to natural laws she might secure uninterrupted health and happiness for herself and mould future generations to her will. When we consider all a mother's influence over her child, antenatal as well as educational, we see her power is second only to that of God himself....

There is no such sacredness and responsibility in any other human relation as in that of the mother. Give her then a voice in the laws that regulate our social conditions, that we may learn how to live, how to marry, how to educate ourselves and children for the reproduction, not only of the mortal but immortal part of our natures. There is a good deal said rather deploringly about the small families of the American people. When we begin to weigh the momentous consequences of bringing badly organized children into the world, there will be fewer still. To simply propagate our kind is a mere animal function that we share in common with the beasts of the field, but when in self-denial, a pure chaste beautiful life, obedient to every law of soul and body, a mother can give the world one noble, healthy, happy man or woman, a perpetual blessing in the home, the church and the state, she will do a better work for humanity than in adding numbers alone with but little regard for quality....

Home life to the best of us has its shadows and sorrows, and because of our ignorance this must needs be.... The day is breaking. It is something to know that life's ills are not showered upon us by the Good Father from a kind of Pandora's box, but are the results of causes that we have the power to control. By a knowledge and observance of law the road to health and happiness opens before [us]: a joy and peace that passeth all understanding shall yet be ours and Paradise regained on earth. When marriage results from a true union of intellect and spirit and when Mothers and Fathers give to their holy offices even that preparation of soul and body that the artist gives to the conception of his poem, statue or landscape, then will marriage, maternity and paternity acquire a new sacredness and dignity and a nobler type of manhood and womanhood will glorify the race!!

Document 17

Anthony, "Homes of Single Women," October, 1877

In this very interesting speech, Anthony combined the Victorian reverence for domesticity with her own intense commitment to economic independence for women. She described the first generation of fully self-supporting women, many of them her friends, whose economic independence was marked by a new level of personal freedom, in particular their ability to own their own homes. Anthony herself was part of an earlier generation; she lived with her parents and sister and did not establish her own household until she was seventy. Anthony believed that the difference between the women she described and the great masses of wage-earning women was only a matter of degree, and she offered these "exceptional women" as "models" for "the average woman we everyday meet." "Homes of Single Women" was not a popular speech, or one of Anthony's own favorites. She gave it very few times and thought it "stale, flat and unprofitable."[37]

Susan B. Anthony Papers, Library of Congress

A home of one's own is the want, the necessity of every human being, the one thing above all others longed for, worked for. Whether the humblest cottage or the proudest palace, a home of our own is the soul's dream of rest, the one hope that will not die until we have reached the very portals of the everlasting home.

Probably none of us will attempt to question the superiority of the time-honored plan of making a home by the union of one man and one woman in marriage. But in a country like ours where such considerable numbers of men, from choice or necessity, fail to establish matrimonial homes, there is no way of escape; vast numbers of women must make homes for themselves, or forego them altogether. In Massachusetts, alone, there are, to-day, 70,000 more women than men, wives and sisters of soldiers and sailors, miners and stockmen, lumber-men and mountain-men, who in their search for wealth have forgotten the loved of their youth. To these deserted women, necessity has proved the mother of invention. And as you pass from village to village, you will see lovely white cottages, wreathed in vines, nestled midst gardens of vegetables and flowers, fruit and shade trees, each a little Paradise save the presence of the historic Adam before whom woman reverently says, "God thy law, thou mine!!" For homes like these, the passer-by is wont to heave a pitying sigh, as there rises before him the sad panorama of crushed affections, blighted hopes, bereaved hearts. But these are homes of exceeding joy and gladness, compared with the myriads of ill-assorted marriage homes, where existence, by night and by day, is but a living death!!

It has been said that the man of the nineteenth century insists upon having for a wife a woman of the seventeenth century. It is perhaps nearer the truth to say that he demands the spirit of the *two* centuries combined in one woman: the activity and liberality of thought which characterize the present era, with the submission to authority which belonged to the past. In woman's transition from the position of subject to sovereign, there must needs be an era of self-sustained self-supported homes, where her freedom and equality shall be unquestioned. As young women become educated in the industries of the world, thereby learning the sweetness of independent bread, it will be more and more impossible for them to accept the Blackstone marriage limitation that "husband and wife are one, and that one the husband." ....

Even when man's intellectual convictions shall be sincerely and fully on the side of Freedom and equality to woman, the force of long existing customs and laws will impel him to exert authority over her, which will be distasteful to the self-sustained, self-respectful woman. The habit of the ages cannot, at once, be changed. Not even amended constitutions and laws can revolutionize the practical relations of men and women, immediately, any more than did the Constitutional freedom and franchise of Black men, transform white men into practical recognition of the civil and political rights of those who were but yesterday their legal slaves. Constitutional equality only gives to all the aid and protection of the law, while they educate and develop themselves, while they grow into the full stature of freemen. It simply allows equality of *chances* to *establish equality.*

Not until women shall have practically demonstrated their claim to equality in the world of work, in agriculture, manufactures, mechanics, inventions, the arts and sciences, not until they shall have established themselves in education, literature and politics and are in actual possession of the highest places of honor and emolument, by the industry of their own hands and brains, and by election or appointment; not until they shall have actually won equality at every point, morally, intellectually, physically, politically, will the superior sex really accept the fact and lay aside all assumptions, dogmatic or autocratic.

Meanwhile, "the logic of events" points, inevitably, to an *epoch of single women.* If women will not accept marriage *with subjection,* nor men proffer it *without,* there is, there can be, *no alternative.* The women who will *not be ruled* must live without marriage. And during this transition period, wherever, for the maintenance of self-respect on the one side, and education into recognition of equality on the other, single women make comfortable and attractive homes for themselves, they furnish the best and most efficient object lessons for men.

Fanny Fern, in her inimitable way, pictures the Modern "Old Maid" thus: "No, sir, she don't shuffle round in skimpy raiments, awkward shoes, cotton gloves, with horn side-combs fastening six hairs to her temples. She don't ... keep a cat, a snuff box, or go to bed at dark, or scowl at little children, or gather catnip, not a bit of it. She wears nicely fitting dresses and becoming bits of color in her hair; and she goes to concerts and parties and suppers and lectures, and she don't go alone, either! She lives in a good house earned by herself, and she gives nice, little teas in it. She don't work for no wages and bare toleration, day and night; no sir. If she has no money, she teaches or she lectures or she writes books or poems, or she is a book-keeper, or she sets type, or she does anything but depend on somebody else's husband; and she feels well and independent, in consequence, and holds up her head with the best, and asks no favor, and woman's rights has done it." ....

Mary Clemmer very truly says, "The secret of the rare material success which attended the Cary sisters is to be found in the fact that from the first they began to make a home." ... The sisters were deeply interested in the cause of equal rights to all; and the subject of woman's enfranchisement was frequently the topic of conversation. While at that time Mr. Greeley, almost always present, advocated warmly the right of women to equal educational and industrial advantages, he stoutly opposed their demand for suffrage. It was his habit to say, "The best women I know do not want to vote." The charming Alice would as often put the question to each of the distinguished women at her table, "Do you want to vote, Miss Booth?" "Yes," and "Do you want to vote Mrs. Allen?" "Yes." "Do you want to vote, Miss Dickenson?" "Yes." And each and every one as invariably replied, "Yes." Yet at the very next reception, Mr. Greeley would again repeat his stereotype "settler" of the question. He died in the delusion that "the best women do not want to vote." ....

Another delightful home of women alone is that of Mary L. Booth, the successful editor of *Harper's Bazaar,* and Mrs. Wright, in a beautiful four story brown front on 59th Street.... Of this co-partnership, Miss Booth is so purely a woman of literary pursuits and outside affairs, that she gives over all domestic details, and largely too all those of her own wardrobe, to the care of Mrs. Wright, whom the world would call more feminine in her character. Yet, I have been told that she was the wife of a Captain of a ship, and that once, when on a voyage with her husband, he was taken very ill, and his mates and other officers proving inefficient, she bravely took command, and brought the vessel safely into port....

A woman's home all must love and honor is that of the President of the National Woman Suffrage Association, Dr. Clemence S. Lozier, a very mother in Israel to every woman struggling for an honest subsistence. For twenty and more years, her house has been the home of one or more poor young women studying medicine at the College she herself founded, and in the maintenance of which she has invested between fifteen and twenty thousand dollars of her own earnings. She is often heard to say, in public and in private, "All my success, professionally, and financially, I owe to the 'Woman's Rights Movement.' It is but my duty, therefore, to help it, and thereby help all other women who shall come after me."

The marriage of Dr. Lozier's youth was a very happy, but brief one, her husband dying early, leaving her the mother of one child. Her second experiment was exceedingly unfortunate; the man not only leaving her to support herself and young son, by sewing and teaching and nursing, but he himself *fed* on the scanty earnings of her hands.... Mrs. Lozier's eye chanced to rest on a letter of Elizabeth Cady Stanton's read at the first New York State Women's Temperance Convention, held at Albany in 1852, urging the right of divorce for drunkenness, and clearly setting forth the crime of the mother who stamped her child with the drunkard's appetite for rum. That letter shocked Mrs. Lozier into her first thought, not only of her right, but her solemn duty to cease to be the *wife* of such a man. She quickly obtained a legal separation from bed and board, which was all the laws of New York, then or now, allow for drunkenness, [and] set about studying medicine....

What numbers of the wayfaring advocates of reform, will with me bear grateful testimony to that haven of rest, that coziest home of the Mott sisters, in Albany, New York City. For thirty years and more, in that stolidly conservative old Dutch City, those two women stood almost the *sole* representatives of the then unpopular movements for Temperance, Peace, Anti-Slavery, and Woman's Rights. At different periods during those years, those sisters earned their living by teaching, boardinghouse keeping, and skirt-manufacturing. They were the most self respecting women I ever knew, always ennobling whatever work they laid their hands on.

Do any of you Gentlemen and Ladies doubt the truth of my picturings of the homes of unmarried women? Do any of you still cling to the old theory, that single women, women's rights women, professional women, have no home instincts? ... All this is done from pure love of home; no spurious second-hand domesticity affected for the praise of some man, or conscientiously maintained for the comfort of the one who furnishes the money;

nor because she has nothing else to busy herself about, but her one impelling motive is from the true womanly home instinct, unsurpassed by that of any of the women who "have all the rights they want."

... The charm of all these women's homes is that their owners are "settled" in life; that the men, young or old, who visit them, no more count their hostesses' chances in the matrimonial market, than when guests in the homes of the most happily married women. Men go to these homes as they do to their gentlemen's clubs, to talk of art, science, politics, religion and reform.... They go to meet their equals in the proud domain of intellect, laying aside for the time being at least, all of their conventional "small talk for the ladies."

But, say you, all these beautiful homes are made by exceptional women; the few women of superior intellect, rare genius, or masculine executive ability, that enables them to rise above the environments of sex, to lean on themselves for support and protection, to amass wealth, to win honors and emoluments. They are not halves, needing complements, as are the masses of women; but evenly balanced well rounded characters; therefore are they models to be reached by the average women we everyday meet....

Part Three
1880–1906

Introduction

*Anthony and the Consolidation
of the Women's Movement*

The major context for the political role that Stanton and Anthony played in the last decades of the nineteenth century was the tremendous expansion in women's reform activities. In the years after Reconstruction, middle- and upper-class American women, white but also Black, formed and joined an extraordinary number of socially conscious, all-female organizations. These organizations ranged from the innumerable women's clubs that sprang up in every town and city to foster study and sociability, to the larger social reform organizations, especially the Woman's Christian Temperance Union (1874) and the Young Woman's Christian Association (1871).[1] The dilemma for suffragists was how to relate their concerns for sexual equality and political power to this proliferation of organized public activity among women. The response of Stanton and Anthony was different, from this approach and from each other. Anthony tried to unify all organized, reform-minded women around the demand for the vote, whatever their differences over other issues. Stanton, aiming for a more comprehensive political unity, insisted on challenging women whenever she thought they were being too conservative on the wide variety of political issues she believed should concern them.

In some ways, the women's organizations of the post Reconstruction years continued the prewar tradition of women's benevolent and moral reform activity. Their leaders tended to stress women's unique virtues and special responsibility to the community, rather than the identity of men's and women's public roles. They placed great emphasis on women's privileged responsibility for domestic life and the rearing of children, and on the moral superiority that they believed flowed from them. Most of the women's organizations of the period, despite nominal non-sectarianism and formal independence from church control, were committed to the organization of society around Christian values. However, traditional womanly virtues like self-sacrifice and responsibility for the unfortunate and dependent appeared in a broader light in the context of the rapid industrialization of American society and the social upheaval and human suffering it produced in this period. The responsibility that middle-class women had once felt for pauper widows and orphans they now expressed for the struggling young wage-earning women of the cities; and the criticisms they had formerly directed against secular and individualist tendencies were now aimed at the relentless drive for money and the reduction of "what was meant to be perennial and sacred" to a matter of price and profit.[2]

The relation between these postwar women's organizations and the suffrage movement was complex. Organizations that emphasized the moral superiority of women in their conception of women's public role were both a reaction against and a product of the women's rights perspective.

On the one hand, many of the leaders of the organizations conceived of them as conservative alternatives to the suffrage movement, and especially to the leadership of Stanton and Anthony. They particularly objected to what they considered excessively radical attacks on femininity and criticisms of the domestic and gender conventions of bourgeois society.[3]

On the other hand, the militant feminism of suffragists had changed the traditions of female reform. Unlike prewar societies, postwar women's organizations were generally free of male control and preached the importance of independence and equality for women. They were assertive about women's capacity to do more than men expected of them and developed techniques for encouraging women to gain wider interests and new skills.[4] Perhaps most important, they no longer insisted that women's influence be limited to the domestic circle and did not consider public life exclusively masculine.

Initially, Anthony was not very enthusiastic about the postwar proliferation of women's organizations and reform activities. It was a cardinal article of faith for her that any work which did not focus on enfranchisement was fruitless for women to pursue. Gradually, however, she began to recognize that there was a great deal of pro-suffrage sentiment latent in the non-suffrage women's organizations.

In this regard, the achievements of Frances Willard in the Woman's Christian Temperance Union (WCTU) especially impressed her. Initially, the leaders of the WCTU had been explicitly opposed to woman suffrage. Willard, who was elected second president of the WCTU in

1879, was a suffragist. In 1881, she risked her presidency to advocate full political equality for women, and won the support of most of the members.[5] She rebranded "woman suffrage," which was too associated with radical activism, as "the home protection ballot," encouraging women to dare to go into the political sphere to protect their homes and families. By the 1890s, WCTU women constituted the majority of suffrage activists in the West and Midwest.

Willard's successes demonstrated that support for suffrage could be made compatible with relatively conventional ideas about the role of women and that it was therefore possible to create a much larger and broader woman suffrage movement than had been built before. Encouraged by Willard's accomplishments, Anthony began to work toward the formation of a broad consensus in favor of woman suffrage among all organized, reform-minded women. "Our intention ... is to make every one ... believe in the grand principles of equality of rights and chances for women...," she wrote in 1884 in an effort to keep Stanton from raising a controversial issue. "Neither you nor I have the right ... to complicate or compromise our question." Anthony even had to abandon the tactical militancy, for which she had always had a strong personal attraction, because it offended women who accepted the rule of respectability.[6] Instead of a movement of women united around an explicit political program for the transformation of society and women's place in it, she began to envision the unification of all women, whatever their social or political beliefs, around their common womanhood and the single goal of political equality. Beginning in the mid–1880s, Anthony began to dedicate her considerable energies and powers of organization to the consolidation of the many postwar women's reform organizations into a single, unified women's reform movement.

Under Anthony's leadership, suffragists took on the work of unifying the various women's organizations. In 1888, the NWSA organized and sponsored a gala, week-long International Council for Women. The initial plan, formulated by Stanton in 1883, had been to convene an international meeting of suffragists, but, two years later, the NWSA voted to expand the council to include "women workers along all lines of social, intellectual or civil progress and reform."[7] Anthony enthusiastically supported the change, hoping that the NWSA's willingness to accommodate itself to the broad range of women's reform interests and their doubts about suffragism would eventually lead to a substantial increase in their support for woman suffrage. However, she refused to authorize an invitation that was so broad that it included women who were opposed to woman suffrage. Instead, she saw to it that the call to the Council expressed her own suffragist conviction that "those active in great philanthropic enterprises [will] sooner or later realize that so long as women are not acknowledged to be the political equals of men, their judgment on public questions will have but little weight."[8]

Anthony's hope for the International Council was that it would be a model of harmony and united womanhood. "I don't want a controversy or a lot of negations," she insisted, "but shall tell each one to give her strongest affirmation."[9] Her goal was to show that, despite women's different political loyalties and various reform affiliations, they could still unite around the fact of their common womanhood. American women representing more than fifty suffrage, temperance, social purity, and general reform organizations attended the Congress. Feminists from nine foreign countries including India also came, many brought at the NWSA's expense. The Council defined "representative women" more broadly than other women's federations of the period. Although white women of the middle and upper classes predominated, other women's voices could be heard. Huldah Loud, head of the Women's Department of the Knights of Labor, was a featured speaker. Even the color bar was crossed as Frances Ellen Harper, a leading Black feminist, spoke in the session on temperance about the obligation of the rich to the poor.[10]

Anthony was extremely proud of the International Council, which was one of the most ambitious projects that the NWSA ever undertook. The 1888 International Council undoubtedly inaugurated an era of organizational consolidation among American women. A permanent National Council of Women was formed, the first multi-reform national women's organization ever founded in the United States. The formation of the National Council of Women was followed within a year by the creation of a second (somewhat competing) national organization, the General Federation of Women's Clubs, and then by the National Council of Jewish Women and the National Association of Colored Women. All of these encouraged the formation of state and local affiliates and did a great deal to increase and consolidate women's ability to control community institutions and affect state and municipal governments.

However, these developments did not generate as much support for woman suffrage as Anthony had hoped. During the 1888 International Council, suffrage was treated very cautiously. The session in which it was discussed was cautiously titled "political conditions" and enfranchisement was not included in the Council's final statement of goals. This reluctance to endorse the demand for the vote was so pronounced that, on the occasion of the third International Council, in 1899 in London, antisuffragists were invited to participate in the session on "political conditions," leading suffragists to withdraw. In the end, the creation of an International Council of Women did so little to advance the suffrage movement worldwide that by 1904 American suffragists had to form an entirely new organization for that purpose, the International Woman Suffrage Alliance.[11] Nor did the General Federation of Women's Clubs support suffrage until 1914, on the very eve of victory, three decades after the WCTU had done so.[12] Anthony was mystified and disappointed by the fact that the consolidation of American women's organizations, to which she had contributed so much, had not done more to benefit woman suffrage. "The Federation of Clubs ... can count forty thousand members ... the Christian Temperance Union ... can report a half-million members; I will tell you frankly and honestly that all we number is seven thousand," she explained in 1893. "...What a hindrance this lack has been. If we could have demonstrated to the Congress that we had a thorough organization back of our demand, we should have had all our demands granted long ago" (see Document 18).

Out of a similar spirit of harmony and the desire to draw together women's organizational power, the suffrage movement itself began to unite. Ever since the initial split in 1869 there had been many calls for the unification of the NWSA, led by Stanton and Anthony, and the AWSA, led by Lucy Stone and Henry Blackwell, but not until the late 1880s were there any initiatives from the leaders of either organization.[13] In 1887, Alice Stone Blackwell, daughter of Stone and Blackwell and corresponding secretary of the AWSA, proposed a joint meeting to consider merger. Later, she explained that the AWSA became willing to merge with the NWSA because "the question of easy divorce" and "persons of notorious immorality" were no longer welcomed on the NWSA's platform.[14] Representatives of the NWSA responded positively to her invitation, formed a committee to discuss unification, and invited the leaders of the American to participate in the International Council, which was the first time the two organizations had cooperated in many years.[15]

Within the NWSA, Anthony was a leading force for merger. From the beginning of the negotiations process, she was convinced that "the best good for women's enfranchisement surely will come through the union of all the friends of woman suffrage into one great and grand National Association...."[16] Her enthusiasm was consistent with her general effort in this period to set aside political differences among women in order to create the largest possible unity around the demand for the vote. "I cannot think of any stipulation I wish to make the basis of union," she wrote, "save that we unite and after that discuss all measures...."[17]

Despite Anthony's authority and her efforts to convince friends and recruits to "stand by Susan once more," she faced opposition that delayed the merger for two years.[18] Leading opponents to the move included veteran suffragists like Olympia Brown and Matilda Joslyn Gage, and younger activists such as Clara Colby and Harriette Shattuck. Linking all their objections was their fear that the essence of the NWSA's expansive approach to suffrage would somehow be lost through unification. They were concerned that merger would lead to the abandonment of the NWSA's strategic focus on federal citizenship and the ideological message it carried of women's full and absolute equality with men. They objected to the proposed plan of organization, which they charged would decentralize organizational activity from the national society to the state and local affiliates.[19] Opponents of the merger believed that a majority of the NWSA members supported them, and moved that the issue be submitted to a vote of the whole organization, but the NWSA's Executive Committee, which was controlled by pro-union forces, refused, and itself made the decision to merge with the AWSA. "The executive sessions ... were the most stormy in the history of the association," Ida Harper, Anthony's biographer, wrote, "and only the unsurpassed parliamentary knowledge of the chairman, May Wright Sewall, aided by the firm cooperation of Miss Anthony, could have harmonized the opposing elements and secured a majority in favor of union."[20] In February 1890, the two organizations met in joint convention and declared themselves the National American Woman Suffrage Association (NAWSA), which led the suffrage movement to its conclusion three decades later.

Like the International Council, the unification of the suffrage movement reflected Anthony's belief that political and ideological differences among women were far less important than, and could be subordinated to, their common struggle for enfranchisement. "The time is past when the mass of the suffrage women will be compromised by any one person's peculiarities!" Anthony wrote Stanton in 1897. "We number over ten thousand women and each one has opinions ... and we can only hold them together to work for the ballot by letting alone their whims and prejudices on other subjects."[21] Thus, although Anthony was personally antiracist, she opposed all efforts to raise the question of discrimination against Black women in the NAWSA because she feared it would anger southern white suffragists.[22]

Eventually, she was forced to face the conflict between her personal and organizational stances, when she met and developed a friendship with the bold African American suffragist, Ida B. Wells. Anthony defended Wells' controversial campaign against the epidemic of lynching of African Americans in the South, even as she ashamedly acknowledged to her new friend her accommodation to southern white suffragists' racism, including an insult to the aging Frederick Douglass (see Document 19).

Anthony's approach to unity within the feminist movement was paralleled by a strategy for winning support outside it that refused to make political distinctions among potential male allies. This "nonpartisan" approach was explicitly articulated at the NAWSA's founding convention, during a session on "Our Attitude Toward Political Parties." "The sentiment was in favor of keeping strictly aloof from all political alliances," Anthony and Ida Harper wrote. "It was shown that suffrage can only be gained through the assistance of men in all parties."[23] The "nonpartisan" posture that Anthony helped to shape remained the official strategy of the NAWSA for the next thirty years.

Stanton's Commitment to Suffrage Radicalism

Elizabeth Stanton's relation to the consolidation of the late nineteenth-century women's movement was far more uneasy than Anthony's. In many ways she was the first victim of the NAWSA's emphasis on unity, hostility to dissent, and implicit conservatism. While Anthony devoted herself to the unification of all women around the demand for the vote, Stanton understood that there were profound political differences that support for woman suffrage and the common fact of gender could not obscure forever. In a movement that was growing in conservatism, she was still temperamentally a radical, eager as she had always been to lead women to the most challenging interpretation of what it meant to be free. She was elected first president of the NAWSA in 1890, not because she represented the spirit of consolidation and "affirmation" that had led to the merger—she did not—but because Anthony insisted that she must have the office and that "every woman ... who has any love for Susan B. Anthony ... don't vote for any human being but Mrs. Stanton."[24] Even so, 40 percent of those voting refused to support Stanton, and she remained in office only two difficult years.

Stanton's leadership was a challenge to the idea, fast becoming the watchword of the suffrage movement, that what women wanted to do with the ballot was irrelevant to their struggle to win it. She raised disturbing questions about what women wanted out of the political process, both for their own emancipation and for the reform of society in general. She challenged the idea that the drive for woman suffrage should—or could—be isolated from political developments in the larger society (see Document 20). Inasmuch as "our demands are to be made and carried like other political questions, by the aid of and affiliation with parties," she insisted, "it is puerile to say 'no matter how we use the ballot the right is ours.'"[25] Stanton believed that feminists must continue to make themselves part of a larger political movement, but must do so from a position of independent strength and ally with the most radical and democratic forces they could find. By the end of the decade, she had identified herself with the growing socialist movement in the United States.[26]

However, Stanton challenged suffrage unity primarily by questioning suffragists' vision for the emancipation of women. She recognized that suffragists disagreed about what constituted the "civil, political, religious, social, educational, industrial rights" of women, and how to use the ballot to gain them.[27] In the face of the growing orthodoxy of the suffrage movement, she insisted on full and open debate. "The fact that we differ on all these points is the very reason we should discuss them," she explained some years later. "If to question is heresy in this Association, the sooner it is rent in twain the better."[28]

Above all, Stanton's systematic critique of Christianity led her to challenge the suffrage mainstream. Although she had always been an anticleric and an opponent of Calvinism, her criticisms of the Christian religion became much more important to her in her later years. She was especially influenced by the secularist movement in the late 1880s in England, where her daughter lived and where she spent a great deal of time. In England, the continued existence of an established church meant that non–Christians could not sit in Parliament until 1858, and that "blasphemy," which was still a civil crime. Stanton's studies in this period were profoundly shaped by intellectual currents such as Positivism, Biblical criticism, and the anthropological study of primitive societies.[29]

Stanton argued that organized religion had a conservative impact on society; it led to tolerance for superstition, inculcated a spirit of submission to authority, looked to divine rather than human action, and encouraged charity rather than rebellion as a response to human suffering. Her particular emphasis, however, was feminist, and she charged Christianity with a special animus toward women (see Document 24). She showed that the status of women in pre–Christian societies had been high, and that the spread of Christianity had debased the position of women. For a long time, Christianity had excluded women from the priesthood, thus identifying the deity solely with the masculine element. However, despite the contribution that Christianity had made to their oppression, she observed that women remained "the chief supporters of the church today," victims of its doctrine of female inferiority.

"It has been through the perversion of [woman's] religious sentiments," Stanton concluded, "that she has been so long held in a condition of slavery."[30]

Her criticisms of Christianity's spiritual claims were closely related to her challenge to existing sexual morality. In contrast to those who believed that Christian ethics were at the root of sexual decency, she argued that Christianity identified women with sexual corruption and was responsible for the double standard which oppressed nineteenth-century women. She did not believe that a universal standard of morality could be ascertained, and she utterly rejected the notion that it had triumphed under modern Christianity. "There never has been any true standard of social morality, and none exists to day," she insisted. "What constitutes chastity changes with time and latitude; its definition would be as varied as is public opinion on other subjects."[31]

At the deepest level, Stanton dissented from the belief that the best way to understand human sexuality was by the larger society's establishing what constituted a proper sexual morality. As such, Stanton's attitude to sexual morality drew strongly on her fundamental belief in individual rights, which, as a feminist, she extended to family and sexual life. In 1883, Frederick Douglass' second marriage to a white woman flaunted a now widespread objection to interracial marriage and set up an uproar from white and Black critics alike. Stanton sought to publish a defense of Douglass' individual right to free choice in such matters, but so uniform was this conviction that despite her intellectual celebrity, Stanton was unable to find a place to publish. Instead, she sent her letter privately to Douglass, who appreciated it deeply (see Document 18).

Still, it needs to be said that Stanton's defense of Douglass' individual rights was based on her conviction that he—like herself—was a unique and superior individual, whom the general rank of society had no right to judge. In these post–Reconstruction years of growing white supremacy and racial inequality, neither her characterological radicalism nor her personal support for Douglass extended to a defense of the rights of African Americans in general. Stanton's previous commitment to universal suffrage now gave way to her belief in the principle of "educated suffrage," an insistence that the ability to read and write in English was a defensible standard for enfranchisement. In the 1890s, as Stanton believed that the influx of European immigrants constituted a new obstacle to women's enfranchisement, her advocacy of educated suffrage extended to her growing nativism (see Document 22).

Stanton's conviction that religion in general and Christianity in particular were at the root of women's oppression ran headlong into the growing power of Christian ideology within the women's movement. Christian feminists (like Frances Willard, who she did not particularly support) believed that the spread of Christianity had profoundly elevated the status of women. They encouraged women's religious convictions as a way to develop their social conscience and their pride in womanhood. They believed that a strong community consensus based on Christian ethics would help to protect women, and they feared that its disintegration would increase women's abuse and exploitation. Nor were these differences merely philosophical; they were political in the most concrete sense of the word. Christian reformers, men and women alike, agitated for a constitutional amendment recognizing Christianity, won state and local laws enforcing Sunday closings, and advocated censorship, anti-divorce, and various other social purity legislation to use the power of the state to enforce Christian morality.[32]

Stanton took every opportunity to challenge the "Christian party in politics," its crusades against sexual immorality, and the influence it was gathering within American feminism. At the founding convention of the NAWSA, she insisted on declaring her opposition to the "women [who] are taking an active part in pressing on the consideration of Congress many narrow sectarian measures," some of whom were sitting alongside her on the platform (see Document 21).[33] She also condemned the efforts of the National Reform Association, a social purity organization, to secure a federal law to reduce the number of divorces by severely limiting the grounds on which they could be obtained.[34] At the 1891 convention, she took the extremely unpopular position of defending the Irish patriot Charles Parnell, who was being hounded by the British and American public because he was an adulterer.[35] And in 1892 she began a campaign that brought her into direct conflict with the WCTU and other Christian reform organizations, to keep the Chicago World's Fair open on Sundays.[36]

Stanton's secularism in particular and her radicalism in general made her very unpopular among many feminists.[37] As president of the NAWSA she had little real power. Anna Howard Shaw, Anthony's protégé and an ordained Methodist minister, strongly opposed Stanton's election as president. "If [Aunt Susan] will crowd Mrs. Stanton down our throats, well we won't have her if we can help it..." she wrote to a friend in 1890. "I have said from the first I will not work under and will work to defeat Mrs. S."[38] Carrie Chapman Catt, who eventually led the suffrage movement to victory, also neither liked Stanton, whom she met in 1890, nor respected Anthony's devotion to her.[39] Stanton's resolutions were often ignored and she took to hiding her authorship in hopes of getting them passed. Finally, in 1892, she succeeded in leaving her office. "It is not good for all our thoughts or interests to run in one groove," she wrote to Olympia Brown. "For this reason I resigned the office I held."[40] Anthony, who had been virtual leader of the NAWSA since its formation, succeeded her as its president, an office she held until 1900. After which she was succeeded by Carrie Chapman Catt and Anna Howard Shaw.

Stanton's most famous speech, "The Solitude of Self," was delivered at the convention at which she resigned the presidency of the NAWSA (see Document 23). It was her swan song as leader of suffragism, and in it she presented the philosophical core of her thought about women's emancipation, as well as the differences between her ideas and those which were coming to dominate the suffrage movement. Her basic message was "the infinite diversity in human character" and the necessity of equal rights for all individuals, themes which had always been central to her feminism. Her approach to women's emancipation, which stressed the liberation of each woman's unique capacities and inclinations, was being eclipsed by an emphasis on that which was allegedly common to all women, the attributes and abilities that women, once freed of male influence, were expected to share. Stanton conceded the claims of gender, the fact that women had common concerns as "mother, wife, sister and daughter," and even more as a sex equal in importance to men. However, in determining women's rights, both of these considerations were less important to her than "the individuality of each human soul," the human condition which simultaneously distinguishes each of us from the other, and is common to us all, women and men alike.

Stanton's individualism had its roots in the past, in classical natural rights thought, but it looked forward as well, to aspects of modern twentieth-century feminism, anticipating what Angelina Grimké had once described as "new forms of truth ... to test the faithfulness of the pioneer minds of the age."[41] The individual of whom Stanton spoke was not just a creature of political philosophy, but of psychology as well. The new note Stanton struck as she insisted on "the solitude of self" was existential. Although she urged women to continue to fight for equality in "the outer conditions of human beings," she also encouraged them to struggle for full development and independence in the inner aspects as well. Even as she was moving toward socialism, and realizing the importance of cooperation as a principle of social organization, her bequest to the women of the future stressed the psychological dimension of freedom and defended the importance of individual self-determination for women.

Four years after Stanton's resignation, the breach between her and other leading suffragists widened. In late 1895, she finally published *The*

Woman's Bible, a feminist commentary first on the Old Testament and three years later on the New Testament. Since 1886, she had been planning an ambitious study of the Bible that would avoid treating it as a "fetish," but would assess what it had to say about women's position, "as [one would] any book of human origin."[42] She tried to interest women of widely differing opinions to join the project, which she hoped would provoke a debate on whether the Bible taught women's inferiority or their equality. She invited leading Christian feminists, including Frances Willard, some of whom were intrigued by the project but ultimately did not participate because they feared their conservative constituencies would see it as an attack on the Bible and be offended by it.[43] Finally, in 1894, Stanton began *The Woman's Bible* on a much less ambitious scale She was assisted mainly by other feminist freethinkers, but also by a few exceptionally courageous religious women, such as the Rev. Phoebe Hanaford. Each commentator, Christian or freethinker, considered various Biblical passages as they supported or contradicted her particular beliefs. In her own commentaries, Stanton praised those few parts of the Bible that she believed depicted women as courageous and self-respecting, and criticized the many passages which seemed to her to degrade women and teach men to have contempt for them (see Document 24).

Within the women's movement and especially in the NAWSA, the publication of *The Woman's Bible* raised a storm of protest. Anthony tried to establish a truce between Stanton's critics and her supporters but failed. Instead, at the 1896 NAWSA convention, there was "animated and at times rather personal" debate over *The Woman's Bible.* Corresponding secretary (and Anthony protégé) Rachel Foster Avery denounced the book in her annual report. "[It is] a volume with a pretentious title ... without either scholarship or literary value, set forth in a spirit which is neither that of reverence or inquiry," Avery declared. "I recommend that we take some action by resolution to show that the Association is not responsible for the individual actions of its officers." (Stanton was not an officer.) Other suffragists spoke in Stanton's defense, including Charlotte Perkins Stetson (later Gilman), who was attending her first national suffrage convention, and Lillie Devereux Blake, who charged that only a minority of the critics of *The Woman's Bible* had even read it. Despite their arguments, a resolution was introduced declaring the NAWSA a "nonsectarian"—not nonreligious—organization and disavowing any connection with *The Woman's Bible.* The resolution passed, fifty-three to forty-one.[44]

Anthony was profoundly disturbed by the convention's attack on *The Woman's Bible.* She left the chair to join the debate and defended Stanton with great passion. Anthony rejected the resolution both because she believed that "the right of individual opinion" must be protected, and because the convention's repudiation of "one who has stood for half a century the acknowledged leader of progressive thought ... in regard to ... the absolute freedom of women'" was a victory for conservatism (see Document 24). Yet Anthony herself had built the organization that had turned against Stanton. Every one of the younger women she had recruited into suffrage work voted against *The Woman's Bible*, and several—Rachel Foster Avery, Harriet Taylor Upton, Anna Howard Shaw—spearheaded the drive to repudiate it. The entire affair caused Anthony "great agony of spirit," and she briefly considered resigning, but in the end she rejected the idea and returned to her vision of a single-minded, "nonpartisan" suffrage movement, free of "entanglements" and implicitly inhospitable to radicalism.[45]

Through all this, Anthony's personal attachment to Stanton remained strong. "I never expect to know any joy in this world equal to that of going up and down the land ... engaging halls and circulating Mrs. Stanton's speeches," she said. "If I ever have had any inspiration, she has given it to me."[46] Yet, despite her tremendous respect for Stanton and her tendency to portray herself as her intellectual dependent, a mere "hewer of wood and drawer of water" for a great philosopher and stateswoman, Anthony had found her own way politically, and this way, although it was sometimes difficult for her to acknowledge, was different from Stanton's. While Stanton believed (in Anthony's words) that "women should take up ... public questions which so evidently need the combined wisdom of men and women in their solution," Anthony was convinced that the controversies that resulted would "create animosities and alienate supporters of a cause which can achieve victory only through the assistance of all religious bodies and political parties."[47] When Anthony retired from the presidency of the NAWSA in 1900, and identified Carrie Chapman Catt as her successor, Stanton and other insurgents supported a rival candidate.[48] Despite their enduring friendship, Stanton and Anthony were no longer united by a common political perspective and had ceased to provide American feminism with unified leadership.

The *Woman's Bible* incident greatly accelerated Stanton's alienation from the suffrage movement in the last years of her life. She had always demanded the suffrage, both because she thought it was women's right, and because she believed women would be a liberal and democratic force in politics. Now, she wrote, "Much as I desire the suffrage I would rather never vote than to see the policy of our government at the mercy of the religious bigotry of such women. My heart's desire is to lift women out of all these dangerous and degrading superstitions, and to this end will I labor my remaining days on earth." Deposed from leadership and increasingly aware that she had very little time left, she searched for ways to get her ideas across to American women. "I want to publish and scatter many good things on all questions before I leave this planet," she wrote two years before her death.[49] In 1898 she published her autobiography, *Eighty Years and More,* which, she complained, the suffrage press did not adequately review. For years she had resisted Anthony's efforts to issue a volume of her speeches and writings, but now she searched desperately for financial backing for an edition. She wrote to Carnegie and Rockefeller for money, but got only $500 from the latter.[50] The volume never appeared. This last disappointment left her uncharacteristically bitter. "If my suffrage coadjutors had ever treated me with the boundless generosity they have my friend Susan, I could have scattered my writings abundantly," she wrote to Elizabeth Boynton Harbert, one of the few young suffragists who continued to support her. "They have given Susan thousands of dollars, jewels, laces, silks and satins, and me criticisms for my radical ideas."[51]

Stanton died in 1902, Anthony four years later (see Document 25). After their deaths, they were remembered quite differently. Many devoted followers carefully preserved Anthony's memory, literally making her a suffrage saint. Her home was made into a museum, her papers were collected in repositories on the East and West Coasts, and the story of her life was told in several honorific biographies.[52] Stanton was nowhere near as glorified. Her children issued a single volume of her letters, but otherwise no effort was made to collect her writings or remember her to later generations of women. She was not even the subject of a full-length biography until 1940.[53] The extraordinary breadth of her historical contribution—her interest in divorce reform and her passionate secularism, as well as her advocacy of the vote—was largely forgotten. In general, Stanton was honored only for her earliest accomplishments, in particular the Seneca Falls convention, while Anthony was identified with the whole history—and eventual triumph—of the woman suffrage movement. In the twenty-first century, her memory has received considerable public attention, primarily for her racist and nativist outbursts.[54]

The uneven honor paid Stanton and Anthony is understandable. By the end of their lives, their common conviction about the importance of enfranchising women had developed into two quite different approaches to building the woman suffrage movement. Stanton's insistence that suffragists have a common political program for social reform and women's emancipation had been discredited. Instead, Anthony's belief that no other issue must be allowed to intrude on the question of political equality for women had come to predominate. The twentieth-century suffrage movement pursued this strategic direction. Suffrage leaders who followed Anthony succeeded in unifying enormous numbers of women around the demand for the vote and marshaling their power to overcome opposition and force the enfranchisement of women. Twentieth-century suffragism no longer connected itself explicitly with the transformation of the sexual order and the emancipation of women from coercive sexual stereotypes, a project which shifted to a newly emerging movement which named itself "feminism."[55] Inasmuch as Stanton and Anthony advocated different paths for suffragism, Anthony's path triumphed, and enfranchisement was eventually won, the victory has been laid at Anthony's feet and it is her leadership that the historical record commemorates.

However, remembering Anthony while forgetting Stanton is an historical half-truth, a serious obstacle to assessing the full impact of women's enfranchisement. More than any other leader of the woman suffrage movement, Stanton had urged that women's solidarity be based on an explicit political program for social reform and women's emancipation.

Stanton's vision for the power of women's votes reappeared decades after enfranchisement, when a "political gender gap"[56] emerged, and when women's votes—especially the votes of women of color, whom Stanton had never fully recognized—carried the hope for social change, and even for American democracy itself.

Document 18

Stanton on Frederick Douglass' Second Marriage; Douglass Response, 1884

A decade and a half after the Fifteenth Amendment controversy, news of Frederick Douglass' second marriage broke. After the death of his first wife Anna, an illiterate, a free-born Black woman, Douglass married Helen Pitts, a white woman twenty years his junior. Their families were neighbors, her parents were abolitionists, and she worked as a clerk in his office as Recorder of Deeds for the District of Columbia. As interracial marriages were widely condemned, a firestorm broke out among the public, white and Black both.

Stanton was determined to issue a public defense of Douglass' right to marry whom he chose. In addition to her personal relationship with Douglass, she was motivated by her fundamental devotion to the principle of personal liberty—that individuals rather than society should make decisions about how to lead their private lives.

Anthony, as angry as she had ever been at Stanton, tried to stop her. "The *Douglass* question, of *the intermarriage of the races*!" was a matter of science, she argued, the truth of which was not yet settled and which affected men and women equally. Stanton had the right to her own opinions, she said, but not to say anything which would be charged against the entire suffrage movement.[57]

Nevertheless, Stanton persisted. As she so often did when expressing her most radical opinions, she turned to satire. Inverting the attacks against an "inferior" Black man marrying a "superior" white woman, she portrayed Douglass instead as a "full fledged citizen" who had deigned to marry a creature with no rights at all. However, she was unable to find any newspaper willing to publish her public defense of Douglass' actions. Sending it on to him privately, she wrote that she would not give those who held "these contemptible prejudices" the satisfaction of knowing the full extent of her rage.

Document 18. Stanton on Douglass' Second Marriage

Excerpted from Gordon, *Select Papers*, vol. 4, 353–57.

Johnstown Fulton Co New York
May 27th [1884]

My dear Douglass

I enclose you a little piece of America history. When the hue & cry began at your marriage, I resolved to "pitch in" & defend your action in public as I did everywhere in private. I wrote two articles sent one to a friend in the New York press & one to Washington, intended as an open letter to you ridiculing this ridiculous prejudice of color. Both parties kept them declaring I should not mix in that controversy on the eve of the Woman suff[rage] convention. I did feel strongly about the matter, for just at that time there was another fuss about burying a colored man in a "white" cemetery,[58] ... & I did feel as if I would like to fire ten pounds of dynamite at the heels of all contemptible prejudices as to sex & color. But they were too small for an outlay of dynamite so I took ridicule. I send you enclosed that you may know my sympathies were with you as they have always been. But the colored people in their late conventions have behaved as badly as those who call themselves white. Well Douglass I have suffered all my life, just as you have, you have endured one curse I another. I do not believe you have passed through a shade of feeling that I do not understand. To be the equals yea the superiors of those who have the impudence to prescribe our spheres is enough to exasperate a saint. I know that with your intense pride & self respect that you have suffered more perhaps than any other American slave that ever trod this planet. I know I have more than any other women [sic] I ever met. I have always been in a chronic condition of rebellion. If I had not naturally a sunny temperament & good health, I should have been the princess of feminine devils.

... Well my friend if it is any comfort for you to know that there is another soul that though absent, is walking the vine press with you, know that every squib about your marriage brought the blood to my face & quickened my pulses, just as the vulgar squibs do about my sex. I have never been able to find words to express my indignation, when I think of woman's position. I have so little patience left when I meet these jackasses in the opposition, that I sit so silent & apparently indifferent that they do not even have the satisfaction to know that I care what they say. Well, well my best wishes for you & your wife sincerely yours, Elizabeth Cady Stanton

Enclosure, January 27, 1884

Frederick Douglass Esteemed Friend,

Allow me to congratulate you, on your recent marriage, & express my sincere wish, that all the happiness possible in a true union may be yours.

In view of all you have suffered & all you have achieved, the sunset of your life should be one of peace & enjoyment, but the days of your persecution seen [sic] not yet to be ended.

I hear much hostile criticism on your condescension in marrying a *white woman*. After all the terrible battles, & political upheavals we have had in expurgating our constitutions of that odious adjective "white" it is really remarkable that you of all men should have stooped to do it honor. "The white" feature of this contract is bad enough, but "the woman" is still worse.

To think that you a full fledged citizen of this republic, one of the male aristocracy, a sovreign [sic] in your own right, who can make & unmake Presidents, Senators, & Congressmen, amend constitutions, capable as a scholar & statesmen of occupying the loftiest position in the gift of the American people, to think that you should unite your future destiny with "a woman."

In choosing a domestic companion from this anomalous order of being, did you forget that according to some authorities, a woman is not yet "a person," much less "a citizen," ranked with idiots, lunatics, & criminals in our state constitutions, an outlaw, a pariah, not fit according to the present Solicitor of the Treasury[59] to pilot a little steamboat, up the muddy Mississippi? No wonder your large circle of admiring friends protest against such self-sacrifice on your part.

In defence of the right to pilot ships or marry whom we please we might quote some of the basic principles of our government, we might suggest that in some things individual rights, & tastes should control.

If a woman wishes to perfect herself in the science of navigation, it might be said that unbounded liberty to do so is her inalienable right. If a good man from.... Maryland sees fit to marry a disfranchised woman from New York, there being no legal impediments to the union, full liberty of choice in such relations should be conceded.

But alas! If we settle all these questions on the principle of right & justice, what is to become of our time honored customs, prejudices & sentimentalisms? ....

If we press Mrs. Miller her steamboat, Mr. Douglass & his wife into the compass of a syllogism, & prove logically that "United States citizens" have a right to choose their own wives & employments, half the writing & speaking in this country ... as to class privileges might be ended. I hail the day when in the discussion of human rights exact & equal justice will be ... demanded for all without distinction of race or sex. With my kind regards to your wife, & my best wishes for your happiness, very sincerely yours Elizabeth Cady Stanton

Douglass wrote back that as he expected, Stanton's "love of Liberty" had brought her to his defense.

Document 18. Stanton on Douglass' Second Marriage

Washington D.C. May 30, 1884

My dear Mrs. Stanton:

I am very glad to find, as I do find by your kind good letter, that I have made no mistake in respect of your feeling concerning my marriage. I have known you and your love of Liberty so long and well, that without one word from you on the subject, I had recorded your word and vote against the clamor raised against my marriage to a white woman. To those who find fault with me on this account I have no apology to make. My wife and I have simply obeyed the convictions of our own minds and hearts in a matter wherein we along were concerned and about which no body has any right to interfere. I could never have been at peace with my own soul or held up my head among men had I allowed the fear of popular clamor to deter me from following my convictions as to this marriage. I should have gone to my grave a self accused and a self convicted moral coward. Much as I respect the good opinion of my fellow men, I do not wish it at expense of my own self-respect. Circumstances have during the last forty years thrown me much more into white society than in that of colored people. While true to the rights of the colored race my nearest personal friends owning to association and common sympathy and aims have been white people—and as men choose their wives from friends and associates, it is not strange that I have chosen my wife and that she has chosen me. You, Dear Mrs. Stanton, could have found a straight smooth and pleasant road through the world had you allowed the world to decide for you your sphere in life—that is had you allowed it to link your moral and intellectual individuality into nonentity. But you have nobly asserted your own and the rights of your sex—and the world will know here after that you have lived and worked beneficently in the world.

You have made both Mrs Douglass and myself very glad and happy by your letter and we both give you our warmest thanks for it. Helen is a braver woman than I am a man and bears the assaults of popular prejudice more serenely than I do. No sign or complaint escapes her. She is steady firm and strong and meets the gaze of the world with a tranquil heart and unruffled brow. I am amazed by her heroic bearing and am greatly strengthened by it. She has sometimes said she would not regret though the storm of opposition were ten times greater.

I would like to write you a long letter, but I must be off to the Chicago Convention[60] and must leave this to be folded and directed by Helen. How good it is to have a wife who can read and write, and who can as Margaret Fuller says cover one in all his range. Always truly yours Fredk Douglass

Douglass died in 1895, Stanton eight years later. Anthony became a friend of Helen Douglass.

DOCUMENT 19

Anthony, "Organization Among Women," Columbian Exposition, 1893

Unlike the 1876 Centennial World's Fair, the grand Columbian Exposition held in Chicago in 1893 gave women and their achievements pride of place, centered on an elegant Woman's Building, designed by a woman architect. Although Anthony had played a role in gaining congressional funding, the Exposition's Board of Lady Managers feared what they considered the radical tendencies of suffragists, who they largely excluded. Eventually suffrage leaders were able to organize a "World's Congress of Representative Women," which drew one of the largest audiences at the entire Exposition. Stanton, not fit enough to attend, nonetheless sent several papers which were read for her. Anthony however made several appearances and was widely celebrated, enjoying for the first time recognition for her leadership. In this context, it is interesting that in the following speech she voiced discontent at the overshadowing of her own movement by other organized activities of women, some of which she herself had championed.

May Wright Sewall, ed., *World Congress of Representative Women*, (Chicago: Rand, McNally & Co., 1894) vol. 2, pp. 462–65.

During the week of the presentation of the work of the various organizations that have been represented in this Congress, organizations from the Old World and the New, I have been curious to learn that "all roads lead to Rome." That is to say, it doesn't matter whether an organization is called the King's Daughters, the partisan, or non-partisan Woman's Christian Temperance Union; whether it is called a Portia club, a sorosis, or a federation of clubs; a missionary society to reclaim the heathen of the Fiji Islands or an educational association; whether it is of the Jewish, of the Catholic, of the Protestant, of the Liberal, or the other sort of religion;

somehow or other, everybody and every association that has spoken or reported has closed up with the statement that what they are waiting for is the ballot.

Another curious thing I have noted as I have listened to their reports is, that one association, the Federation of Clubs, which is only three years old—not old enough to vote yet—can count forty thousand members; that the Relief Associations of Utah, which is perhaps a quarter of a century old, reports thirty thousand members; that the Christian Temperance Union, which is yet but a little past its second decade, can report a half-million members; that the King's Daughters, only seven years old, can report two hundred thousand members; and so I might run through with all the organizations of the Old and the New worlds that have reported here, and I will venture to say that there is scarcely one of them that does not report a larger number than the Woman's Suffrage Association of the United States. Now why is it? I will tell you frankly and honestly that all we number is seven thousand. This is the number that reported this year to the national organization, which is an association composed of all the State societies and local societies that are united and that pay a little money. These other societies have a fee, or I suppose they do. But I want to say that all this great national suffrage movement that has made this immense revolution in this country, has done the work of agitation, and has kept up what Daniel Webster called it, "this rumpus of agitation," probably represents a smaller number of women, and especially represents a smaller amount of money to carry on its work than any other organization under the shadow of the American flag. We have known how to make the noise, you see, and how to bring the whole world to our organization in spirit, if not in person. I would philosophize on the reason why. It is because women have been taught always to work for something else than their own personal freedom; and the hardest thing in the world is to organize women for the one purpose of securing their political liberty and political equality. It is easy to congregate thousands and hundreds of thousands of women to try to stay the tide of intemperance; to try to elevate the morals of a community; to try to educate the masses of the people; to try to relieve the poverty of the miserable; but it is a very difficult thing to make the masses of women, any more than the masses of men, congregate in great numbers to study the cause of all the ills of which they complain, and to organize for the removal of that cause; to organize for the establishment of great principles that will be sure to bring about the results which they so much desire.

Now, friends, I can tell you a great deal about what the lack of organization means, and what a hindrance this lack has been in the great movement with which I have been associated. If we could have gone to our State legislatures saying that we had numbered in our association the vast masses of the women; five millions of women in these United States who sympathize with us in spirit, and who wish we might gain the end; if we could have demonstrated to the Congress of the United States, and to the legislatures of the respective States, that we had a thorough organization back of our demand, we should have had all our demands granted long ago, and each one of the organizations which have come up here to talk at this great congress of women would not have been compelled to climax its report with the statement that they are without the ballot, and with the assertion that they need only the ballot to help them carry their work on to greater success. I want every single woman of every single organization of the Old World and the New that has thus reported, and that does feel that enfranchisement, that political equality is the underlying need to carry forward all the great enterprises of the world—I want each one to register herself, so that I can report them all at Washington next winter, and we will carry every demand which you want....

Document 20

Anthony and Ida B. Wells, Friendship, 1894–1895

Anthony's roots in abolitionism were much deeper than those of her partner Elizabeth Cady Stanton, and her connection to Ida B. Wells was part and parcel of her sustained devotion to African American women and men. Anthony admired Wells not only as an outstanding individual but as an exceptional leader of her race. Anthony actively supported the anti-lynching campaign which Wells had brought back from England to the U.S.

However, Gilded Age racism had deep sexual undertones. These were a problem for Anthony, while Stanton stood up against such popular opinions when she publicly defended Douglass' interracial marriage (see Document 21). When she met Anthony, Wells had become embroiled in a controversy with WCTU leader Frances Willard, in which sexual matters were crucial. Willard accepted at face value the rampant claims of Black men's sexual violence against white women, while Wells knew that such charges were largely fabricated excuses for discrimination and violence. Even though she supported Wells' campaign against lynching, Anthony, who was very conventional when it came to sexual matters (as well as unwilling to threaten her alliance with the WCTU) would not support Wells in her conflict with Willard.

Anthony's discomfort with the way Wells conducted her home life after her marriage to Ferdinand Barnett, which is documented in the last of these excerpts, raises similar issues. Wells, like other African American activists of her generation, pioneered the new practice of women combining personal and professional lives. Her path-breaking decision to hyphenate her family name with that of her husband's signaled this more modern approach. She rejected the assumption of Anthony's generation that women were obligated to choose between personal and public duties. Anthony criticized her—as she had Stanton long before—for letting family responsibilities interfere with political ones, and vice versa.

Anthony's first meeting with Wells took place in April 1895, a turning point year for both. Frederick Douglass, Wells' mentor, had died in February. Wells returned from her second English tour, determined to ignite an anti-lynching movement in the U.S. African American women in Brooklyn organized to defend her against the fierce racist reaction to her anti-lynching campaign, which became the seed of the Black women's club movement. Wells came to Rochester after stops in San Francisco, Los Angeles and Chicago and after publishing *A Red Record*, her carefully documented analysis of the scope of deadly southern lynchings.

Meanwhile, Anthony had just returned from the 1895 suffrage meetings in Atlanta, which had been replete with racial tensions. Even as she visited several African American churches and organizations in the area, she yielded to the attitudes of the southern white suffragists she was courting to keep Black women out of their movement. As her subsequent confession to Wells indicates, she was ashamed but even so continued to defend the pragmatism of her decision.

On March 31, three days after Wells arrived in Rochester, having already spoken to African American audiences, she came to speak before Plymouth Church. Wells spoke, after which, Anthony described the racial practices she had witnessed in Atlanta. It is unclear whether Anthony did object to Black women being relegated to the galleries at the Atlanta suffrage convention.

This account draws on numerous sources, including Wells' autobiography, published posthumously by her daughter

---

From the *Rochester Democrat and Chronicle,* April 1, 1895, p. 8, "Wrongs of the Negro":

Miss Anthony then addressed the people present, relating incidents brought to her notice during her recent travels in the South. She expressed herself as being surprised and shocked at observing the extent to which the "color line" was carried; notably in travel, where certain cars bore the placard announcing that "This car is for white persons only," or at the stations in which separate waiting rooms were used for the accommodation of the negro. Miss Anthony told her experiences at suffrage conventions in the Southern cities, at which the colored women were compelled to seek the galleries, much to her annoyance, and concluded by eulogizing the memory of the late Frederick Douglass, and expressing herself as considering it a most honorable privilege in being allowed to attend his funeral services.

The two women were together again four days later at Rochester's premier

Document 20. Anthony and Ida B. Wells, Friendship

suffrage association, the Political Equality Club. Anthony, who was president, may well have arranged for the event. In response to what they learned from Wells, the group passed a strongly worded anti-lynching resolution.

> From *Rochester Democrat and Chronicle*, April 5, 1895:
>
> Whereas reliable information has reached us through the personal knowledge of our friend of human rights, Miss I. B. Wells, that the barbarous practice of lynching, not only men, but women, without judge or jurors—on suspected, not proven crime, and sometimes without even a charge of crime, is still in practice in the South and West ....
> Resolved, That the Woman's Political Equality Club of Rochester deplore and denounce such degraded and neglected conditions of any portion of our people as admit of such atrocities without arousing speedy retribution and reform by our governmental officials, through a thorough investigation, and the application of strong measures for the protection of the disfranchised portion of our people, who are thus rendered helpless and without redress, and also for the safety of our whole community.

Three days later, on April 7, Wells spoke before another mixed-race church audience, at which time she was confronted by a hostile southerner. The incident was widely reported, and eventually included in Anthony's journal and official biography. However, Anthony's version omitted two details included in this contemporary newspaper account. Wells emphasized the sexual dimension of southern anti–Black law; and she also added important information about the debt peonage suffered by Black southern agricultural workers. The young Black Rochester girl, whose mistreatment Anthony described, was the daughter of Wells' local hostess, Anna Morse.

> From *Asheville North Carolina Citizen Times*, April 8, 1895:
>
> Last evening at the First Baptist church Miss Ida Wells said negro lynching had increased in the South in a marked degree; that between 1882 and 1892 1000 colored people were lynched on slight pretexts, and, in many cases, when they were known to be innocent. She gave a number of illustrations, bearing upon her conclusion, when a theological student, who said he hailed from Texas, arose and said: "Do you assume that all the negroes that have been lynched in the South since the war have been innocent?" "I never said that," replied Miss Wells. "I simply claim they were innocent in the eyes of the law. No man is guilty until found so by trial." Miss Wells then resumed her lecture. She said it was a crime for negroes to intermarry with whites; that this was manifestly unjust to the colored

women of the South. She insisted that if it was illegal for white men to marry colored women, it should also be illegal for them to form alliances with them. A white man might live with a colored woman with impunity, but if he should marry her it would be a crime.

Here the Texan, in evident excitement, said, "Do the negroes want to marry white folks? If the negroes are so badly treated in the South, why do they not come North or go West or to some more congenial clime?"

"They are not able to emigrate," replied Miss Wells, "because they are always in debt to their landlords, being paid in checks for provisions only good at plantation stores. I would remain in the South myself had I not been forbidden to come back on pain of losing my life."

Miss Anthony, who was present, could restrain herself no longer. She jumped to her feet, and with fire in her eye, said, "The colored people receive no better treatment in the North than in the South. That is why they do not come here. In our city only last week a dance was to be given in No. 3 school for the benefit of children in the seventh grade, and tickets were issued to children for 10 cents. Now it happened that there was a colored girl in that grade, who wanted to get in as well as white children, and her mother gave her the money. But when she went to the teacher, Miss Stuart, she was told that if she insisted on attending, none of the white children would go, and the affair would be given up; so the poor child was turned away. I consider that outrage on the feelings of that colored girl was the result of the same spirit that inspires lynching in the South." Miss Anthony's denunciation of these distinctions among Christian people of the North as well as the South was dramatic, and the theological student from Texas subsided in the outburst of approval on the part of the audience that followed.

On the evening of April 8, Anthony inivited Wells to dinner and to spend the night at her home. There she learned that racial discrimination occurred in her own home. In her autobiography, Wells included the story of Anthony's secretary's refusal to take dictation from her. Anthony's official biography also includes the incident.

Excerpted from *Select Papers of Stanton and Anthony*, vol. 5, p. 691.

April 8, 1895: Ida B. Wells of Memphis—guest—... Told typewriter Anna Dorsey—to ask Miss Wells if she would like to dictate her letters & have them written on the type writer—When I returned—I found Miss Wells scribbling away—& said couldn't you dictate & let Anny type write for you—"oh yes—if I had a chance"—then I went to my room & said—"You didn't understand me did you to ask Mrs W."—["]Yes—she said—but I didn't choose to write for a colored woman"—I engaged to work for *you!*

Well—when I ask an employee to do a favor to a guest I expect her to comply—so the little fatherless & homeless girl of 20—left.

Wells' memories of Anthony were written much later, after her own days of fiery activism were behind her. The reference to Frances Willard has to do with their conflict because the WCTU's leader had insisted that lynching was vindicated by Black men's sexual predatory behavior (see p. 163 above).

From *Crusade for Justice*, ed. Alfreda Duster, pp. 229–30:

Those were precious days in which I sat at the feet of this pioneer and veteran in the work of women's suffrage. She had endeavored to make me see that for the sake of expediency one had often to stoop to conquer on this color question. This was when we discussed Miss Willard's attitude, and of course, I could not see what she was trying to make clear to me. She added that she, too, belonged to Miss Willard's class, for she had done that very same thing in the Women's Equal Suffrage Association. "… [W]hen the Equal Suffrage Association went to Atlanta, Georgia, knowing the feeling of the South with regard to Negro participation on equality with whites, I myself asked Mr. Douglass not to come. I did not want to subject him to humiliation, and I did not want anything to get in the way of bringing the southern white women into our suffrage association, now that their interest had been awakened. Not only that," said Miss Anthony, "but when a group of colored women came and asked that I come to them and aid them in forming a branch of the suffrage association among the colored women I declined to do so, on the ground of that same expediency. And you think I was wrong in so doing?" she asked. I answered uncompromisingly yes, for I felt that although she may have made gains for suffrage, she had also confirmed white women in their attitude on segregation.

I suppose Miss Anthony had pity on my youth and inexperience for she never in any way showed resentment of my attitude. She gave me rather the impression of a woman who was eager to hear all sides of any question, and that I am sure is one of the reasons for her splendid success in the organization which did so much to give the women of this country an equal share in all the privileges of citizenship.

On another point we were not always in agreement. Whatever the question up for discussion as to wrongs, injustices, inequality, maladministration of the law, Miss Anthony would always say, "Well, now when women get the ballot all that will be changed." So I asked her one day, "Miss Anthony, do you really believe that the millennium is going to come when women get the ballot? Knowing women as I do, and their petty outlook on life, although I believe that it is right that they should have the vote, I do not believe that the exercise of the vote is going to change women's nature nor the political situation." Miss Anthony seemed a little bit startled, but she did not make any contention on that point.

Three years later, in the fall 1898, Wells (now Wells-Barnett and the mother of two) returned to Rochester at the invitation of T. Thomas Fortune to reestablish the Afro-American League.

Ibid., p. 255:

Again I was the guest of Susan B. Anthony. I had been with her several days before I noticed the way she would bite out my married name in addressing me. Finally I said to her, "Miss Anthony, don't you believe in women getting married?" She said, "Oh, yes, but not women like you who had a special call for special work. I too might have married but it would have meant dropping the work to which I had set my hand." She said, "I know of no one in all this country better fitted to do the work you had in hand than yourself. Since you have gotten married, agitation seems practically to have ceased. Besides, you have a divided duty. You are here trying to help in the formation of this league and your eleven-month-old baby needs your attention at home. You are distracted over the thought that maybe he is not being looked after as he would be if you were there, and that makes for a divided duty."

Although it was a well-merited rebuke from her point of view, I could not tell Miss Anthony that it was because I had been unable, like herself, to get the support which was necessary to carry on my work that I had become discouraged in the effort to carry on alone. For that reason I welcomed the opportunity of trying to help unite our people so that there would be a following to help in the arduous work necessary.

Document 21

Stanton, "Address to the Founding Convention of the National American Woman Suffrage Association," February 1890

Stanton's speech on the occasion of the merger of the National and American suffrage associations was very controversial. In it, she began to challenge the newly achieved unity of the suffrage movement by exposing some of the political differences hidden beneath it. At one level, she was trying to influence suffragists' opinions on current political issues such as the separation of church and state and divorce legislation. But even deeper, she was trying to shape the entire political perspective of the new suffrage organization. She continued to believe that the goal of the woman suffrage movement was not simply to win the vote for women but to build women into a force for radical political change. However, many of the new, younger leaders disagreed with her, and their approach soon came to dominate the National American Woman Suffrage Association.

Elizabeth Cady Stanton Papers, Library of Congress.

... The chief barriers in the way to a more pronounced success in our movement have been: 1st, the apathy and indifference of society to all reforms. 2ndly, Our lack of thorough and widespread organization.... [As] to organization, for many years, we had no forces to organize. Each individual was a free lance to say or do whatsoever she liked.... [N]ow after twenty years of grand work in different lines, we have come to the conclusion that in Union there is strength, and added power in thorough organization. In uniting all our forces to-day under one banner, with the hearty cooperation of every friend of the movement, victory might soon be ours.... Isolated effort is of little value in carrying any great measure.... With all our forces molded together and concentrated on one point, our influence on the near future will, I know, prove irresistible....

In view of the many vital questions now up for consideration in which women are especially interested, it seems to me that the time has come for more aggressive measures, more self assertion on our part than was ever manifested before....

For fifty years we have been Plaintiffs at the bar of justice, and three generations of statesmen, Judges, and reformers have exhausted their able arguments and eloquent appeals in the courts and before the people. But as the Bench, the Bar and the Jury are all men, we are non-suited every time, and yet, some men tell us we must be patient and persuasive, that we must be womanly. My friends, what is man's idea of womanly? It is to have a manner that pleases him, quiet, deferential, submissive, that approaches him as a subject does a master. He wants no self assertion on our part, no defiance, no vehement arraigning of him as a robber and a criminal. While the grand motto, "resistance to tyrants is obedience to God," has echoed and reechoed around the globe electrifying the lovers of liberty in every latitude and making crowned heads tremble on their thrones, while every right achieved by the oppressed has been wrung from tyrants by force, while the darkest page of human history is the outrages on women, shall men tell us to-day to be patient, persuasive, womanly? What do we know as yet as to what is womanly? The women we have seen thus far have been with rare exceptions the mere echoes of men.... Patience and persuasiveness are beautiful virtues in dealing with children and the feeble minded adults, but with those who have the gift of reason and understand the principles of justice, it is our duty to compel them to act up to the highest light that is in them and as promptly as possible....

As women are taking an active part in pressing on the consideration of Congress many narrow sectarian measures, such as more rigid Sunday laws, to stop travel and distribution of the mail on that day, and intend to introduce the name of God into the Constitution, this action on the part of some women is used as an argument for the disfranchisement of all. I hope this convention will declare that the Woman's Suffrage Association is opposed to all Union of Church and State and pledges itself as far as possible, to maintain the secular nature of our government. As Sunday is the only day the laboring man can escape from the cities, to stop the street cars, omnibusses and rail roads would indeed be a lamentable exercise of arbitrary authority. No, no, the duty of the state is to protect those who do the work of the world in the largest liberty and instead of shutting them up in their gloomy tenement houses on Sunday, we should open wide the parks, horticultural gardens, the museums, the libraries, the galleries of art and the music halls, where they can listen to the divine melodies of the great masters. All these are questions of legislation and what influence women will exert as voters is already being canvassed, hence the importance of this Association expressing its opinions on all questions in which woman's social, civil, religious, and political rights are involved. Consider the thousands of women with babies in their arms year after year who have no change to the dull routine of their lives, except on Sunday when their husbands can go with them on some little excursion by land or sea, suddenly compelled to stay at home by passage of a rigid Sunday law, secured by the votes of those who can drive about at pleasure in their own carriages and go wherever they may desire. It is puerile to say "no matter how we use the ballot the right is ours," but if the presumption that we will use it wisely enters into the chance of our obtaining it, it is desirable for the public to know our opinions on practical questions of morals and politics.

We must demand a voice too in another field of labor, thus far bounded, fenced and tilled by man alone, where according to his own statistics one may now gather more thorns and thistles than fruits and flowers. And this is the home. Many propositions are now floating about as to the laws regulating our family relations.... The message I should like to go out from this convention is that there should be no further legislation on the questions of Marriage and Divorce until woman has a voice in the state and national governments. Surely here is a relation in which above all others there should be equality; a relation in which woman really has a deeper interest than man and if the laws favor either party it should be the wife and mother. Marriage is a mere incident in a man's life. He has business interests and ambitions in other directions, but as a general thing it is all of life to woman where all her interests and ambitions centre. And if the conditions of her surroundings there are discordant and degrading, she is indeed most unfortunate and needs the protection of the laws to set her free rather than hold her in bondage.

And yet it is proposed to have a national law restricting the right of divorce to a narrower basis.... Congress has already made an appropriation for a Report on the Question which shows that there are 10,000 divorces annually in the United States and other statisticians say the majority asked for by women. If liberal divorce laws for wives are what Canada was for the slaves, a door of escape from bondage, we had better consult the women before we close the avenues to freedom. Where discontent is rocked in every cradle and complaints to heaven going up with every prayer, talk not of the sacredness of such relations, nor of the best interests of society requiring their permanent establishment. The best interests of society and the individual always lie in the same direction, hence the state as well as the family is interested in building the home on solid foundation.

Some may say that none of these questions legitimately belong on this platform, but as they always have been discussed on the women's rights platform from the beginning they probably always will be. Wherever and whatever any class of women suffer whether in the home, the church, the courts, in the world of work, or on the statute books, a voice in their behalf should be heard in our conventions. We must manifest a broad catholic spirit for all shades of opinion in which we may differ and recognize the equal right of all parties sects and races tribes and colors. Colored women, Indian women, Mormon women Christian infidels and women from every quarter of the globe have been heard in these Washington conventions and I trust they always will be. The enfranchisement of woman is not a question to be carried by political clap-trap, by strategem or art, but by the slow process of education, by constant agitation and in new directions attacking in every turn stronghold of the enemy.... Let us ... stir up a whole group of new victims from time to time, by turning our guns on new strongholds. Agitation is the advance guard of education. When any principle or question is up for discussion, let us seize on it and show its connection, whether nearly or remotely, with woman's disfranchisement. There is such a thing as being too anxious lest someone "hurt the cause" by what he or she may say or do; and perhaps the very thing you fear is exactly what should be done. It is impossible for any one to tell what people are ready to hear....

Another question demanding consideration on our platform is the race problem that was supposed to be settled a quarter of a century ago by the proclamation of emancipation.... How comes it ... that the race problem is again up for discussion in Congress and the civil rights bill in our hotels? Because every fundamental principle by which [the freedman] was emancipated and enfranchised was immediately denied in its application to women.... The denial of principle in the case of women at the North has reacted in the denial of the same principle in the case of the Freedman of the South. And now our statesmen are at their wits' end to know what to do with the Freedmen and are actually proposing to colonize him. If the Russian system is to be adopted and all discontented citizens are to be sent to some Siberia, our turn will come next. Hence we had better make a stand on the Freedman and demand justice for him as well as ourselves. It is justice, and that alone that can end the impossible conflict between freedom and slavery going on in every nation on the globe. That is all the Nihilists, the socialists, the Communists ask, and that is all Ireland asks, and the Freedmen and women of this Republic ask no more.

Document 22

Stanton, "Educated Suffrage Justified"; Harriot Stanton Blatch, "An Open Letter to Mrs. Stanton," 1894

In the 1890s, as European immigrants poured into the nation's cities, political forces in favor of voter restriction grew. Stanton had first suggested requiring English-language literacy for enfranchisement in 1877. She argued that since an individual could with effort become literate, her proposal did not contradict the principle of universal suffrage. In 1894, a suffrage campaign for an amendment to the New York State constitution, in which Stanton was heavily involved, failed. (The entire constitutional revision, not just the woman suffrage amendment, that year failed.) This article, the first of three she wrote for the *Woman's Journal*, is laced through with the resentment of the native-born to new immigrants, whom she blamed for the state amendment's defeat.

Stanton was not alone in her advocacy of an English literacy qualification for the franchise. Many reformers, including African American leaders such as W. E. B. Du Bois and Mary Church Terrell, also called for education requirements for suffrage.[61] Stanton's rage, however, also reflected personal factors, the way in which her feminism could emerge, unqualified by any other democratic sentiment, a reaction that recurred throughout her career (see Document 11).

Stanton invited a response from Harriot Stanton Blatch, her daughter, who was now living near London. It is included to indicate the close bond between mother and daughter, as well as the historical differences between them. The socialist politics to which Blatch was exposed in England frame her reaction. As indicated by Blatch's repeated use of the term "proletariat," Blatch's socialism was much more based in working class politics than her mother's.

After her mother's death, when she returned to the U.S., Blatch took up leadership of the U.S. suffrage movement, into which she brought a new level of awareness of class differences and the importance of working-class women.

Stanton, "Educated Suffrage Justified," *Woman's Journal*, November 3, 1894; from Gordon, et al., *The Selected Papers of Stanton and Anthony*, vol. 5, pp. 655–58.

"Universal suffrage Is the first truth and only basis of a genuine republic."[62] There may be certain restrictions, however, for the exercise of this right, without denying the general principle.

We have had, at different times, in the several States, eleven different classes disqualified for the suffrage, namely, idiots, lunatics. criminals, paupers, minors, men who bet on elections, clergymen (by custom not constitution) those not possessing $250, those who could neither read nor write, all black men, and all women black and white. Nine of these are surmountable qualifications, supposed to exist for the best interests of the State, but from which the citizen, with time and effort, may easily escape.

By modern scientific appliances, the idiot may develop sufficient intelligence to provide for his own wants and protect this rights. The lunatic may become sane. The criminal may be pardoned and reform. The pauper may become capable of self-support. The minor may come of age. The men who bet on elections may awake to the dishonor of violating the State Constitution, which every good citizen is bound to support. The penniless by thrift may acquire $250. The ignorant may learn to read and write. The clergy can change their profession, or convince the people (as they have done) that an interest in the State in no way conflicts with holy mission to save the souls of their people.

But for the remaining two classes the disqualifications are insurmountable. Neither time nor effort can change sex or color; hence such qualifications are indeed opposed to every principle of a true republic. Regulating the suffrage is one thing; denying it absolutely is another.

It seems to me the proposition for "educated suffrage" made and reiterated in the WOMAN'S JOURNAL, is preeminently wise and timely.[63] A law providing that after 1898 those who vote must be able to read and write the English language would be an immense advantage to the individual and the State. With the ignorant and impecunious from the Old World landing on our shores by hundreds every day, we must have some restrictions of the suffrage for our own safety and for their education before they take part in the administration of the government. Every man of them should be compelled to read and write the English language before they are allowed to register themselves as voters. This would be a double blessing—to them and to the State.

A knowledge merely of the elements of learning would give a man greater aptitude for his duties in all relations of life. What is learned in the primary department in school is the foundation for all that is achieved in the higher classes. If a foreigner can read and write the English language intelligently, he has taken the first step towards understanding the spirit of our institutions and the duties of citizenship. In reply to Mr. Garrison I would say[64]: Instead of repealing the educational law of Massachusetts, which he deems a mere travesty, I would draw the line a little higher, at intelligent reading and writing. To acquire this would take the ignorant foreigner at least two years, so we should be sure that he did not go straight from the steerage to the polls.

The proposition, as stated in the WOMAN'S JOURNAL, involves no injustice to women, but provides that all educated men and women shall vote on the same basis. True, we cannot take the suffrage from the ignorant men who already exercise it, not because they prize it so highly, but because no political party dare make the experiment. If Mr. Garrison belonged to a disfranchised class he might more keenly feel the humiliation of a foreign yoke, such as educated women endure to-day: tried in the courts by foreign jurors and witnesses, who scarcely understand the language in which the advocate pleads the case and the judge gives the charge.

... [A] law that would compel all American citizens to acquire a knowledge of their own language before exercising the suffrage, would surely be a stimulus in the right direction. A law compelling all our foreign citizens to read and write the English language would make our whole people more homogeneous and united.

The greatest block in the way of woman's enfranchisement is the fear of the "ignorant vote" being doubled. Wise men see what a strain it is on our institutions to-day, and object to any further experimenting in that direction. I do not see that the ignorant classes need the suffrage more than the enlightened, but just the reverse. When a vessel is in danger on a stormy sea, we need skill and intelligence on the bridge and at the wheel, to protect those who are ignorant of the science of navigation. Just so in the State we need the highest intelligence and morality to govern a nation with justice and wisdom. "The first desire of every enlightened mind," says Matthew Arnold, "is to take part in the great work of government."

Harriot Stanton Blatch responded: "An Open Letter to Mrs. Stanton," *Woman's Journal*, December 22, 1894.

My honored Mother:

A few days since, you wrote asking my opinion of a letter of yours in the WOMAN'S JOURNAL of Nov. 3. As you represent a growing body of opinion in America, and addressed the wide constituency of the JOURNAL, I beg leave to express my thoughts in an equally public way.

When I opened the JOURNAL of the third instant, my eye caught the column headed "Ignorant Suffrage no Failure," and as I read the convincing quotations from Frederick Douglass, thinking you were the person quoting them, I was filled with a spirit of self-gratification, that the previous arguments we had had on this subject had evidently told upon your former position. Imagine my humiliation when I found at the bottom of the article, not your name, but William Lloyd Garrison's. My chagrin while reading the next letter, which was really yours, was only saved from being of a most painful character by the thought that I could claim Mr. Garrison as one of my personal friends, at least.

People are ever raising to themselves fetiches [sic] to worship in government, as in everything else. No sooner is one Golden Calf,—as, for Instance, that it is only the man with a money-bag who has a stake in the country,—been torn down, than another is erected. The idea of restricting the suffrage to those who can read and write is another fetich. Now, my dear mother, if you have the heart to re-read the letter in which you invite us to fall down and worship this fetich, you will find that throughout you imply that if a person can read and write, he is "enlightened" and "educated," and if he cannot read and write, he is "ignorant." I am sure, if you will frankly appeal to your knowledge of the world, you will be forced to admit that many a person who could satisfy you in the "intelligence" of his reading, nay, more, who could satisfy a board of examiners of his collegiate accomplishments, is lamentably ignorant; while many a man, without a sign of the three Rs about him, is gifted with the sterling commonsense and abiding honesty which the school of life's experience teaches.

But you go still further, and call every American citizen who was born in Europe and who cannot read or write the English language, an "ignorant foreigner." Perhaps you forgot that the nations of Europe have their public school systems. Take Germany, for instance; probably not a son of the Fatherland arrives in New York who has not had quite as good a common school education as the average man of the proletariat born in the United States. I think I am right in saying that you cannot read, write, or speak a word of German. Now, I not only affirm that you would not be an "ignorant foreigner," if you landed in Germany, but I declare, if you were given the franchise there, you would be the most Intelligent voter in the whole Empire on women's questions. Of course I do not mean to contend that every foreigner in America is as well-informed as you would be in Germany; but I do say that the proletariat, whether able to read or not, can give a more valuable opinion than any other class upon such a question, for example, as the housing of the poor. As our ability to feel our own needs is not bounded by our linguistic accomplishments, neither should our power to remedy them through government be so bounded. Because you overlook the fact that the conditions of the poor are so much harder than yours or mine, you are led to argue that "the ignorant classes do not need the suffrage more than the enlightened, but just the reverse." Every working man needs the suffrage more than I do, but there is another who needs it more than he does, just because conditions are more galling, and that is the working woman.

You warn us that "Wise men see what a strain it (the ignorant vote) is on our institutions." I here derive great comfort that you did not quote wise women in support of your contentions, but left the burden to men. As you omit to name these wise men, I cannot challenge their right to the title; but, certain it is, their wisdom is free of any historical basis. The heaviest strain on American institutions was the Civil War and all the upheaval that preceded it; but surely the "ignorant vote" was not then the disturbing cause. And has not a government by an aristocracy of "intellect" been tried? Why, my dear mother, right in our own country a government of the "educated" ruled over a wide area for generations. Before the war, the whole southern section of the United States was ruled by its men who could "read and write." They had it all their own way, and what did they do with their power? No, no, we are ever vainly trying to get morals and character out of intellect, but they grow on quite other soil. ....

But do not understand that, if it were possible to separate the truthful, the upright, the conscientious and the loving from their weaker fellow men, I would advocate a government of an aristocracy of the moral; for I would not, and on this ground, that government is not the end of man, but merely a method of expressing collective thought, and achieving concerted action. And the thought is not collective if any human being capable of thought is excluded. We cannot escape the law that society is never stronger than its weakest link. Hence the wisdom of having the weakest link brought out in full light of day, freely showing its weakness, so that flaws may be corrected. If the strong links never were made to feel the detriment to themselves, individually and collectively, of the existence of the weak, nothing would be done to improve the feeble. Let the illiterate man express himself, he is not ignorant on all sides; and let the mistakes which arise from his limitations stand as stumbling blocks in the paths of the wise, so that his power for evil may bring conviction of his need for help.

Again, you assert that "if a foreigner can read and write the English language intelligently, he has taken the first step towards understanding the spirit of our institutions and the duties of citizenship." Let me assure you the spirit of freedom is not a treasure hidden in America, but is everywhere throbbing in the heart of growing Democracy. I do not call the man ignorant or wanting in an understanding of Republican principles who, under the grinding, economic conditions of the Old World, stints himself to lay by, little by little, his passage money across the Atlantic, hoping to find in America a broader freedom for himself; but I do call ignorant, and a real danger to the State, the educated man, born and bred in a republic, who devotes his highest energies to money getting and neglects his every duty as a citizen. Monarchy is the true government for the lazy; a Republic calls for energy, and true it is that the actual voters will form the government. And if the "reading and writing," "intelligent," "enlightened," "educated," "wise," "moral" American won't soil his hands with politics, let him at least be thankful that he has the "ignorant" masses to give him that necessary thing—a government.

Yours ever devotedly,
HARRIOT STANTON BLATCH.

Document 23

Stanton, "The Solitude of Self," January 18, 1892

Stanton delivered "The Solitude of Self" in 1892, at the convention at which she resigned the presidency of the suffrage movement. Anthony did not like the speech at first, but Stanton thought it "the best thing I have ever written" and it remains one of the most moving statements of feminism of any age.[65] Stanton's advanced age and her political isolation help to explain the speech's sad, wearied tone, but her ultimate message was a triumphant one, a powerful defense of the feminist philosophy by which she had lived her life and made most of her political decisions.

The essence of Stanton's feminism was the belief that, ultimately, life placed the same demands on women as on men, required the same resources of them, and therefore, in justice, should provide them with the same individual rights. In this speech, however, her emphasis was shifting from individualism as a political philosophy to individualism as a description of the inner experience common to men and women. As such, Stanton anticipated the existentialist philosophy associated with the rebirth of modern feminism and its concern with the "personal" elements of women's experience.

The Woman's Journal, January 1892, pp. 1–2:

The point I wish plainly to bring before you on this occasion is the individuality of each human soul; our Protestant idea, the right of individual conscience and judgment; our republican idea, individual citizenship. In discussing the rights of woman, we are to consider, first, what belongs to her as an individual, in a world of her own, the arbiter of her own destiny, an imaginary Robinson Crusoe, with her woman, Friday, on a solitary island. Her rights under such circumstances are to use all her faculties for her own safety and happiness.

Secondly, if we consider her as a citizen, as a member of a great nation, she must have the same rights as all other members, according to the fundamental principles of our Government.

Thirdly, viewed as a woman, an equal factor in civilization, her rights and duties are still the same; individual happiness and development.

Fourthly, it is only the incidental relations of life, such as mother, wife, sister, daughter, which may involve some special duties and training....

The strongest reason for giving woman all the opportunities for higher education, for the full development of her faculties, forces of mind and body; for giving her the most enlarged freedom of thought and action; a complete emancipation from all forms of bondage, of custom, dependence, superstition; from all the crippling influences of fear-is the solitude and personal responsibility of her own individual life. The strongest reason why we ask for woman a voice in the government under which she lives; in the religion she is asked to believe; equality in social life, where she is the chief factor; a place in the trades and professions, where she may earn her bread, is because of her birthright to self-sovereignty; because, as an individual, she must rely on herself. No matter how much women prefer to lean, to be protected and supported, nor how much men desire to have them do so, they must make the voyage of life alone, and for safety in an emergency, they must know something of the laws of navigation. To guide our own craft, we must be captain, pilot, engineer; with chart and compass to stand at the wheel; to watch the winds and waves, and know when to take in the sail, and to read the signs in the firmament over all. It matters not whether the solitary voyager is man or woman; nature, having endowed them equally, leaves them to their own skill and judgment in the hour of danger, and, if not equal to the occasion, alike they perish.

To appreciate the importance of fitting every human soul for independent action, think for a moment of the immeasurable solitude of self. We come into the world alone, unlike all who have gone before us; we leave it alone, under circumstances peculiar to ourselves. No mortal ever has been, no mortal ever will be like the soul just launched on the sea of life. There can never again be just such a combination of prenatal influences; never again just such environments as make up the infancy, youth and manhood of this one. Nature never repeats herself, and the possibilities of one human soul will never be found in another. No one has ever found two blades of ribbon grass alike, and no one will ever find two human beings alike. Seeing, then, what must be the infinite diversity in human character, we can in a measure appreciate the loss to a nation when any large class of the people is uneducated and unrepresented in the government.

We ask for the complete development of every individual, first, for his own benefit and happiness. In fitting out an army, we give each soldier his own knapsack, arms, powder, his blanket, cup, knife, fork and spoon. We provide alike for all their individual necessities; then each man bears his own burden.

Again, we ask complete individual development for the general good; for the consensus of the competent on the whole round of human interests, on all questions of national life; and here each man must bear his share of the general burden. It is sad to see how soon friendless children are left to bear their own burdens, before they can analyze their feelings; before they can even tell their joys and sorrows, they are thrown on their own resources. The great lesson that nature seems to teach us at all ages is self-dependence, self-protection, self-support....

In youth our most bitter disappointments, our brightest hopes and ambitions, are known only to ourselves. Even our friendship and love we never fully share with another; there is something of every passion, in every situation, we conceal. Even so in our triumphs and our defeats....

We ask no sympathy from others in the anxiety and agony of a broken friendship or shattered love. When death sunders our nearest ties, alone we sit in the shadow of our affliction. Alike amid the greatest triumphs and darkest tragedies of life, we walk alone. On the divine heights of human attainment, eulogized and worshipped as a hero or saint, we stand alone. In ignorance, poverty and vice, as a pauper or criminal, alone we starve or steal; alone we suffer the sneers and rebuffs of our fellows; alone we are hunted and hounded through dark courts and alleys, in by-ways and highways; alone we stand in the judgment seat; alone in the prison cell we lament our crimes and misfortunes; alone we expiate them on the gallows. In hours like these we realize the awful solitude of individual life, its pains, its penalties, its responsibilities; hours in which the youngest and most helpless are thrown on their own resources for guidance and consolation. Seeing, then, that life must ever be a march and a battle, that each soldier must be equipped for his own protection, it is the height of cruelty to rob the individual of a single natural right.

To throw obstacles in the way of a complete education is like putting out the eyes; to deny the rights of property, like cutting off the hands. To refuse political equality is to rob the ostracized of all self-respect; of credit in the market place; of recompense in the world of work, of a voice in choosing those who make and administer the law, a choice in the jury before whom they are tried, and in the judge who decides their punishment. What a picture ... of woman's position! Robbed of her natural rights, handicapped by law and custom at every turn, yet compelled to fight her own battles, and in the emergencies of life to fall back on herself for protection....

The young wife and mother, at the head of some establishment, with a kind husband to shield her from the adverse winds of life, with wealth, fortune and position, has a certain harbor of safety, secure against the ordinary ills of life. But to manage a household, have a desirable influence in society, keep her friends and the affections of her husband, train her children and servants well, she must have rare common sense, wisdom, diplomacy, and a knowledge of human nature. To do all this, she needs the cardinal virtues and the strong points of character that the most successful statesman possesses. An uneducated woman trained to dependence, with no resources in herself, must make a failure of any position in life. But society says women do not need a knowledge of the world, the liberal training that experience in public life must give, all the advantages of collegiate education; but when for the lack of all this, the woman's happiness is wrecked, alone she bears her humiliation; and the solitude of the weak and the ignorant is indeed pitiable. In the wild chase for the prizes of life, they are ground to powder.

In age, when the pleasures of youth are passed, children grown up, married and gone, the hurry and bustle of life in a measure over, when the hands are weary of active service, when the old arm chair and the fireside are the chosen resorts, then men and women alike must fall back on their own resources. If they cannot find companionship in books, if they have no interest in the vital questions of the hour, no interest in watching the consummation of reforms with which they might have been identified, they soon pass into their dotage. The more fully the faculties of the mind are developed and kept in use, the longer the period of vigor and active interest in all around us continues. If, from a life-long participation in public affairs, a woman feels responsible for the laws regulating our system of education, the discipline of our jails and prisons, the sanitary condition of our private homes, public buildings and thoroughfares, an interest in commerce, finance, our foreign relations, in any or all these questions, her solitude will at least be respectable, and she will not be driven to gossip or scandal for entertainment.

The chief reason for opening to every soul the doors to the whole round of human duties and pleasures is the individual development thus attained, the resources thus provided under all circumstances to mitigate the solitude that at times must come to everyone.

... Inasmuch, then, as woman shares equally the joys and sorrows of time and eternity, is it not the height of presumption in man to propose to represent her at the ballot box and the throne of grace, to do her voting in the State, her praying in the church, and to assume the position of High Priest at the family altar?

Nothing strengthens the judgment and quickens the conscience like individual responsibility. Nothing adds such dignity to character as the recognition of one's self-sovereignty; the right to an equal place, everywhere conceded; a place earned by personal merit, not an artificial attainment by inheritance, wealth, family and position. Conceding, then, that the responsibilities of life rest equally on man and woman, that their destiny is the same, they need the same preparation for time and eternity. The talk of sheltering woman from the fierce storms of life is the sheerest mockery, for they beat on her from every point of the compass, just as they do on man, and with more fatal results, for he has been trained to protect himself, to resist, and to conquer. Such are the facts in human experience, the responsibilities of individual sovereignty. Rich and poor, intelligent and ignorant, wise and foolish, virtuous and vicious, man and woman; it is ever the same, each soul must depend wholly on itself.

Whatever the theories may be of woman's dependence on man, in the supreme moments of her life, he cannot bear her burdens. Alone she goes to the gates of death to give life to every man that is born into the world; no one can share her fears, no one can mitigate her pangs; and if her sorrow is greater than she can bear, alone she passes beyond the gates into the vast unknown.

From the mountain-tops of Judea long ago, a heavenly voice bade his disciples, "Bear ye one another's burdens"; but humanity has not yet risen to that point of self-sacrifice; and if ever so willing, how few the burdens are that one soul can bear for another! ....

So it ever must be in the conflicting scenes of life, in the long, weary march, each one walks alone. We may have many friends, love, kindness, sympathy and charity, to smooth our pathway in everyday life, but in the tragedies and triumphs of human experience, each mortal stands alone.

But when all artificial trammels are removed, and women are recognized as individuals, responsible for their own environments, thoroughly educated for all positions in life they may be called to fill; with all the resources in themselves that liberal thought and broad culture can give; guided by their own conscience and judgment, trained to self-protection, by a healthy development of the muscular system, and skill in the use of weapons and defence; and stimulated to self-support by a knowledge of the business world and the pleasure that pecuniary independence must ever give; when women are trained in this way, they will in a measure be fitted for those hours of solitude that come alike to all, whether prepared or otherwise. As in our extremity we must depend on ourselves, the dictates of wisdom point to complete individual development.

In talking of education, how shallow the argument that each class must be educated for the special work it proposes to do, and that all those faculties not needed in this special work must lie dormant and utterly wither for want of use, when, perhaps, these will be the very faculties needed in life's greatest emergencies! Some say, "Where is the use of drilling girls in the languages, the sciences, in law, medicine, theology? As wives, mothers, housekeepers, cooks, they need a different curriculum from boys who are to fill all positions. The chief cooks in our great hotels and ocean steamers are men. In our large cities, men run the bakeries; they make our bread, cake and pies. They manage the laundries; they are now considered our best milliners and dressmakers. Because some men fill these departments of usefulness, shall we regulate the curriculum in Harvard and Yale to their present necessities? If not, why this talk in our best colleges of a curriculum for girls who are crowding into the trades and professions, teachers in all our public schools, rapidly filling many lucrative and honorable positions in life?"

... Women are already the equals of men in the whole realm of thought, in art, science, literature and government.... The poetry and novels of the century are theirs, and they have touched the keynote of reform, in religion, politics and social life. They fill the editor's and professor's chair, plead at the bar of justice; walk the wards of the hospital and speak from the pulpit and the platform. Such is the type of womanhood that an enlightened public sentiment welcomes to-day, and such the triumph of the facts of life over the false theories of the past.

Is it, then, consistent to hold the developed woman of this day within the same narrow political limits as the dame with the spinning-wheel and knitting-needle occupied in the past? No, no! Machinery has taken the labors of woman, as well as man, on its tireless shoulders; the loom and the spinning-wheel are but dreams of the past; the pen, the brush, the easel, the chisel, have taken their places, while the hopes and ambitions of women are essentially changed.

We see reason sufficient in the outer conditions of human beings for individual liberty and development, but when we consider the self-dependence of every human soul, we see the need of courage, judgment and the exercise of every faculty of mind and body, strengthened and developed by use, in woman as well as man.

Whatever may be said of man's protecting power in ordinary conditions, amid all the terrible disasters by land and sea, in the supreme moments of danger, alone woman must ever meet the horrors of the situation. The Angel of Death even makes no royal pathway for her. Man's love and sympathy enter only into the sunshine of our lives. In that solemn solitude of self, that links us with the immeasurable and the eternal, each soul lives alone forever. A recent writer says: "I remember once, in crossing the Atlantic, to have gone upon the deck of the ship at midnight, when a dense black cloud enveloped the sky, and the great deep was roaring madly under the lashes of demoniac winds. My feeling was not of danger or fear (which is a base surrender of the immortal soul) but of utter desolation and loneliness; a little speck of life shut in by a tremendous darkness."

And yet, there is a solitude which each and every one of us has always carried with him, more inaccessible than the ice-cold mountains, more profound than the midnight sea; the solitude of self. Our inner being which we call ourself, no eye nor touch of man or angel has ever pierced. It is more hidden than the caves of the gnome; the sacred adytum of the oracle; the hidden chamber of Eleusinian mystery, for to it only Omniscience is permitted to enter.

Such is individual life. Who, I ask you, can take, dare take on himself the rights, the duties, the responsibilities of another human soul?

Document 24

Stanton, "Introduction" and Commentaries on Genesis, Chapters 1–4, *The Woman's Bible*; Anthony, Response to the NAWSA Resolution Disavowing *The Woman's Bible*; Stanton, Draft of "Criticism of Bigotry of Women"

Stanton's lifelong interest in the relation of Christianity to the idea of women's inferiority grew stronger in the 1880s and 1890s, in reaction to the growing influence of organized religion in the women's movement in particular and in American politics in general. *The Woman's Bible* was the most enduring product of the secularism that concerned her in her later years. It was also part of the general scholarly effort to interpret the Bible as an historical document, rather than as divine revelation. From her unique feminist perspective, Stanton argued that the historical impact of Christian ideas, particularly about sexuality and maternity, had been to degrade women. The body of the book was organized as a series of commentaries, deliberately informal and irreverent, on Biblical passages which mentioned or affected women. In these commentaries, Stanton and her collaborators criticized the Bible for its irrationalities and superstitions, but she also encouraged the development of a new, "rational" religion, deliberately designed "in harmony with science, common sense and the experience of mankind in natural laws." Soon after the publication of *The Woman's Bible*, the National American Woman Suffrage Association, horrified by the controversy the book raised, passed a resolution disavowing any connection with it. The objections of Anthony to this action are also included.

Stanton, *The Woman's Bible*, Excerpts

The Woman's Bible, Part 1 (New York: European Publishing Co., 1895), pp. 1–33:

From the inauguration of the movement for woman's emancipation the Bible has been used to hold her in the "divinely ordained sphere," prescribed in the Old and New Testaments. The canon and civil law; church and state; priests and legislators; all political parties and religious denominations have alike taught that woman was made after man, of man, and for man, an inferior being, subject to man. Creeds, codes, Scriptures and statutes, are all based on this idea. The fashions, forms, ceremonies and customs of society, church ordinances and discipline all grow out of this idea....

The Bible teaches that woman brought sin and death into the world, that she precipitated the fall of the race, that she was arraigned before the judgment seat of Heaven, tried, condemned and sentenced. Marriage for her was to be a condition of bondage, maternity a period of suffering and anguish, and in silence and subjection, she was to play the role of a dependent on man's bounty for all her material wants, and for all the information she might desire on the vital questions of the hour, she was commanded to ask her husband at home. Here is the Bible position of woman briefly summed up.

Those who have the divine insight to translate, transpose and transfigure this mournful object of pity into an exalted, dignified personage, worthy our worship as the mother of the race, are to be congratulated as having a share of the occult mystic power of the eastern Mahatmas.

The plain English to the ordinary mind admits of no such liberal interpretation. The unvarnished texts speak for themselves. The canon law, church ordinances and Scriptures, are homogeneous, and all reflect the same spirit and sentiments.

These familiar texts are quoted by clergymen in their pulpits, by statesmen in the halls of legislation, by lawyers in the courts, and are echoed by the press of all civilized nations, and accepted by woman herself as "The Word of God." So perverted is the religious element in her nature, that with faith and works she is the chief support of the church and clergy; the very powers that make her emancipation impossible. When, in the early part of the Nineteenth Century, women began to protest against their civil and political degradation, they were referred to the Bible for an answer. When they protested against their unequal position in the church, they were referred to the Bible for an answer.

This led to a general and critical study of the Scriptures. Some, having made a fetish of these books and believing them to be the veritable "Word of God," with liberal translations, interpretations, allegories and symbols, glossed over the most objectionable features of the various books and clung to them as divinely inspired. Others, seeing the family resemblance between the Mosaic code, the canon law, and the old English common law, came to the conclusion that all alike emanated from the same source; wholly human in their origin and inspired by the natural love of domination in the historians. Others, bewildered with their doubts and fears, came to no conclusion. While their clergymen told them on the one hand, that they owed all the blessings and freedom they enjoyed to the Bible, on the other, they said it clearly marked out their circumscribed sphere of action: that the demands for political and civil rights were irreligious, dangerous to the stability of the home, the state and the church. Clerical appeals were circulated from time to time conjuring members of their churches to take no part in the anti-slavery or woman suffrage movements, as they were infidel in their tendencies, undermining the very foundations of society. No wonder the majority of women stood still, and with bowed heads, accepted the situation.

Listening to the varied opinions of women, I have long thought it would be interesting and profitable to get them clearly stated in book form ... a large committee has been formed, and we hope to complete the work within a year.

Those who have undertaken the labor are desirous to have some Hebrew and Greek scholars, versed in Biblical criticism, to gild our pages with their learning. Several distinguished women have been urged to do so, but they are afraid that their high reputation and scholarly attainments might be compromised by taking part in an enterprise that for a time may prove very unpopular. Hence we may not be able to get help from that class.

Others fear that they might compromise their evangelical faith by affiliating with those of more liberal views, who do not regard the Bible as the "Word of God," but like any other book, to be judged by its merits. If the Bible teaches the equality of Woman, why does the church refuse to ordain women to preach the gospel, to fill the offices of deacons and elders, and to administer the Sacraments, or to admit them as delegates to the Synods, General Assemblies and Conferences of the different denominations? They have never yet invited a woman to join one of their Revising Committees, nor tried to mitigate the sentence pronounced on her by changing one count in the indictment served on her in Paradise.

The large number of letters received, highly appreciative of the undertaking, is very encouraging to those who have inaugurated the movement, and indicate a growing self-respect and self-assertion in the women of this generation. But we have the usual array of objectors to meet and answer. One correspondent conjures us to suspend the work, as it is "ridiculous" for "women to attempt the revision of the Scriptures." I wonder if any man wrote to the late revising committee of Divines to stop their work on the ground that it was ridiculous for men to revise the Bible. Why is it more ridiculous for women to protest against her present status in the Old and New Testament, in the ordinances and discipline of the church, than in the statutes and constitution of the state? Why is it more ridiculous to arraign ecclesiastics for their false teaching and acts of injustice to women, than members of Congress and the House of Commons? Why is it more audacious to review Moses than Blackstone, the Jewish code of laws, than the English system of jurisprudence? Women have compelled their legislators in every state in this Union to so modify their statutes for women that the old common law is now almost a dead letter. Why not compel Bishops and Revising Committees to modify their creeds and dogmas? ....

Others say it is not politic to rouse religious opposition. This much-lauded policy is but another word for cowardice. How can woman's position be changed from that of a subordinate to an equal, without opposition, without the broadest discussion of all the questions involved in her present degradation? For so far-reaching and momentous a reform as her complete independence, an entire revolution in all existing institutions is inevitable.

Let us remember that all reforms are interdependent, and that whatever is done to establish one principle on a solid basis, strengthens all. Reformers who are always compromising, have not yet grasped the idea that truth is the only safe ground to stand upon. The object of an individual life is not to carry one fragmentary measure in human progress, but to utter the highest truth clearly seen in all directions, and thus to round out and perfect a well balanced character....

Again there are some who write us that our work is a useless expenditure of force over a book that has lost its hold on the human mind. Most intelligent women, they say, regard it simply as the history of a rude people in a barbarous age, and have no more reverence for the Scriptures than any other work. So long as tens of thousands of Bibles are printed every year, and circulated over the whole habitable globe, and the masses in all English-speaking nations revere it as the word of God, it is vain to belittle its influence. The sentimental feelings we all have for those things we were educated to believe sacred, do not readily yield to pure reason....

The only points in which I differ from all ecclesiastical teaching is that I do not believe that any man ever saw or talked with God, I do not believe that God inspired the Mosaic code, or told the historians what they say he did about woman, for all the religions on the face of the earth degrade her, and so long as woman accepts the position that they assign her, her emancipation is impossible. Whatever the Bible may be made to do in Hebrew or Greek, in plain English it does not exalt and dignify woman....

There are some general principles in the holy books of all religions that teach love, charity, liberty, justice and equality for all the human family, there are many grand and beautiful passages, the golden rule has been echoed and re-echoed around the world. There are lofty examples of good and true men and women, all worthy our acceptance and imitation whose lustre cannot be dimmed by the false sentiments and vicious characters bound up in the same volume. The Bible cannot be accepted or rejected as a whole, its teachings are varied and its lessons differ widely from each other. In criticising the peccadilloes of Sarah, Rebecca and Rachel, we would not shadow the virtues of Deborah, Huldah and Vashti. In criticising the Mosaic code we would not question the wisdom of the golden rule and the fifth Commandment....

The canon law, the Scriptures, the creeds and codes and church discipline of the leading religions bear the impress of fallible man, and not of our ideal great first cause, "the Spirit of all Good," that set the universe of matter and mind in motion, and by immutable law holds the land, the sea, the planets, revolving round the great centre of light and heat, each in its own elliptic, with millions of stars in harmony all singing together, the glory of creation forever and ever.

THE BOOK OF GENESIS.
CHAPTER I.
Genesis i: 26, 27, 28.

26 And God said, let us make man in our image, after our likeness: and let them have dominion over the fish of the sea, and over the fowl of the air, and over the cattle, and over all the earth, and over every creeping thing that creepeth upon the earth.

27 So God created man in his *own* image, in the image of God created he him; male and female created he them.

28 And God blessed them, and God said unto them, Be fruitful, and multiply, and replenish the earth, and subdue it; and have dominion over the fish of the sea, and over the fowl of the air, and over every living thing that moveth upon the earth.

Here is the sacred historian's first account of the advent of woman; a simultaneous creation of both sexes, in the image of God. It is evident from the language that there was consultation in the Godhead, and that the masculine and feminine elements were equally represented. Scott in his commentaries says, "this consultation of the Gods is the origin of the doctrine of the trinity." But instead of three male personages, as generally represented, a Heavenly Father, Mother, and Son would seem more rational.

The first step in the elevation of woman to her true position, as an equal factor in human progress, is the cultivation of the religious sentiment in regard to her dignity and equality, the recognition by the rising generation of an ideal Heavenly Mother, to whom their prayers should be addressed, as well as to a Father.

If language has any meaning, we have in these texts a plain declaration of the existence of the feminine element in the Godhead, equal in power and glory with the masculine. The Heavenly Mother and Father! "God created man in his own image, male and female." Thus Scripture, as well as science and philosophy, declares the eternity and equality of sex—the philosophical fact, without which there could have been no perpetuation of creation, no growth or development in the animal, vegetable, or mineral kingdoms, no awakening nor progressing in the world of thought. The masculine and feminine elements, exactly equal and balancing each other, are as essential to the maintenance of the equilibrium of the universe as positive and negative electricity, the centripetal and centrifugal forces, the laws of attraction which bind together all we know of this planet whereon we dwell and of the system in which we revolve.

In the great work of creation the crowning glory was realized, when man and woman were evolved on the sixth day, the masculine and feminine forces in the image of God, that must have existed eternally, in all forms of matter and mind. All the persons in the Godhead are represented in the Elohim the divine plurality taking counsel in regard to this last and highest form of life. Who were the members of this high council, and were they a duality or a trinity? Verse 27 declares the image of God male and female. How then is it possible to make woman an afterthought? We find in verses 5–16 the pronoun "he" used. Should it not in harmony with verse 26 be "they," a dual pronoun? We may attribute this to the same cause as the use of "his" in verse 11 instead of "it." The fruit tree yielding fruit after "his" kind instead of after "its" kind. The paucity of a language may give rise to many misunderstandings.

The above texts plainly show the simultaneous creation of man and woman, and their equal importance in the development of the race. All those theories based on the assumption that man was prior in the creation, have no foundation in Scripture.

As to woman's subjection, on which both the canon and the civil law delight to dwell, it is important to note that equal dominion is given to woman over every living thing, but not one word is said giving man dominion over woman.

Here is the first title deed to this green earth giving alike to the sons and daughters of God. No lesson of woman's subjection can be fairly drawn from the first chapter of the Old Testament....

CHAPTER II.

Genesis ii: 21–25.

21 And the Lord God caused a deep sleep to fall upon Adam, and he slept; and he took one of his ribs, and closed up the flesh thereof.

22 And the rib which the Lord God had taken from man, made he a woman, and brought her unto the man.

23 And Adam said, This is now bone of my bone, and flesh of my flesh: she shall be called Woman, because she was taken out of man.

24 Therefore shall a man leave his father and his mother, and shall cleave unto his wife; and they shall be one flesh.

25 And they were both naked, the man and his wife, and were not ashamed.

As the account of the creation in the first chapter is in harmony with science, common sense, and the experience of mankind in natural laws, the inquiry naturally arises, why should there be two contradictory accounts in the same book, of the same event? It is fair to infer that the second version, which is found in some form in the different religions of all nations, is a mere allegory, symbolizing some mysterious conception of a highly imaginative editor.

The first account dignifies woman as an important factor in the creation, equal in power and glory with man. The second makes her a mere afterthought. The world in good running order without her. The only reason for her advent being the solitude of man.

There is something sublime in bringing order out of chaos; light out of darkness; giving each planet its place in the solar system; oceans and lands their limits; wholly inconsistent with a petty surgical operation, to find material for the mother of the race. It is on this allegory that all the enemies of women rest their battering rams, to prove her inferiority. Accepting the view that man was prior in the creation, some Scriptural writers say that as the woman was of the man, therefore, her position should be one of subjection. Grant it, then as the historical fact is reversed in our day, and the man is now of the woman, shall his place be one of subjection?

The equal position declared in the first account must prove more satisfactory to both sexes; created alike in the image of God—The Heavenly Mother and Father.

Thus, the Old Testament, "in the beginning," proclaims the simultaneous creation of man and woman, the eternity and equality of sex; and the New Testament echoes back through the centuries the individual sovereignty of woman growing out of this natural fact. Paul, in speaking of equality as the very soul and essence of Christianity, said, "There is neither Jew nor Greek, there is neither bond nor free, there is neither male nor female; for ye are all one in Christ Jesus." With this recognition of the feminine element in the Godhead in the Old Testament, and this declaration of the equality of the sexes in the New, we may well wonder at the contemptible status woman occupies in the Christian Church of to-day.

All the commentators and publicists writing on woman's position, go through an immense amount of fine-spun metaphysical speculations, to prove her subordination in harmony with the Creator's original design.

It is evident that some wily writer, seeing the perfect equality of man and woman in the first chapter, felt it important for the dignity and dominion of man to effect woman's subordination in some way. To do this a spirit of evil must be introduced, which at once proved itself stronger than the spirit of good, and man's supremacy was based on the downfall of all that had just been pronounced very good. This spirit of evil evidently existed before the supposed fall of man, hence woman was not the origin of sin as so often asserted....

CHAPTER III.

Genesis iii: 1–24.

1 Now the serpent was more subtle than any beast of the field which the Lord God had made. And he said unto the woman, Yea, hath God said, Ye shall not eat of every tree of the garden?

2 And the woman said unto the serpent, We may eat of the fruit of the trees of the garden:

3 But of the fruit of the tree which is in the midst of the garden, God hath said Ye shall not eat of it, neither shall ye touch it, lest ye die.

4 And the serpent said unto the woman, Ye shall not surely die:

5 For God doth know that in the day ye eat thereof then your eyes shall be opened, and ye shall be as gods, knowing good and evil.

6 And when the woman saw that the tree was good for food, and that it was pleasant to the eyes, and a tree to be desired to make one wise, she took of the fruit thereof, and did eat and gave also unto her husband with her; and he did eat.

7 And the eyes of them both were opened, and they knew that they were naked; and they sewed fig leaves together, and made themselves aprons.

8 And they heard the voice of the Lord God walking in the garden in the cool of the day; and Adam and his wife hid themselves from the presence of the Lord God amongst the trees in the garden.

9 And the Lord God called unto Adam, and said unto him, Where art thou?

10 And he said, I heard thy voice in the garden, and I was afraid, because I was naked; and I hid myself.

11 And he said, Who told thee that thou wast naked? Hast thou eaten of the tree, whereof I commanded thee that thou shouldst not eat?

12 And the man said, The woman whom thou gavest to be with me, she gave me of the tree, and I did eat.

13 And the Lord God said unto the woman, What is this that thou hast done? And the woman said, The serpent beguiled me, and I did eat.

14 And the Lord God said unto the serpent, Because thou hast done this, thou art cursed above all cattle, and above every beast of the field; upon thy belly shalt thou go, and dust shalt thou eat all the days of thy life:

15 And I will put enmity between thee and the woman, and between thy seed and her seed; it shall bruise thy head and thou shalt bruise his heel.

16 Unto the woman he said, I will greatly multiply thy sorrow and thy conception; in sorrow thou shalt bring forth children: and thy desire shall be to thy husband, and he shall rule over thee.

17 And unto Adam he said, Because thou hast hearkened unto the voice of thy wife, and hast eaten of the tree, of which I commanded thee, saying, Thou shalt not eat of it; cursed is the ground for thy sake; in sorrow shalt thou eat of it all the days of thy life;

18 Thorns also and thistles shall it bring forth to thee; and thou shalt eat the herb of the field;

19 In the sweat of thy face shalt thou eat bread till thou return unto the ground; for out of it wast thou taken; for dust thou art, and unto dust shalt thou return.

20 And Adam called his wife's name Eve; because she was the mother of all living.

21 Unto Adam also and to his wife did the Lord God make coats of skins and clothed them.

22 ¶ And the Lord God said, Behold the man is become as one of us, to know good and evil; and now, lest he put forth his hand, and take also of the tree of life, and eat, and live for ever;

23 Therefore the Lord God sent him forth from the garden of Eden, to till the ground from whence he was taken.

24 So he drove out the man: and he placed at the east of the garden of Eden cherubim, and a flaming sword which turned every way, to keep the way of the tree of life.

Adam Clarke, in his commentaries, asks the question, "is this an allegory?" He finds it beset with so many difficulties as an historical fact, that he inclines at first to regard it as a fable, a mere symbol, of some hidden truth. His mind seems more troubled about the serpent than any other personage in the drama. As snakes cannot walk upright, and have never been known to speak, he thinks this beguiling creature must have been an ourang-outang, or some species of ape. However, after expressing all his doubts, he rests in the assumption that it must be taken literally, and that with higher knowledge of the possibilities of all living things, many seeming improbabilities will be fully realized.

A learned professor in Yale College,[66] before a large class of students, expressed serious doubts as to the forbidden fruit being an apple, as none grew in that latitude. He said it must have been a quince. If the serpent and the apple are to be withdrawn thus recklessly from the tableaux, it is feared that with advancing civilization the whole drama may fall into discredit. Scientists tell us that "the missing link" between the ape and man, has recently been discovered, so that we can now trace back an unbroken line of ancestors to the dawn of creation.

As out of this allegory grows the doctrines of original sin, the fall of man, and woman the author of all our woes, and the curses on the serpent, the woman, and the man; the Darwinian theory of the gradual growth of the race from a lower to a higher type of animal life, is more hopeful and encouraging. However, as our chief interest is in woman's part in the drama, we are equally pleased with her attitude, whether as a myth in an allegory, or as the heroine of an historical occurrence.

In this prolonged interview, the unprejudiced reader must be impressed with the courage, the dignity, and the lofty ambition of the woman. The tempter evidently had a profound knowledge of human nature, and saw at a glance the high character of the person he met by chance in his walks in the garden. He did not try to tempt her from the path of duty by brilliant jewels, rich dresses, worldly luxuries or pleasures, but with the promise of knowledge, with the wisdom of the Gods. Like Socrates or Plato, his powers of conversation and asking puzzling questions, were no doubt marvellous, and he roused in the woman that intense thirst for knowledge, that the simple pleasures of picking flowers and talking with Adam did not satisfy. Compared with Adam she appears to great advantage through the entire drama. The curse pronounced on woman is inserted in an unfriendly spirit to justify her degradation and subjection to man. With obedience to the laws of health, diet, dress, and exercise, the period of maternity should be one of added vigor in both body and mind, a perfectly natural operation should not be attended with suffering. By the observance of physical and psychical laws the supposed curse can be easily transformed into a blessing. Some churchmen speak of maternity as a disability, and then chant the Magnificat in all their cathedrals round the globe. Through all life's shifting scenes, the mother of the race has been the greatest factor in civilization.

We hear the opinion often expressed, that woman always has, and always will be in subjection. Neither assertion is true. She enjoyed unlimited individual freedom for many centuries, and the events of the present day all point to her speedy emancipation. Scientists now give 85,000 years for the growth of the race. They assign 60,000 to savagism, 20,000 to barbarism, and 5,000 to civilization. Recent historians tell us that for centuries woman reigned supreme. That period was called the Matriarchate. Then man seized the reins of government, and we are now under the Patriarchate. But we see on all sides new forces gathering, and woman is already abreast with man in art, science, literature, and government. The next dynasty, in which both will reign as equals, will be the Amphiarchate, which is close at hand....

CHAPTER IV.

Genesis iv: 1–12, 19, 23.

1 And Adam knew Eve his wife; and she conceived, and bare Cain, and said, I have gotten a man from the Lord.

2 And she again bare his brother Abel. And Abel was a keeper of sheep, but Cain was a tiller of the ground.

3 And in process of time it came to pass, that Cain brought of the fruit of the ground an offering unto the Lord.

4 And Abel, he also brought of the firstlings of his flock and of the fat thereof. And the Lord had respect unto Abel and to his offering.

5 But unto Cain and to his offering he had not respect. And Cain was very wroth, and his countenance fell.

6 And the Lord said unto Cain, Why art thou wroth? and why is thy countenance fallen?

7 If thou doest well, shalt thou not be accepted: and if thou doest not well, sin lieth at the door: and unto thee shall be his desire, and thou shalt rule over him.

8 And Cain talked with Abel his brother; and it came to pass, when they were in the field, that Cain rose up against Abel his brother, and slew him.

9 And the Lord said unto Cain, where is Abel thy brother? And he said, I know not: Am l my brother's keeper?

10 And he said, What hast thou done? the voice of thy brother's blood crieth unto me from the ground.

11 And now art thou cursed from the earth which hath opened her mouth to receive thy brother's blood from thy hand.

12 When thou tillest the ground, it shall not henceforth yield unto thee her strength; a fugitive and a vagabond shalt thou be in the earth.

19 ¶ And Lamech took unto him two wives: the name of the one *was* Adah, and the name of the other Zillah.

23 And Lamech said unto his wives, Adah and Zillah, hear my voice; ye wives of Lamech, hearken unto my speech.

... The manner in which the writer of these chapters presents the women so in conflict with Chapters i and v, which immediately precede and follow, inclines the unprejudiced mind to relegate the ii, iii and iv chapters to the realm of fancy as no part of the real history of creation's dawn.

The curse pronounced on Cain is similar to that inflicted on Adam, both were to till the ground, which was to bring forth weeds abundantly. Hale's statistics of weeds show their rapid and widespread power of propagation. "A progeny," he says, "more than sufficient in a few years to stock every planet of the solar system." In the face of such discouraging facts, Hale coolly remarks. "Such provisions has the just God made to fulfil the curse which he promised on man."

It seems far more rational to believe that the curses on both woman and man were but figments of the human brain, and that by the observance of natural laws, both labor and maternity may prove great blessings.

With all the modern appliances of steam and electricity, and the new inventions in machinery, the cultivation of the soil is fast coming to be a recreation and amusement. The farmer now sits at ease on his plough, while his steed turns up the furrows at his will. With machinery the sons of Adam now sow and reap their harvests, keep the wheels of their great manufactories in motion, and with daily increasing speed carry on the commerce of the world. The time is at hand when the heavy burdens of the laborer will all be shifted on the shoulders of these tireless machines. And when the woman, too, learns and obeys the laws of life, these supposed curses will be but idle dreams of the past. The curse falls lightly even now on women who live in natural conditions, and with anaesthetics is essentially mitigated in all cases.

When these remedial agents were first discovered, some women refused to avail themselves of their blessings, and some orthodox physicians refused to administer them, lest they should interfere with the wise provisions of Providence in making maternity a curse.

Anthony, Response to NAWSA Resolution

Ida Harper, *Life of Anthony,* Vol. 2, pp. 853–54.

The one distinct feature of our association has been the right of individual opinion for every member. We have been beset at each step with the cry that somebody was injuring the cause by the expression of sentiments which differed from those held by the majority. The religious persecution of the ages has been carried on under what was claimed to be the command of God. I distrust those people who know so well what God wants them to do, because I notice it always coincides with their own desires. All the way along the history of our movement there has been this same contest on account of religious theories. Forty years ago one of our noblest men said to me, "You would better never hold another convention than allow Ernestine L. Rose on your platform"; because that eloquent woman, who ever stood for justice and freedom, did not believe in the plenary inspiration of the Bible. Did we banish Mrs. Rose? No, indeed!

Every new generation of converts threshes over the same old straw. The point is whether you will sit in judgment on one who questions the divine inspiration of certain passages in the Bible derogatory to women. If Mrs. Stanton had written approvingly of these passages you would not have brought in this resolution for fear the cause might be injured among the *liberals* in religion. In other words, if she had written *your* views, you would not have considered a resolution necessary. To pass this one is to set back the hands on the dial of reform.

What you should say to outsiders is that a Christian has neither more nor less rights in our association than an atheist. When our platform becomes too narrow for people of all creeds and of no creeds, I myself can not stand upon it. Many things have been said and done by our *orthodox* friends which I have felt to be extremely harmful to our cause; but I should no more consent to a resolution denouncing them than I shall consent to this. Who is to draw the line? Who can tell now whether these commentaries may not prove a great help to woman's emancipation from old superstitions which have barred its way?

Lucretia Mott at first thought Mrs. Stanton had injured the cause of all woman's other rights by insisting upon the demand for suffrage, but she had sense enough not to bring in a resolution against it. In 1860 when Mrs. Stanton made a speech before the New York Legislature in favor of a bill making drunkenness a ground for divorce, there was a general cry among the friends that she had killed the woman's cause. I shall be pained beyond expression if the delegates here are so narrow and illiberal as to adopt this resolution. You would better not begin resolving against individual action or you will find no limit. This year it is Mrs. Stanton; next year it may be I or one of yourselves, who will be the victim.

If we do not inspire in women a broad and catholic spirit, they will fail, when enfranchised, to constitute that power for better government which we have always claimed for them. Ten women educated into the practice of liberal principles would be a stronger force than 10,000 organized on a platform of intolerance and bigotry. I pray you vote for religious liberty, without censorship or inquisition. This resolution adopted will be a vote of censure upon a woman who is without a peer in intellectual and statesmanlike ability; one who has stood for half a century the acknowledged leader of progressive thought and demand in regard to all matters pertaining to the absolute freedom of woman.

Stanton, Draft of "Criticism"

Unpublished manuscript draft, Stanton Papers, Library of Congress.

... Three different conventions of women have passed resolutions against "The Women's [sic] Bible." As if a Revising Committee of thirty women had not as good a right to express their opinion of what is taught in the Scriptures as a Committee of Bishops.

There is no persecution so bitter as that in the name of religion. I published a leaflet in favor of opening the Worlds Fair on Sunday. Five hundred copies by chance fell into the hands of one of my devout friends, as sweet a woman as I ever knew in other respects. She threw them all into the fire. Dear, said I, you have committed a state prison offence. However, I shall not incarcerate you, but if you had lived in the time of Calvin you would as readily burned me and thought you did God service.

Much as I desire the suffrage, I would rather never vote, than to see the policy of our government at the mercy of the religious bigotry of such women. My hearts desire is to lift women out of all these dangerous and degrading superstitions and to this end will I labor my remaining days on earth.

Seeing the danger of a union in state and church in the old world, our fathers determined to lay the foundations of our republic in the equal rights of all citizens, without regard to sect or creed, Quaker, Baptist, Jew, Catholic, Protestant, Infidel, Agnostic all enjoying the same freedom. All encroachments on this principle should be firmly resisted.

ELIZABETH CADY STANTON

Document 25

Anna Howard Shaw, "The Passing of Aunt Susan"; Helen Gardener, "Elizabeth Cady Stanton"

Stanton died in 1902, at the age of eighty-seven, Anthony in 1906, when she was eighty-six. Their eulogies suggest several important comparisons between the political leadership each woman provided. The tribute to Anthony was written by Anna Howard Shaw, the first woman ordained as a Methodist minister and her successor as president of the National American Woman Suffrage Association. Stanton's obituary was written by an atheist, published in a secularist magazine, and stressed the challenges Stanton had mounted against religious authority. Shaw's account of Anthony shows us a woman totally identified with the organized women's movement. Helen Gardener's portrait of Stanton is that of a political independent and thoroughgoing radical, an individualist who was often the only one "great enough to be honest with her own soul." Gardener went from being a radical devotee of Stanton's theories about women's intellectual equality to become a grand pragmatist, negotiating between the movement's leaders and the president of the United States.

Above all, it is the last minutes of the lives of Stanton and Anthony that provide us with a striking contrast and perfect complement: Anthony, the organizer, murmuring the names of "an endless, shadowy review" of women, famous and unknown; Stanton, the philosopher, composing her last address.

Anna Howard Shaw, *Story of a Pioneer* (New York: Harper and Brothers, Publishers, 1915), pp. 221–35.

In 1906, when the date of the annual convention of the National American Woman Suffrage Association in Baltimore was drawing near, she became convinced that it would be her last convention. She was right. She showed a passionate eagerness to make it one of the greatest conventions ever held in the history of the movement; and we, who loved her and saw that the flame of her life was burning low, also bent all our energies to the task of realizing her hopes. In November preceding the convention she visited me and her niece, Miss Lucy Anthony, in our home in Mount Airy, Philadelphia, and it was clear that her anxiety over the convention was weighing heavily upon her. She visibly lost strength from day to day. One morning she said abruptly, "Anna, let's go and call on President M. Carey Thomas, of Bryn Mawr."

I wrote a note to Miss Thomas, telling her of Miss Anthony's desire to see her, and received an immediate reply inviting us to luncheon the following day. We found Miss Thomas deep in the work connected with her new college buildings, over which she showed us with much pride....

"We want your co-operation, and that of Miss Garrett," began Miss Anthony, promptly, "to make our Baltimore Convention a success. We want you to persuade the Arundel Club of Baltimore, the most fashionable club in the city, to give a reception to the delegates; and we want you to arrange a college night on the programme—a great college night, with the best college speakers ever brought together."

These were large commissions for two extremely busy women, but both Miss Thomas and Miss Garrett—realizing Miss Anthony's intense earnestness—promised to think over the suggestions and see what they could do. The next morning we received a telegram from them stating that Miss Thomas would arrange the college evening, and that Miss Garrett would reopen her Baltimore home, which she had closed, during the convention. She also invited Miss Anthony and me to be her guests there, and added that she would try to arrange the reception by the Arundel Club.

"Aunt Susan" was overjoyed. I have never seen her happier than she was over the receipt of that telegram. She knew that whatever Miss Thomas and Miss Garrett undertook would be accomplished, and she rightly regarded the success of the convention as already assured....

From beginning to end the convention was probably the most notable yet held in our history. Julia Ward Howe and her daughter, Florence Howe Hall, were also guests of Miss Garrett, who, moreover, entertained all the speakers of "College Night." Miss Anthony, now eighty-six, arrived in Baltimore quite ill, and Mrs. Howe, who was ninety, was taken ill soon after she reached there. The two great women made a dramatic exchange on the programme, for on the first night, when Miss Anthony was unable to speak, Mrs. Howe took her place, and on the second night, when Mrs. Howe had succumbed, Miss Anthony had recovered sufficiently to appear for her....

On the 15th of February we left Baltimore for Washington, where Miss Anthony was to celebrate her eighty-sixth birthday.... "Aunt Susan" should not have attempted the Washington celebration, for she was still ill and exhausted by the strain of the convention. But notwithstanding her sufferings and the warnings of her physicians, she insisted on being present; so Miss Garrett sent the trained nurse to Washington with her, and we all tried to make the journey the least possible strain on the patient's vitality....

The birthday celebration that followed our executive meeting was an impressive one. It was held in the Church of Our Father, whose pastor, the Rev. John Van Schaick, had always been exceedingly kind to Miss Anthony. Many prominent men spoke. President Roosevelt and other statesmen sent most friendly letters, and William H. Taft had promised to be present. He did not come, nor did he, then or later, send any excuse for not coming—an omission that greatly disappointed Miss Anthony, who had always admired him. I presided at the meeting, and though we all did our best to make it gay, a strange hush hung over the assemblage—a solemn stillness, such as one feels in the presence of death. We became more and more conscious that Miss Anthony was suffering, and we hastened the exercises all we could. When I read President Roosevelt's long tribute to her, Miss Anthony rose to comment on it.

"One word from President Roosevelt in his message to Congress," she said, a little wearily, "would be worth a thousand eulogies of Susan B. Anthony. When will men learn that what we ask is not praise, but justice?"

At the close of the meeting, realizing how weak she was, I begged her to let me speak for her. But she again rose, rested her hand on my shoulder, and, standing by my side, uttered the last words she ever spoke in public, pleading with women to consecrate themselves to the Cause, assuring them that no power could prevent its ultimate success, but reminding them also that the time of its coming would depend wholly on their work and their loyalty. She ended with three words—very fitting words from her lips, expressing as they did the spirit of her lifework—*"Failure is impossible."*

The next morning she was taken to her home in Rochester, and one month from that day we conducted her funeral services.... During the first three weeks of her last illness, ... I did what she wished me to do—I continued our work, trying to do hers as well as my own. But all the time my heart was in her sick-room, and at last the day came when I could no longer remain away from her. I had awakened in the morning with a strong conviction that she needed me, and at the breakfast-table I announced to her niece, Miss Lucy Anthony, the friend who for years has shared my home, that I was going at once to "Aunt Susan." ....

When I reached my friend's bedside one glance at her face showed me the end was near; and from that time until it came, almost a week later, I remained with her; while again, as always, she talked of the Cause, and of the life-work she must now lay down. The first thing she spoke of was her will, which she had made several years before, and in which she had left the small property she possessed to her sister Mary, her niece Lucy, and myself, with instructions as to the use we three were to make of it. Now she told me we were to pay no attention to these instructions, but to give every dollar of her money to the $60,000 fund Miss Thomas and Miss Garrett were trying to raise. She was vitally interested in this fund, as its success meant that for five years the active officers of the National American Woman Suffrage Association, including myself as president, would for the first time receive salaries for our work....

During the last forty-eight hours of her life she was unwilling that I should leave her side. So day and night I knelt by her bed, holding her hand and watching the flame of her wonderful spirit grow dim. At times, even then, it blazed up with startling suddenness. On the last afternoon of her life, when she had lain quiet for hours, she suddenly began to utter the names of the women who had worked with her, as if in a final roll call. Many of them had preceded her into the next world; others were still splendidly active in the work she was laying down. But young or old, living or dead, they all seemed to file past her dying eyes that day in an endless, shadowy review, and as they went by she spoke to each of them.

Not all the names she mentioned were known in suffrage ranks; some of these women lived only in the heart of Susan B. Anthony, and now, for the last time, she was thanking them for what they had done. Here was one who, at a moment of special need, had given her small savings; here was another who had won valuable recruits to the Cause; this one had written a strong editorial; that one had made a stirring speech. In these final hours it seemed that not a single sacrifice or service, however small, had been forgotten by the dying leader. ... Then, after lying in silence for a long time with her cheek on my hand, she murmured: "They are still passing before me—face after face, hundreds and hundreds of them, representing all the efforts of fifty years. I know how hard they have worked. I know the sacrifices they have made. But it has all been worth while!"

Helen Gardener, Obituary of Elizabeth Cady Stanton, *Free Thought Magazine*, January, 1903, pp. 6–9.

One of the most versatile of women she was, and yet, for so many years her tongue and pen led the contest in this and other countries for what is commonly called the rights of woman—that is, for woman's right to stand as a unit among other units of the race—so it happens that her name naturally is fixed in the general public mind as belonging to that step of progress alone. Indeed, in one of the most intelligently appreciative editorials I have yet seen on her life and death, which editorial appeared in a leading New York daily paper, she was spoken of as "a woman with one idea—suffrage—to which she had held, steadfastly, for fifty years."

This might be said of many of her associates, perhaps, either in praise or criticism; but a woman of one idea was precisely what Mrs. Stanton was not. Hers was a wonderfully well-rounded mentality, poised and strong on every side. Fearless and truth-loving, sincere and frank. But she did not allow her frankness to degenerate into rudeness. Her truth-loving never led her to disregard the feelings and rights of those who did not agree with her. She never mistook a loud voice and a sharp retort for argument, or for proof of the justice of her position.

She wished her body to be cremated. This, also, was because of her firm conviction of the right and value to the living, of this method of disposing of the dead.

She hugged to her breast no superstitions that prevented her from thinking first and always of the highest good to the living—to those who come after. Many of her constituents in the suffrage work deeply deplored her activity in free religious lines; but she calmly replied that woman would never be fit for freedom, nor understand its benefits and bearing until she ceased to hold to her bosom the primary cause of her degradation—her religious superstitions, which bind her to the degraded status assigned her as "the will of God" in all accepted "revelations." ....

So, for the past few years, much of Mrs. Stanton's time and literary energy have been spent in an effort to bring women up to this vantage ground—in a contest against religious superstitions, rather than against purely political ones, which she perceived had their basis and origin in the religious ones. Like Wendell Phillips, in the anti-slavery work, she believed in striking at the root, rather than in breaking of the branches of a fundamental wrong in the hope to eradicate it. She was deeply blamed by some of her old associates for putting out what she called "The Woman's Bible." That is to say, she gathered together all of the passages in the Bible which related especially to woman, and interpreted them (as man had done with all of them relating to himself—and to woman, also) in the light of modern thought.

For eighteen years past it has been my good fortune to be a close friend of this wonderful woman. I have hundreds of letters from her on the work of this "Woman's Bible," and on other topics, and I believe I may claim to know her aims and intent in it as well as any other person. In fact, I was one of the original "revision committee," and while the usual objection made to it by her critics is that it is too radical, my own objection was, always, that it was not radical enough! But to neither criticism did she give heed. She had her own ideal and plan and she went steadily about it without fear and without bigotry.

In 1887 she wrote me from England thus: "Think of it, she (referring to a fine suffrage leader) says she wishes to break down the material slavery of woman. If she wanted to get the Turkish women out of the harem, would she begin with arguments on republican government? No, indeed; she would know that they are held in sexual slavery by the power of their religion—and so are we. If women were emancipated from their religious superstitions they would understand their interests in the things of this life more readily. But believing that all things here are regulated by the finger of God, the Bible written by him, expressing his will, how can you rouse them to a desire for or belief in their social and political freedom until you first show them that all these things are the outgrowth of man's thought and selfishness, largely based upon his own superstitions and ignorance of Nature's laws, and resulting in woman's degradation and subjection? Do write whenever you have time. We enjoy your good, wholesome common sense. You, at least, never aim at one thing and try thereby to hit another."

Gladstone was called "the grand old man" because it was believed by many of his constituents that he had the faculty of always seeing and dealing with any new subject or difficulty wisely and ably.

I always called Elizabeth Cady Stanton "My Mother Superior," but she may well be known as "the grand old woman," for upon almost every social and political question of her time, her voice and pen expressed her clear and lucid thought in luminous language, and never once did she fail to face toward the light; never once did her steady eye look away from Justice, Freedom and Fair-dealing for all.

She asked no privileges and opposed those who did.

What she sought for herself, she sought, also, for others. She did not believe that mistakes, however hoary, were sacred. She believed in progress—in rectifying the blunders of the past. The last bubble punctured by her keen pen was done, as I say, only three days before she died. It was in the interest of a clean, wholesome, happy home life—in the interest of honest, loving parenthood, in the interest of a child—life spent in an atmosphere of harmony and freed from one of pretense and domestic warfare—a plea, in short, for the right of children to be born of love and reared in its pure light. It was the last protest of this clear, fearless brain against the sophistries of those who hold that it is for the dignity and honor of woman and home that a mistake should be made perpetual—that the "Almighty" has joined together two who hate each other and on this theory they must continue to live out the farce to the bitter end. Her last printed utterance was an able protest against this absurdity, and was an honor to both head and heart of one who, seeing clearly, is not afraid to express her thought even though she be (as she was in this case) the only champion whose bugle note did not quaver behind the mists and fogs of past ideas and lose its values in the defective acoustics of rock-bound superstitions.

Harriot Stanton Blatch, worthy daughter of this splendid mother, writes me of her last hours: "None of us knew mother was so near her end 'til Sunday really (the day she died). She had been suffering from shortness of breath lately, from time to time, and from that cause felt under the mark. On Saturday she said to the doctor, very emphatically, 'Now, if you can't cure this difficulty of breathing, and if I am not to feel brighter and more like work again, I want you to give me something to send me pack-horse speed to heaven.'" And I can just see the twinkle in her eye when she said it.

Her daughter continues: "Two hours before her death (on Sunday) she said she wished to stand up. She was sitting in her arm chair in the drawing-room, not dressed, but in her dressing-gown, and with her hair all arranged as usual." In those beautiful white puffs, like a halo around her massive head—how well we all know and love them! "She had told her maid earlier in the day to dress her hair, and when it was finished she said: 'Now, I'll be dressed.' But I dissuaded her, seeing she was weary. The trained nurse (who had only been summoned an hour earlier), and the doctor, when she asked to stand, helped her to rise and stood on either side of her. I placed a table for her to rest her hands on. She drew herself up very erect (the doctor said the muscular strength was extraordinary) and there she stood for seven or eight minutes, steadily looking out, proudly before her. I think she was mentally making an address. When we urged her to sit down she fell asleep. Two hours later, the doctor thinking her position constrained in her chair, we lifted her to her bed, and she slipped away peacefully in a few minutes." And so passed from our sight and touch that splendid all-embracing personality. Could any death be more ideally beautiful—more what she would have wished? I can see her now, standing there in her last hours, with that delicate halo of soft, white curls around her death-touched face, pleading once again the cause of the mothers of the race, before an imaginary audience of sons and fathers of those who have lost in her their most eloquent, far-reaching voice.

For in her the world has lost its greatest woman, its noblest mother, its clearest thinker. She embraced in her motherhood all who were under the ban of oppression; she thought for the thoughtless of whatever sex; she was great enough to be honest with her own soul, and to walk in the light of the sun, hand in hand with the naked Truth! And in this she stood almost alone.

Other women there are and were, who walked side by side with her on certain planes, it is true. But none kept perfect step. Not one matched her in all-around ability, in versatility, in the capacity to be supremely clear and strong in every field of thought, in every line of progress.

Chapter Notes

Introduction to the Third Edition

1. "The Last Suffragist: An Intellectual and Political Biography," in *Woman Suffrage, Women's Rights* (New York: New York University Press, 1998), pp 1–29.
2. "Mapping the Margins: Intersectionality, Identity Politics, and Violence Against Women of Color," *Stanford Law Review* #43 (1991), pp. 1241–99.
3. "Outgrowing the Compact of the Fathers: Equal Rights, Woman Suffrage, and the U.S. Constitution, 1820–1878," *Woman Suffrage, Women's Rights*, pp. 81–113.
4. Most influentially, Brent Staples, "When the Suffrage Movement Sold Out to White Supremacy," *New York Times*, February 2, 2019, and "How the Suffrage Movement Betrayed Black Women," *ibid.*, July 28, 2018.

Part One. 1815–1861

1. Mary Wollstonecraft, *Vindication of the Rights of Woman* (New York: W.W. Norton, 1967), pp. 145, 9–10, 7, 148–49, 168–73.
2. Clarence Cook, ed., *A Girl's Life Eighty Years Ago: Letters of Eliza Southgate Bowne* (New York: G. Scribner's Sons, 1887) cited by Nancy F. Cott, ed., *Root of Bitterness* (New York: E.P. Dutton & Co., 1972), pp. 107–08. Nicholas McGuinn, "George Eliot and Mary Wollstonecraft," *The Nineteenth Century Woman*, eds. Sara Delamont and Lorna Duffin (London: Croom Helm, 1978).
3. Hannah Mather Crocker, *Observations of the Real Rights of Women, and their Appropriate Duties, Agreeable to Scripture, Reason and Common Sense* (Boston: By the Author, 1818); Emma Hart Willard, *Address to the Public: Particularly to the Members of the Legislature of New York, Proposing a Plan for Improving Female Education* (Albany: I.W. Clark, 1819); both excerpted in *Up From the Pedestal: Selected Writings in the History of American Feminism*, ed. Aileen S. Kraditor (Chicago: Quadrangle Books, 1968), pp. 40, 43–44, 82.
4. Alice S. Rossi, "Woman of Action: Frances Wright," in *The Feminist Papers from Adams to de Beauvoir* (New York: Columbia University Press, 1973); the quotation is cited on p. 93. Also see Frances Wright, *Course of Popular Lectures* (New York: Office of *The Free Enquirer*, 1830).
5. On Rose and Hertell, see Yuri Suhl, *Ernestine Rose and the Battle for Human Rights* (New York: Reynal and Company, 1959), pp. 53–55. On Robert Dale Owen, see *History of Woman Suffrage*, Vol. 1, eds. Elizabeth Cady Stanton, Susan B. Anthony, and Matilda J. Gage (Rochester: Susan B. Anthony, 1881), p. 293 (hereafter referred to as *HWS*). In Massachusetts, Mary Upton Ferrin agitated both for married women's property legislation and divorce reform; see *HWS*, Vol. 1, p. 208.
6. The phrase is Nancy Cott's, from *The Bonds of Womanhood: "Woman's Sphere" in New England, 1780–1835* (New Haven: Yale University Press, 1977), p. 202.
7. Catharine E. Beecher, *A Treatise on*

Domestic Economy (New York: Schocken Books, 1977), especially chap. 15 and pp. 9 and 183.

8. Barbara Berg, *The Remembered Gate: Origins of American Feminism* (New York: Oxford University Press, 1978), especially p. 210; also Carroll Smith Rosenberg, "Beauty, the Beast and the Militant Woman: A Case Study in Sex Roles and Social Stress in Jacksonian America," *American Quarterly*, Vol. 23 (1971), pp. 562–84.

9. Louis Filler, *The Crusade Against Slavery, 1830–1860* (New York: Harper and Brothers, 1960), p. 129.

10. Catharine E. Beecher, *An Essay on Slavery and Abolitionism with Reference to the Duty of American Females* (Philadelphia: Henry Perkins, 1837), pp. 100–02.

11. Angelina Grimké, *Letters to Catharine E. Beecher in Reply to an Essay on Slavery and Abolitionism* (Boston: Isaac Knapp, 1838), pp.115–16; Sarah Grimké, *Letters on the Equality of the Sexes and the Condition of Women Addressed to Mary S. Parker* (Boston: Isaac Knapp, 1838), pp. 16 and 54.

12. As a young woman, Stanton mentioned her weight in a letter to Elizabeth Smith Miller, her cousin, June 24, 1860, Autograph Collection, Vassar College Library. For the 240 lb. figure, see Stanton to Miller, September 11, 1888, Theodore Stanton Papers, Douglass College Library, as cited by Elisabeth Griffith, "Elizabeth Cady Stanton: Grand Old Woman" (unpublished manuscript, 1978). For her attitude toward female sexuality, see her comments about Walt Whitman in her September 6, 1883, diary entry in *Elizabeth Cady Stanton as Revealed in Her Letters, Diary and Reminiscences*, eds. Theodore Stanton and Harriot Stanton Blatch (New York: Harper & Brothers Publishers, 1922), p. 210 (hereafter referred to as *Stanton Letters*).

13. "Interview with Elizabeth Cady Stanton," *Sunday New York Herald*, January 22, 1899.

14. Elizabeth Cady Stanton, *Eighty Years and More: Reminiscences, 1815–1897* (New York: Simon and Schuster, 2020), pp. 43–44.

15. Stanton described herself as "reading law" in a questionnaire she filled out for the Troy Seminary many years later.

16. Elizabeth Cady Stanton to Elisabeth Pease, as cited by Alma Lutz, *Created Equal: A Biography of Elizabeth Cady Stanton* (New York: The John Day Company, 1940), p. 36.

17. Angelina Grimké Weld to Gerrit and Anne Smith, June 18, 1840, *Letters of Theodore Dwight Weld, Angelina Grimké Weld, and Sarah Grimké, 1822–1844*, Vol. 2, eds. Gilbert H. Barnes and Dwight L. Dumond (New York: Appleton-Century Company, 1934), p. 842.

18. *HWS*, Vol. 1, p. 419.

19. As quoted in *James and Lucretia Mott, Life and Letters*, ed. Anna D, Hallowell (Boston: Houghton, Mifflin and Company, 1884), p. 186.

20. Mott to Stanton, March 16, 1855, Elizabeth Cady Stanton Papers, Library of Congress; and Mott to Richard Webb, September 5, 1855, in Hallowell, *James and Lucretia Mott*, p. 357. Melder, *Beginnings of Sisterhood*, p. 145, mentions that Stanton circulated the Grimkés' writings.

21. Stanton's letter is quoted by Mott to Richard and Hannah Webb, February 25, 1842, in Hallowell, *James and Lucretia Mott*, p. 223.

22. This included the Grimkés and Mott. In her first major women's rights speech, delivered in 1849, Mott said, "Far be it from me to encourage women to vote or to take an active part in politics in the present state of our affairs" (cited in Hallowell, *James and Lucretia Mott*, p. 500). The position of the Grimkés, especially Angelina, on politics, was quite ambiguous. In her letters to Catharine Beecher, Angelina wrote that she believed in "woman's right to have a voice in all the laws and regulations by which she is to be *governed*," but she only defended the right to petition and directly asserted the right to vote only later (p. 119).

23. Stanton to Mary Ann Johnson and the Ohio Women's Convention, April 7, 1850. Gordon, et al., *Selected Papers of Elizabeth Cady Stanton and Susan B. Anthony*, Vol. 1 (New Brunswick, NJ: Rutgers University Press, 1995) p. 166.

24. On the plan for petition campaigns, see Elizabeth Cady Stanton to

Amy Post, December 4, 1850, *Stanton Letters*, pp. 24–25.
  25. *HWS*, Vol. 1, p. 833–34.
  26. Lucretia Mott to Stanton, October 3, 1848, Elizabeth Cady Stanton Papers, Library of Congress.
  27. Alma Lutz, *Created Equal*, p. 46.
  28. M.S. Gove Nichols to Stanton, August 21, 1852, *Stanton Letters*, p. 44.
  29. Harriott Hunt to Stanton, June 30, 1852, Elizabeth Cady Stanton Papers, Library of Congress.
  30. Sarah Grimké to Stanton, March 29, 1854, *ibid*.
  31. Lucy Stone to Stanton, August 14, 1853, *ibid*.
  32. Ida Harper, *The Life and Work of Susan B. Anthony*, Vol. 1 (Indianapolis: The Bowen-Merrill Company, 1899), chap. 6. Anthony supervised this two-volume biography and so it is somewhat autobiographical.
  33. For a brief overview of temperance in the 1850s, see Ronald Walters, *American Reformers, 1815–1860* (New York: Hill & Wang, 1978).
  34. From an appeal written by Anthony in 1852, as quoted in Harper, *Life of Anthony*, Vol. 1, p. 71.
  35. *Ibid.*, chap. 6; see also *HWS*, Vol. 1, chap. 14.
  36. *HWS*, Vol. 1, pp. 493–99.
  37. Stanton, *Eighty Years*, p. 187.
  38. *Ibid.*, p. 165.
  39. Harper, *Life of Anthony*, Vol. 2, p. 667.
  40. Harper, *Life of Anthony*, Vol. 1, p. 105.
  41. *HWS*, Vol. 1, pp. 518 and 541–42.
  42. Lucretia Mott to Stanton, n.d., *Stanton Letters*, p. 56.
  43. Stanton's correspondent was probably the Reverend Amory D. Mayo, February 15, 1854, Elizabeth Cady Stanton Papers, Library of Congress.
  44. Stanton to Elizabeth Smith Miller, November 15, 1856, *Stanton Letters*, pp. 68–69.
  45. Stanton to Anthony, December 1857, *ibid.*, p. 71.
  46. Letter to *The Liberator*, May 18, 1860, as cited in *ibid.*, p. 78.
  47. Gordon, et al., *Selected Papers*, vol. 1, p. 94.
  48. Cited in Laura Curtis Bullard, "Elizabeth Cady Stanton," *Our Famous Women: An Authoritative Record of the Lives and Deeds of Distinguished American Women of Our Times* (Hartford, CT: A.D. Worthington, 1886), pp. 617–18.
  49. "Women's Rights Convention Held at Seneca Falls," in Gordon et.al, *Select Papers*, vol. 1, p. 83. There is no contemporary record of any of the speeches delivered at the Seneca Falls Convention.
  50. *Stanton Letters*, p 39.
  51. The four schools that offered coeducational collegiate instruction and degrees to women.
  52. Emily Howland was the daughter of a wealthy merchant, Benjamin Howland, and was born in South Carolina. She organized the lectures by Lucy Stone, James T. Brady, and George William Curtis in 1858.
  53. The older boys, Neil and Kit, attended Dr. Reed's school in Geneva, New York.
  54. Robert Livingston Stanton was born on 13 March 1859 at Seneca Falls.
  55. Daniel Cady died on 31 October at Johnstown. John Brown led a band of twenty-one men against the federal armory at Harper's Ferry on 16 October 1859. Taken prisoner after two days of fighting, he was tried and hanged for treason against the state of Virginia on 2 December 1859. Gerrit Smith was committed to the State Asylum for the Insane at Utica on 7 November and stayed until the end of December. Letters in John Brown's possession at the time of his capture in mid-October exposed Smith's complicity in the raid, as friend and financier, and the risks and guilt of his position drove him temporarily insane.

Part Two. 1863–1878

  1. Stanton, "National Protection for National Citizens," *HWS*, Vol. 3 (Rochester: Susan B. Anthony, 1886), pp. 80–93.
  2. *HWS.*, vol. 2, p.174.
  3. *Feminism and Suffrage: The Emergence of an Independent Women's Movement in America, 1848–1869* (Ithaca: Cornell University Press, 1978) p. 61.
  4. Faye Dudden, *Fighting Chance: The Struggle Over Woman Suffrage and Black*

Suffrage in Reconstruction America (New York: Oxford University Press, 2011).
5. *HWS*, Vol. 2, (Rochester: Susan B. Anthony, 1887), p. 268.
6. "The Revolution for 1870," *The Revolution*, December 6, 1869, p. 360.
7. On the Hester Vaughn case, see *Feminism and Suffrage*, pp. 145–47. The McFarland-Richardson episode is described in Alma Lutz, *Created Equal*, pp. 189–90. The protest meeting against the regulation of prostitution is mentioned in David Pivar, *Purity Crusade: Sexual Morality and Social Control, 1868–1900* (Westport, CT: Greenwood Press, 1973), p. 51.
8. Stanton to Martha Coffin Wright, June 19, 1871, Elizabeth Cady Stanton Papers, Library of Congress.
9. Stanton discusses women's sexual passion in her September 6, 1883, diary entry, in *Stanton Letters*, p. 210.
10. Ellen Carol DuBois, *Harriot Stanton Blatch and the Winning of Woman Suffrage* (New Haven: Yale University Press, 1999).
11. Alice Stone Blackwell to Kitty Blackwell, March 8, 1883, NAWSA Papers, Library of Congress.
12. Anthony, Diary, October 20, 1870, Susan B. Anthony Papers, Library of Congress.
13. Paulina Wright Davis, *A History of the National Woman's Rights Movement for Twenty Years, from 1850 to 1870* (New York: Journeymen Printers' Cooperative Association, 1871), p. 22.
14. This organization, the Working Women's Association, is discussed in *Feminism and Suffrage*, chap. 5.
15. On the free labor ideology of Reconstruction-era labor leaders, see David Montgomery, *Beyond Equality: Labor and the Radical Republicans, 1862–1872* (New York: Vintage, 1967).
16. Stanton to Anthony, June 27, 1870, *Stanton Letters*, p. 127.
17. Stanton, "Editorial Correspondence," *The Revolution*, April 14, 1870, p. 232.
18. "The Revolution for 1870," p. 360.
19. Woodhull's congressional argument is reprinted in *HWS*, Vol. 2, pp. 444–48.
20. Ida Harper, *The Life and Work of Susan B. Anthony*, Vol. 1 (p. 513).

21. Stanton to Martha Coffin Wright, March 21, 1870, Elizabeth Cady Stanton Papers, Library of Congress.
22. *HWS*, Vol. 2, p. 496.
23. For a full list of voting women from 1869 through 1872, see Gordon et al., *Selected Papers*, vol. 2, pp. 645–54.
24. *Ibid.*, p. 680.
25. *Ibid.*, pp. 516–17.
26. See for instance the 1871 letter from Anthony to Stanton quoted in Lutz, *Created Equal*, pp. 207–08. Stanton was not particularly sympathetic to Anthony after her arrest and relatively unenthusiastic about her organizing efforts around her trial; see Stanton to Matilda Gage, June 25, 1873, *Stanton Letters*, pp. 142–43.
27. Lutz, *Created Equal*, p. 217. The comment about spirits refers to Woodhull's spiritualism and her claim that spirits gave her the ideas for her congressional memorial.
28. See Robert Shaplen, *Free Love and Heavenly Sinners* (New York: Alfred A. Knopf, 1954).
29. Peter T. Cominos, "Late Victorian Sexual Respectability and the Social System," *International Review of Social History*, Vol. 8 (1963), pp. 18–48, 216–50.
30. Woodhull to Anthony, January 2, 1873, Alma Lutz Collection, Huntington Library.
31. Stanton to Lucretia Mott, July 6, 1872, *Stanton Letters*, p. 139.
32. DuBois, *Suffrage: Women's Long Battle for the Vote* (New York: Simon and Schuster, 2020), 104.
33. Gordon et al., *Select Papers*, vol. 3, p. 234.
34. *Ibid.*, p. 261.
35. Republicans introduced dozens of resolutions for a fifteenth constitutional amendment in December, most of which guaranteed only manhood suffrage. There were two exceptions. On 7 December 1868, Senator Pomeroy proposed that "[t]he basis of suffrage in the United States shall be that of citizenship, and all native or naturalized citizens shall enjoy the same rights and privileges of the elective franchise." On 8 December, Congressman George W. Julian proposed that "the right of suffrage in the United States shall be based upon citizenship and shall be regulated by Congress;

and all citizens of the United States, whether native or naturalized, shall enjoy this right equally without any distinction or discrimination whatever founded on race, color, or sex."

36. A reference to Senator Henry Wilson, who told the New England Woman Suffrage Association that duty required he "have courage enough" to vote against woman suffrage whenever it was tied to Black suffrage.

37. Katherine Anthony, *Susan B. Anthony: Her Personal History and Her Era* (New York: Doubleday, 1954), p. 337.

Part Three. 1880–1906

1. On the Woman's Christian Temperance Union, see Mary Earhart, *Frances Willard: From Prayers to Politics* (Chicago: University of Chicago Press, 1944). On the club movement see Karen Blair, *The Clubwoman as Feminist: True Womanhood Redefined, 1868–1914* (New York: Holmes and Meier, 1980). Black women formed their own organizations, both because their interests were different and because they were excluded from white women's societies, but their clubs and temperance unions shared many of the same characteristics. See Gerda Lerner, "Early Community Work of Black Club Women," *The Journal of Negro History*, Vol. 59 (1974), pp. 158–67; and Cynthia Neverdon-Morton, "The Black Woman's Struggle for Equality in the South, 1895–1915," in *The Afro-American Woman: Struggles and Images*, eds. Rosalyn Terborg-Penn and Sharon Harley (Port Washington, N.Y.: Kennikat Press, 1978), pp. 43–57.

2. The quotation is from a speech on "The Inviolable Home," by Charlotte Beebe Wilbour, *Association for the Advancement of Women, Papers and Letters* (New York: Mrs. Wm. Ballard, Book & Job Printer, 1874), p. 71. The New England Woman's Club, Young Woman's Christian Association, Women's Educational and Industrial Union, and Sorosis all took an early interest in working girls. By the mid-1880s there was a distinct branch of the club movement, the Working Girls Societies, devoted entirely to these concerns.

3. See, for instance, "An Historical Sketch of the New England Women's Club," 1884, pamphlet, Julia Ward Howe Papers, Schlesinger Library: "Care was to be taken to give the organization such a form as should make it self-protective against disturbing elements, that thus it might become ... a place where women should have opportunity for culture in dignified ... discussion." Also see the very interesting exchange of letters in the *Chicago Tribune*, November 27, 1873, on the social arrangements best suited to coeducation. Frances Willard argued for the necessity of careful supervision of young women to protect their reputations, while Elizabeth Stanton advised against "cribbing and crippling their natural impulses, to make them what is called 'ladylike.'" Undoubtedly, the notoriety of free lover Victoria Woodhull and the Beecher-Tilton scandal exacerbated, but did not create, this concern about the moral character of feminists.

4. Club women, few of whom had any collegiate education, frequently researched and read original papers on literary and cultural topics (Blair, *Clubwoman*). Frances Willard of the WCTU was a spectacularly successful organizer, and stressed the importance of giving as many women as possible individual responsibility; see Frances Willard, *Women and Temperance* (Hartford, CT: Park Publishing Co., 1883), chap. 35.

5. "Miss Willard is doing noble work but I cannot coincide with her view. Miss Willard, in fact, has a lever but she has no fulcrum upon which to place it" ("Female Suffrage: An Interview with Susan B. Anthony," *Chicago Tribune*, December 10, 1879, p. 3).

6. Harper, *Life of Anthony*, Vol. 2 (p. 586. The issue was Fredrick Douglass' marriage to a white woman, which Stanton believed that the suffrage movement should defend. See Document 18. Anthony believed that she was not invited to the founding meeting of the Association for the Advancement for Women in 1873, while Stanton was, because of her arrest and trial for illegal voting earlier that same year. Later in her life, Anthony seemed to take particular pleasure when honor was paid her by wealthy and respectable women.

7. International Council of Women, *Women in a Changing World: The Dynamic Story of the International Council of Women since 1888* (London: Routledge and Kegan Paul, 1966), p. 11.
8. *Ibid.*
9. Harper, *Life of Anthony*, Vol. 2, p. 634; Anthony was especially pleased that "very many conservative associations have appointed delegates" (Anthony to Elizabeth Smith Miller, January 26, 1888, Smith Family Papers, New York Public Library).
10. *Report of the International Council of Women*. pp. 119, 143.
11. Richard J. Evans, *The Feminists* (London: Croom Helm, 1977), p. 251; also see Edith F. Hurwitz, "The International Sisterhood," in *Becoming Visible: Women in European History*, eds. Renate Bridenthal and Claudia Koontz (Boston: Houghton Mifflin Company, 1977), p. 332.
12. Blair, *Clubwoman*, p. 112.
13. See for instance Martha Coffin Wright to Lucy Stone, December 21, 1874, Garrison Family Papers, Smith College; and Antoinette Brown Blackwell to Lucy Stone, January 9, 1886, Blackwell Family Papers, Schlesinger Library.
14. Alice Stone Blackwell, *Lucy Stone, Pioneer of Women's Rights* (Boston: Little, Brown and Company, 1930), p. 229.
15. "Negotiations Between the American and National Associations in Regard to Union," ed. Rachel Foster Avery, pamphlet, Boston Public Library; Rachel Foster Avery to Olympia Brown, January 6, 1888, Olympia Brown Papers, Schlesinger Library.
16. Anthony to Rachel Foster, cited in Harper, *Life of Anthony*, Vol. 2, p. 628.
17. Anthony to Foster, cited in Katherine Anthony, *Susan B. Anthony*, p. 390.
18. Anthony to Mrs. Osborn, February 5, 1890, Garrison Family Papers, Smith College.
19. Harriet H. Robinson and Harriette Robinson Shattuck, "The Union, 1889," unpublished manuscript notebook, Harriet Robinson Papers, Schlesinger Library; Olympia Brown, "A Statement of Facts," privately printed pamphlet, 1889, Olympia Brown Papers, Schlesinger Library.
20. Harper, *Life of Anthony*, Vol. 2, p. 632.
21. Anthony to Stanton, 1897, Clara Colby Papers, Huntington Library.
22. At the 1899 NAWSA convention Anthony opposed a resolution condemning racial discrimination in public transportation; this incident is cited in Aileen Kraditor, *Ideas of the Woman Suffrage Movement, 1890-1920* (New York: Columbia University Press, 1965), p. I 72.
23. *HWS*, Vol. 4, p. 173.
24. Harper, *Life of Anthony*, Vol. 2, pp. 631-32.
25. Stanton addressed these questions in a written dissent to the discussion on political parties (Stanton, "What Should Be Our Attitude Toward Political Parties," unpublished manuscript, Elizabeth Cady Stanton Papers, Library of Congress).
26. "I have just had an article in the Sun in which I recommend our friends to join the People's Party. If the Prohibitionists, the Populists, the labor organizations and the women would all unite, we should be in the majority" (Diary entry, August, 1894, *Elizabeth Cady Stanton as Revealed in Her Letters, Diary and Reminiscences*, eds. Theodore Stanton and Harriot Stanton Blatch [New York: Harper & Brothers, Publishers, 1922], p. 307). On socialism, to an 1898 NAWSA convention, she wrote, "Those who have eyes to see recognize the fact that the period for all ... fragmentary reforms has ended. Agitation of the broader question of philosophical socialism is now in order. This next step in progress ... is now being agitated by able thinkers and writers in all civilized countries" (manuscript letter, Susan B. Anthony Papers, University of Rochester).
27. Stanton, "What Should Be Our Attitude."
28. Stanton, "Open Letter to the Suffrage Convention, 1898," unidentified clipping, Elizabeth Cady Stanton Papers, Library of Congress.
29. Stanton, *Eighty Years and More*, especially chaps. 22-26. Stanton's concerns with religion permeate her autobiography.
30. Stanton, "Has Christianity Benefited Woman?" *North American Review*, Vol. 140 (1885), pp. 389-99.
31. Stanton, "Patriotism and Chastity," *Westminster Review*, Vol. 135 (1891), pp. 1-5.

32. David Pivar, *Purity Crusade*; Sidney Warren, *American Freethought, 1860–1914* (New York: Columbia University Press, 1943).

33. Frances Willard was active in the Prohibition Party, which supported a constitutional amendment and stricter blue laws; Mary Livermore, Julia Ward Howe, Antoinette Brown Blackwell, and others were very involved in the social purity movement and its efforts to restrict divorce legislation (Pivar, *Purity Crusade*).

34. *HWS*, Vol. 4, p. 165; also see Stanton, "Divorce Versus Domestic Warfare," *Arena*, Vol. 5 (1890), pp. 560–69.

35. Stanton, *Eighty Years and More*, 422–23.

36. Stanton, "Sunday at the World's Fair," *North American Review*, Vol. 154 (1892), pp. 254–56; in 1893, Stanton also produced a leaflet, "Open the World's Fair on Sunday," which she distributed widely (See Document 24).

37. Other freethinkers in the suffrage movement included Matilda J. Gage, Olympia Brown, Josephine Henry, and Clara Colby; also see *Heroines of Freethought*, by Sara Underwood (New York: Charles B. Somerby, 1876).

38. Shaw to Lucy Anthony, January 20, 1890, Mary Earhart Dillon Collection, Schlesinger Library.

39. Carrie Chapman Catt to Alice Stone Blackwell, September 18, 1930, Carrie Chapman Catt Papers, Huntington Library; also see Katherine Anthony, *Susan B. Anthony*, p. 438.

40. Stanton to Olympia Brown, November 11, 1892, Olympia Brown Papers, Schlesinger Library.

41. Angelina Grimké Weld to Stanton, reprinted in *The Lily*, October, 1851, p. 75.

42. Stanton to Elizabeth Boynton Harbert, September 15, n.y., Elizabeth Boynton Harbert Papers, Huntington Library.

43. Mary Livermore to Stanton, September 1, 1886, Elizabeth Cady Stanton Papers, Library of Congress; Lady Henry Somerset to Stanton, June 5, 1895, *ibid*.

44. *The Washington Post*, January 28, 1896, and January 29, 1896, clippings in the Susan B. Anthony Papers, Library of Congress; also "The Washington Convention," *Woman's Journal*, February 1, 1896, p. 1. Despite the suffragists' repudiation of *The Woman's Bible*, it went through three editions in the United States and England; in 1898, Stanton issued a second volume, covering the New Testament.

45. Harper, *Life of Anthony*, Vol. 2, pp. 855–57.

46. *Ibid*., p. 667. Anthony made her remarks in 1890, at the celebration of her seventieth birthday.

47. Anthony, "Women's Half-Century of Evolution," *North American Review*, Vol. 175 (1902), p. 807.

48. Lois Banner, *Elizabeth Cady Stanton: A Radical for Women's Rights* (Boston: Little, Brown & Co., 1980), pp. 171–72.

49. Stanton to Elizabeth Boynton Harbert, , June 7, 1900, Elizabeth Boynton Harbert Papers, Huntington Library.

50. Stanton to Harbert, September 30, 1902, *ibid*.

51. Stanton to Harbert, June 7, 1900, *ibid*.

52. On the West Coast, Anthony memorabilia was collected by Una Winter and housed initially at the Los Angeles Public Library and later at the Huntington Library. On the East Coast, collections were established by the Susan B. Anthony Memorial, Inc., and housed in Anthony's home, now a museum, and at the Rochester Public Library. The University of Rochester has since established its own collection. Biographies of Anthony include Ida Husted Harper, *The Life and Work of Susan B. Anthony* (3 volumes): Katherine Anthony, *Susan B. Anthony: Her Personal History and Her Era*; Rheta Childe Dorr, *Susan B. Anthony: The Woman Who Changed the Mind of a Nation* (New York: Frederick A. Stokes, 1928); Alma Lutz, *Susan B Anthony: Rebel, Crusader, Humanitarian* (Boston: Beacon, 1959); and Kathleen Barry, *Susan B. Anthony: Biography of a Singular Feminist* (Ballantine Books, 1987). In 1990, Congress passed a bill designating Stanton's home, the church where the first women's rights convention was held, and other sites in Seneca Falls, New York, as a national historic park for women's rights.

53. Alma Lutz, *Created Equal*. Sub-

sequent important biographies are: Lois Banner, *Elizabeth Cady Stanton: A Radical for Women's Rights* (HarperCollins, 1980); Elisabeth Griffith, *In Her Own Right: The Life of Elizabeth Cady Stanton* (Oxford University Press, 1984); Lori Ginsberg, *Elizabeth Cady Stanton: An American Life* (Hill and Wang, 2009; Vivian Gornick, *The Solitude of Self: Thinking about Elizabeth Cady Stanton* (Farrar Straus and Giroux, 2005).

54. Brent Staples, "How The Suffrage Movement Betrayed Black Women," New York Times, July 28, 2018; followed by many others.

55. Nancy F. Cott, *The Grounding of Modern Feminism* (New Haven: Yale University Press, 1987) chap. 1.

56. Carol M. Mueller, *The Politics of the Gender Gap: The Social Construction of Political Influence* (New York: Sage Publications, 1988).

57. Anthony to Stanton, January 27, 1884, Gordon et al., *Select Papers*, vol. 4, 323–24.

58. At the time Stanton wrote her original letter to Douglass in January, newspapers carried the story of the Hackensack Cemetery Company in New Jersey refusing to bury Sam Bass, an African American sexton of the first Baptist church of Hackensack (*New York Times*, 26, 19 January 1884).

59. Kenneth Rayner (1808–1884) was appointed solicitor of the Treasury by President Hayes in 1877 and served until his death on 6 March 1884.

60. The Republican National Convention met in Chicago from June 3 to 6, and Douglass was in attendance.

61. Ann D. Gordon, "Stanton and the Right to Vote: On Account of Race or Sex," in *Elizabeth Cady Stanton: Feminist as Thinker*, eds. Ellen DuBois and Richard Candida Smith (New York: New York University Press, 2007), p. 123.

62. From Charles Sumner, "Equal Rights of All."

63. Contributors and editors of the *Woman's Journal* carried on the discussion of universal and educated suffrage. Henry Blackwell's editorial on 20 October 1894 reminded readers that woman suffragists in Massachusetts had always supported the state's educational qualification for voting and sought the vote only for women who met that qualification. On October 27, he countered supporters of universal suffrage with examples from cities where immigrants made up a substantial part of the population and political corruption flourished; to provide universal suffrage in those circumstances produced slavery of the masses to political bosses, and a bastard aristocracy of thieves, liquor-sellers and gamblers, and of bribed and brutal policemen."

64. William Lloyd Garrison, Jr., became the designated defender of universal suffrage as the debate continued, and the editors allowed him to respond to other contributors before their essays and letters were published. In the issue of October 20, he briefly challenged some points made by Henry Blackwell and Stanton.

65. *Stanton, Letters*, p. 280.

66. Daniel Cady Eaton, her nephew.

Bibliography

Primary Source Collections

Alma Lutz Collection, Huntington Library
Autograph Collection, Vassar College
Blackwell Family Papers, Schlesinger Library
Carrie Chapman Catt Papers, Library of Congress
Clara Colby Papers, Huntington Library
Elizabeth Boynton Harbert Papers, Huntington Library
Elizabeth Cady Stanton Papers, Library of Congress
Elizabeth Cady Stanton Papers, Vassar College
Elizabeth Smith Miller Scrapbooks, New York Public Library
Garrison Family Papers, Smith College
Harriet Robinson Papers, Schlesinger Library
Ida H. Harper Papers, Huntington Library
Julia Ward Howe Papers, Schlesinger Library
Lillie Devereux Blake Papers, Missouri Historical Society
Mary Earhart Dillon Papers, Schlesinger Library
NAWSA Papers, Library of Congress
Olympia Brown Papers, Schlesinger Library
Susan B. Anthony Papers, Library of Congress
Theodore Stanton Papers, Douglas College

Primary Sources

Association for the Advancement of Women, Papers and Letters. New York: Mrs. Wm. Ballard, Book & Job Printer, 1874.

Barnes, Gilbert H., and Dwight L. Dumond, eds. *Letters of Theodore Dwight Weld, Angelina Grimké Weld, and Sarah Grimké, 1822–1844,* Vol. 2. New York: Appleton-Century Company, 1934.

Beecher, Catharine E. *An Essay on Slavery and Abolitionism with Reference to the Duty of American Females.* Philadelphia: Henry Perkins, 1837.

Beecher, Catharine E. *A Treatise on Domestic Economy.* New York: Schocken Books, 1977.

Bullard, Laura Curtis. *Our Famous Women: An Authoritative Record of the Lives and Deeds of Distinguished American Women of Our Times.* Hartford, CT: A. D. Worthington, 1886.

Cook, Clarence, ed. *A Girl's Life Eighty Years Ago: Letters of Eliza Southgate Bowne.* New York: G. Scribner's Sons, 1887.

Crocker, Hannah Mather. *Observations of the Real Rights of Women, and their Appropriate Duties, Agreeable to Scripture, Reason and Common Sense.* Boston: By the Author, 1818.

Davis, Paulina Wright. *A History of the National Woman's Rights Movement for Twenty Years, from 1850 to 1870.* New York: Journeymen Printers' Cooperative Association, 1871.

Duniway, Abigail Scott. *Pathbreaking: An Autobiographical History of the Woman Suffrage Movement in the Pacific Coast States.* Portland, OR: James, Herns and Abbott, 1914.

Fuller, Margaret. *Woman in the Nineteenth Century.* New York: Greeley & McElrath, 1845.

Gordon, Ann D., et al. *Selected Papers of*

Elizabeth Cady Stanton and Susan B. Anthony, vols. 1–4. New Brunswick, NJ: Rutgers University Press, 1995–98.
Grimké, Angelina. *Letters to Catharine E. Beecher in Reply to an Essay on Slavery and Abolitionism*. Boston: Isaac Knapp, 1838.
Grimké, Sarah. *Letters on the Equality of the Sexes and the Condition of Women Addressed to Mary S. Parker*. Boston: Isaac Knapp, 1838.
Hallowell, Anna D., ed. *James and Lucretia Mott, Life and Letters*. Boston: Houghton, Mifflin and Company, 1884.
Harper, Ida H. *The Life and Work of Susan B. Anthony*, Vol. 1. Indianapolis: The Bowen-Merrill Company, 1899.
Kraditor, Aileen S., ed. *Up from the Pedestal: Selected Writings in the History of American Feminism*. Chicago: Quadrangle Books, 1968.
Sachs, Emanie. *The Terrible Siren*. New York: Harper and Brothers, 1928.
Stanton, Elizabeth Cady. *Eighty Years and More: Reminiscences, 1815–1897*. New York: Simon & Schuster, 2020.
Stanton, Elizabeth Cady, Susan B. Anthony, and Matilda J. Gage, eds. *History of Woman Suffrage*, Vol. l. Rochester: Susan B. Anthony, 1881.
Stanton, Theodore, and Harriot Stanton Blatch, eds. *Elizabeth Cady Stanton as Revealed in Her Letters, Diary and Reminiscences*. New York: Harper & Brothers Publishers, 1922.
Stern, Madeline, ed. *The Victoria Woodhull Reader*. Weston MA: M. & S. Publishers, 1974.
Underwood, Sara. *Heroines of Freethought*. New York: Charles B. Somerby, 1876.
Willard, Emma Hart. *Address to the Public: Particularly to the Members of the Legislature of New York, Proposing a Plan for Improving Female Education*. Albany: I. W. Clark, 1819.
Willard, Frances. *Woman and Temperance*. Hartford, CT: Park Publishing Co., 1883.
Wollstonecraft, Mary. *Vindication of the Rights of Woman*. New York: W.W. Norton, 1967.
Wright, Frances. *Course of Popular Lectures*. New York: Office of *The Free Enquirer*, 1830.

Books: Secondary Sources

Anthony, Katherine. *Susan B. Anthony: Her Personal History and Her Era*. New York: Doubleday, 1954.
Banner, Lois. *Elizabeth Cady Stanton: A Radical for Women's Rights*. Boston: Little, Brown & Co., 1980.
Berg, Barbara. *The Remembered Gate: Origins of American Feminism*. New York: Oxford University Press, 1978.
Blackwell, Alice Stone. *Lucy Stone, Pioneer of Women's Rights*. Boston: Little, Brown and Company, 1930.
Blair, Karen. *The Clubwoman as Feminist: True Womanhood Redefined, 1868–1914*. New York: Holmes and Meier, 1980.
Budd, Susan. *Varieties of Unbelief: Atheists and Agnostics in English Society, 1850–1960*. London: Hinemann, 1977.
Cahill, Cathleen. *Recasting the Vote: How Women of Color Transformed the Suffrage Movement*. Chapel Hill: University of North Carolina Press, 2020.
Cott, Nancy F. *The Bonds of Womanhood: "Woman's Sphere" in New England, 1780–1835*. New Haven: Yale University Press, 1977.
Cott, Nancy F., ed. *Root of Bitterness*. New York: E. P. Dutton & Co., 1972.
Dorr, Rheta Childe. *Susan B. Anthony: The Woman Who Changed the Mind of a Nation*. New York: Frederick A. Stokes, 1928.
DuBois, Ellen Carol. *Feminism and Suffrage: The Emergence of an Independent Women's Movement in America, 1848–1869*. Ithaca: Cornell University Press, 197.
DuBois, Ellen Carol. *Harriot Stanton Blatch and the Winning of Woman Suffrage*. New Haven: Yale University Press, 1999.
DuBois, Ellen Carol. *Suffrage: Women's Long Battle for the Vote*. New York: Simon & Schuster, 2020.
DuBois, Ellen Carol. *Woman Suffrage, Women's Rights*. New York: New York University Press, 1998.
DuBois, Ellen Carol, and Richard Candida Smith, eds. *Elizabeth Cady Stanton: Feminist as Thinker*. New York: New York University Press, 2007.
Dudden, Faye. *Fighting Chance: The Struggle Over Woman Suffrage and*

Black Suffrage in Reconstruction America. New York: Oxford University Press, 2011.

Earhart, Mary. *Frances Willard: From Prayers to Politics*. Chicago: University of Chicago Press, 1944.

Epstein, Barbara. *The Politics of Domesticity: Women, Evangelism and Temperance in Nineteenth Century America*. Middletown, CT: Wesleyan University Press, 1981.

Evans, Richard J. *The Feminists*. London: Croom Helm, 1977.

Filler, Louis. *The Crusade Against Slavery, 1830–1860*. New York: Harper and Brothers, 1960.

Flexner, Eleanor. *Century of Struggle: The Women's Rights Movement in the United States*. New York: Schocken Books, 1977.

Fought, Leigh. *Women in the World of Frederick Douglass*. New York: Oxford University Press, 2017.

Frank, Linda. *An Uncommon Union: Henry B. Stanton and the Emancipation of Elizabeth Cady*. Auburn, NY: Upstate New York History, 2016.

Ginzberg, Lori D. *Untidy Origins: A Study of Women's Rights in Antebellum New York*. Chapel Hill: University of North Carolina Press, 2005.

Goldsmith, Barbara. *Other Powers: The Age of Suffrage, Spiritualism and the Scandalous Victoria Woodhull*. New York: Knopf, 1998.

Gordon, Linda. *Woman's Body, Woman's Right: A Social History of Birth Control*. New York: Grossman, 1976.

International Council of Women. *Women in a Changing World: The Dynamic Story of the International Council of Women since 1888*. London: Routledge and Kegan Paul, 1966.

Irwin, Inez H. *The Story of the National Woman's Party*. New York: Harcourt, 1921.

Jones, Martha S. *Vanguard: How Black Women Broke Barriers, Won the Vote, and Insisted on Equality for All*. New York: Basic Books, 2020.

Kern, Kathi. *Mrs. Stanton's Bible*. Ithaca, NY: Cornell University Press, 2001.

Kraditor, Aileen. *Ideas of the Woman Suffrage Movement, 1890–1920*. New York: Columbia University Press, 1965.

Lutz, Alma. *Susan B. Anthony: Rebel, Crusader, Humanitarian*. Boston: Beacon, 1959.

McMillen, Sally. *Seneca Falls and the Origins of the Women's Rights Movement*. New York: Oxford University Press, 2008.

Montgomery, David. *Beyond Equality: Labor and the Radical Republicans, 1862–1872*. Urbana: University of Illinois Press, 1967.

O'Neill, William. *Everyone Was Brave*. Chicago: Quadrangle Books, 1969.

Pivar, David. *Purity Crusade: Sexual Morality and Social Control, 1868–1900*. Westport, CT: Greenwood Press, 1973.

Rossi, Alice S., ed. *The Feminist Papers from Adams to de Beauvoir*. New York: Columbia University Press, 1973.

Sewall, May Wright, ed. *The World's Congress of Representative Women*. Chicago: Rand McNally & Co., 1894.

Shaplen, Robert. *Free Love and Heavenly Sinners*. New York: Alfred A. Knopf, 1954.

Suhl, Yuri. *Ernestine Rose and the Battle for Human Rights*. New York: Reynal and Company, 1959.

Terborg-Penn, Rosalyn and Sharon Harley, eds. *The Afro-American Woman: Struggles and Images*. Port Washington, N.Y.: Kennikat Press, 1978.

Walters, Ronald. *American Reformers, 1815–1860*. New York: Hill & Wang, 1978.

Warren, Sidney. *American Freethought, 1860–1914*. New York: Columbia University Press, 1943.

Wellman, Judith. *The Road to Seneca Falls: Elizabeth Cady Stanton and the First Women's Rights Convention*. Chicago: University of Illinois Press, 2004.

Women's National Liberal Union: A Report of the Convention for Organization, February 24–25, 1890. Syracuse: Masters and Stone Printers, 1890.

Articles

Anthony, Susan B. "Women's Half-Century of Evolution." *North American Review* 175 (1902), 807.

Cominos, Peter T. "Late Victorian Sexual Respectability and the Social System." *International Review of Social History*, 8 (1963), 18–48.

Crenshaw, Kimberlé. "Mapping the Margins: Intersectionality, Identity Politics, and Violence Against Women of Color." *Stanford Law Review* #43 (1991): pp. 1241–99.

Hurwitz, Edith F. "The International Sisterhood," in *Becoming Visible: Women in European History*, eds. Renate Bridenthal and Claudia Koontz. Boston: Houghton Mifflin Company, 1977.

"Interview with Elizabeth Cady Stanton." *Sunday New York Herald.* January 22, 1899.

Lerner, Gerda. "Early Community Work of Black Club Women." *The Journal of Negro History*, 59 (1974), 158–67.

McGuinn, Nicholas. "George Eliot and Mary Wollstonecraft." *The Nineteenth Century Woman*, eds. Sara Delamont and Lorna Duffin. London: Croom Helm, 1978.

Rosenberg, Carroll Smith. "Beauty, the Beast and the Militant Woman: A Case Study in Sex Roles and Social Stress in Jacksonian America." *American Quarterly* 2, no. 3 (1971), 562–84.

Stanton, Elizabeth Cady. "Divorce Versus Domestic Warfare." *Arena*, 5 (1890) 560–69.

Stanton, Elizabeth Cady. "Has Christianity Benefited Woman?" *North American Review*, Vol. 140 (1885), pp. 389–99.

Stanton, Elizabeth Cady. "Patriotism and Chastity." *Westminster Review* 135 (1891), 1.

Staples, Brent. "When the Suffrage Movement Sold Out to White Supremacy," and "How the Suffrage Movement Betrayed Black Women" *New York Times*, February 2, 2019, and July 28, 2018.

Index

abolitionism 1–3, 11–16, 20–22, 31, 53–36, 53, 56, 67–68, 71–76, 79–81, 92, 100, 104, 117, 136, 156, 163, 186, 202
Afro-American League 168
American Anti-Slavery Society 21–22, 43
American Equal Rights Association 80–81, 96, 100, 104–6
American Revolution 40, 58, 94–95, 110, 115, 198
American Woman Suffrage Association 82, 90, 146, 185
Anglo-Saxon 61, 200–1, 110
Anthony, Lucy 200–2
Anthony, Mary 202
Anthony, Susan B.: economic independence 17, 105–6, 121–26, 133; family 17, 53, 133; racial attitudes 66–68, 146–47, 163–68; Stanton relationship 17–19, 43–57, 63, 71, 79–80, 89, 105, 152–55, 169, 171; trial for voting 3, 88–90, 107–16, 210*n*26
Avery, Rachel Foster 152

Beecher, Catharine 10–11, 21, 48–49, 90
Beecher-Tilton scandal 90
Bible 130, 148, 196, 203; *see also Woman's Bible*
Black codes 79, 100, 104–5
Black suffrage 2, 34, 59, 79–82, 89, 96–97, 104–6, 110, 112–13, 121, 125, 172; conflict with woman suffrage 34, 80–82, 89, 103–6, 125, 172
Blacks 1–2, 3, 36, 105, 149, 164, 173; *see also* slavery
Blackstone, William 134, 188
Blackwell, Alice Stone 145
Blackwell, Antoinette Brown 50–51, 55
Blake, Lillie Devereux 152
Blatch, Harriot Stanton 55, 56, 83, 148, 204–5
Booth, Mary 135
Bright, John 116

Bronte, Charlotte 120
Brown, Antoinette *see* Blackwell, Antoinette Brown
Brown, John 22, 56, 71, 73, 98
Brown, Olympia 146, 151
Burns, Anthony 117
Butler, Benjamin 11

Cady, Daniel 13, 47, 55, 58
Cady, Margaret Livingston 12
capitalism 102, 142
Cary Sisters 135
Catt, Carrie Chapman 150–51, 153
Chapman, Maria Weston 36
Child, Lydia Maria 102, 136
Christianity 26, 28, 72, 75–76, 93, 128, 148–57, 166, 185, 191, 196
citizenship 20, 25, 27, 41, 58–59, 68, 80–81, 87, 89, 91–93, 95, 98, 100–1, 104, 107–16, 119, 146, 156–58, 167, 174–78, 179–80, 199, 210*n*35
civil war 21–22, 84, 92, 94–95, 98, 101, 104, 115, 165, 177
class conflict 9, 110, 113, 174
Clemmer, Mary 135
coeducation 8–9, 49–51, 209*n*51
Colby, Clara 146
Comstock Law 90
Constitution, United States 1, 87, 108–16, 134, 158, 170
Constitutional Amendments: Equal Rights 1; Fifteenth 2, 3, 80, 81, 87, 91, 100–3, 104–6, 113, 16, 156; Fourteenth 80–81, 87, 91, 107, 111–1; Reconstruction 84, 89, 109, 116; Thirteenth 80, 92, 107, 112, 114; woman's suffrage 3, 87, 110
constitutions, state: 16, 40, 58–64, 96–99, 108, 128, 159, 173–74, 188
Couverture 61
Crenshaw, Kimberle 2
Crocker, Hannah 8

Index

Darwinism 193
Daughters of Temperance 17, 18, 37–39
Davis, Andrew Jackson Davis 53–55
Davis, Paulina Wright 16, 84
Declaration of Independence 62, 74, 102, 108–9
Democratic Party 14–15, 79, 92, 116, 123, 125
divorce 9, 15, 18, 37, 39, 41, 43, 46, 82, 84, 86–87, 91, 117–20, 127–30, 136, 145, 150, 154, 169, 171, 197
Douglass, Anna 156
Douglass, Frederick 3, 147, 149–56, 30–33, 81, 100, 104–6, 147, 149, 156–64, 167, 176
Douglass, Helen Pitts 156, 159
Dred Scot 21

education 7–8, 10–11, 12, 14, 24, 28, 49–51, 72, 75, 94, 103, 128, 130, 134–35, 172, 180–84
Eighty Years and More 154
election: of 1872 88–90, 107: of 2016 3
emancipation 34, 79, 88, 92: of slaves 85–86, 98, 115, 121, 146, 172, 180; of women 148, 151, 154–55, 194, 197
Emancipation Proclamation 92, 172
equality of women and men 8, 11, 18, 223, 143, 187, 190–91; *see also* women's rights
Expositions: 1876 Centennial 91, 160; 1893 Columbian 150, 160–62

female element 29, 35, 97–98, 101, 103, 189–91
feminism 2, 3, 9, 12, 15, 18–19, 22, 82, 85, 87, 90, 96, 104, 142, 150–51, 153, 155, 173, 178; *see also* women's rights
Fern, Fanny 135
Finney, Charles 12, 48–49
Foster, Stephen S. 68
Franklin, Benjamin 131–32
free labor 121
free love 8, 16, 19 , 211n3
free soil 13, 15, 21, 27
Fuller, Margaret 3, 159

Gage, Matilda Joslyn 34–36, 91
Gardener, Helen 199
Garrett, Mary 200–2
Garrison, William Lloyd 49, 72–73, 175–76
gender gap 1, 155
Gilman, Charlotte Perkins 152
Grant, Ulysses S. 115, 191
Greeley, Horace 16, 135
Grimké Sisters 11, 13, 17, 36, 79, 151

Hall, Florence Howe 200
Hamilton, Alexander 121
Hanaford, Phoebe 152
Harbert, Elizabeth Boynton 154
Harper, Frances Ellen Watkins 144
Harper, Ida H. 146
Herttell, Thomas 9
History of Woman Suffrage 34–36
home protection ballot 142
Howe Julia Ward 79, 200–1
human rights 74, 116, 158, 165
Hunt, Harriot 17

immigrants 24, 26, 27, 68, 101, 113, 149, 173–78; *see also* Stanton, Elizabeth Cady: nativism
individualism 7, 18, 65, 91, 142, 151, 159, 179–84, 196–97, 199
industrialization 142
International Council of Women 32, 143–44, 146
International Woman Suffrage Alliance 145
intersectionality 2

Jacob, Harriet 79
Jones, Jane Elizabeth 12

Kansas 21, 80, 82, 96–99, 100
Kansas Nebraska Act 21
Kelly, Abby 36
Kemble, Fanny 102
Knights of Labor 144
Know Nothing 68
Ku Lux Klan 79, 104–5

Lawrence, Margaret Stanton 48, 55–56
The Lily 16–17, 37–40, 45
Lincoln, Abraham 22, 92–93, 115
Livermore Mary 79
Loud, Huldah 144
Lozier, Clemence S. 136
lynching 146, 163–67

Madison, James 109
Maine Law 17, 37, 41
male domination 15, 24–27, 127–29, 131, 134, 170, 186, 191
male element 100–1, 148, 189
marriage: contract 9, 20, 60–1, 84, 119, 129–30; inequality of women 15, 44, 53, 60–61, 83–84, 87, 107, 114–15, 117–20, 127–28, 135, 171, 186; interracial 149, 156–59, 163, 165–66
married women's property rights 8, 12, 14, 26, 35, 40, 42, 59, 61, 64, 114–15, 181

McFarland-Richardson affair 83, 117–20, 127
M'Clintock, Mary 14
Mexican American War 14
Mill, John Stuart 97, 107, 120, 128
Minor, Virginia 88, 107
Minor V Happersett 90
moral reform 10–11, 141
Morse, Anna 165
Mosaic Code 188–89
motherhood 15, 20, 44, 61–62, 74, 118–19, 131–32, 136, 141, 185, 186, 196, 203; voluntary 83–84; *see also* Stanton, Elizabeth Cady: motherhood
Mott, James 69
Mott, Lucretia 13–14, 20, 55, 80, 102, 167, 208n22
Mott Sisters 136

National American Woman Suffrage Association 146–47, 150–53, 169–72, 185, 196–98, 199, 202
National Woman Suffrage Association 34, 82, 84, 87, 88, 116, 143–47
natural rights 7, 96, 108, 109, 151, 181
New Departure 87–91
New York State Women's Temperance Society 37–43
Nichols, Mary Gove 16

Owen, Robert Dale 9

Phillips, Wendell 55, 68, 73, 105, 115, 203
positivism 148
prostitution 10, 81, 84, 106, 120

racism 149, 157–58, 164, 166; *see also* Black codes; sexual violence
religion, subordination of women 18, 25, 28, 39, 70, 73–76, 127, 148; *see also* secularism; *Woman's Bible*
reproduction 53–54, 61, 82–84
Republican Party 21–22, 47–48, 79, 81–82, 87, 90, 100, 112, 116
republicanism 58, 62, 74–75, 93–95, 97, 102, 107–12, 128, 177, 179, 203
Revolution 82, 86, 100–3, 105
Rochester 16, 23, 31–33, 38, 43, 45–49, 88, 164–65, 168, 200–1
Roosevelt, Theodore 201
Rose, Ernestine 9, 12, 20, 35, 65–70, 196

Sambo 100, 102, 105
secularism 9–10, 12, 14, 18, 142, 148, 150, 154, 170, 185, 196, 199
self-sovereignty 83–84, 179–84

Seneca Falls 16–17, 31, 37, 58; women's rights convention 22–29, 31–32, 37, 45, 154
Sewall, May Wright 146
sex, aristocracy of 100, 107, 110
sexes, alike and different 20, 23–25, 52–53, 62–63, 100
sexual abuse 2, 10–11, 71, 82, 83, 86–87, 116, 204; *see also* sexual violence
sexual intercourse 44, 74
sexual morality 10, 20, 25, 90, 106, 127, 149–50, 185
sexual rights 9, 82, 84, 85–86, 14
sexual violence 163, 170; and race 81, 104, 163, 165–67
sexuality 9, 11, 12, 16, 17, 19, 41, 84, 149–80; and race 162–65
Shattuck, Harriette 146
Shaw, Anna Howard 15, 150–51, 153, 199–202
single women 17, 85, 132–37, 168
slavery 11, 14, 20, 22, 31–33, 63, 66–69, 72–76, 92, 94, 98, 114, 117–18, 125–28
Smith, Gerrit 13, 22, 26, 56–57, 66
socialism 148, 151, 172, 173
Southgate, Eliza 8
spiritualism 50, 69–70, 210n27
Stanton, Henry Brewster 13–14, 47–48, 52, 55
Stanton, Elizabeth Cady: elitism 2, 29, 59, 75, 101–2, 104, 174–**79**; motherhood 12, 14, 16, 30, 37, 43, 45, 56, 154, 205; nativism 100, 149, 154, 173–78; racial attitudes 2, 70, 74, 81, 100–6, 149, 154, 156–59, 163, 173, 180, 181; and religion 149, 153, 185–98, 203–4
Stanton, Theodore Eaton 43
Stevens, Thaddeus 109
Stone, Lucy 11–12, 20, 21, 46, 50, 52, 68, 79–80, 82, 84, 145
suffrage: educated 149, 173–78, 214n64; manhood 100–3; universal 80–81, 98, 100, 104, 107–16, 149, 173–74; *see also* Black suffrage; woman suffrage
Sumner, Charles 102, 109, 116
Sunday closing 150, 170–71
Supreme Court, U.S. 2, 3, 21, 88, 90, 91, 112, 125

Taft, William Howard 201
taxation 24, 26, 41–42, 59, 64, 98, 102, 108–15
teachers 18, 46, 48–52, 59, 65, 122, 125, 165–66, 184
temperance 11, 16–19, 33–37, 43, 45–46, 58, 65, 82, 97, 136, 144

Thomas, M. Carey 200–2
Tilton, Theodore 105
trade unions 91, 123–24
Train, George Francis 82, 100
trial by jury 59, 108, 116, 118

Upton, Harriet Taylor 153

Vaughn, Hester 83

Washington, George 46, 105
Wells, Ida B. 146, 163–68
Willard, Amelia 49
Willard, Emma 8, 12
Willard, Frances 91, 142, 150, 152, 163, 167, 210*n*
Wollstonecraft, Mary 7–9, 14–15
woman suffrage: arguments for 26–27, 86, 107–16, 170, 181; conflicts within 81–82, 147, 154; expansion 141–47, 155, 169; impact of 167, 197; methods 80–81, 88, 172–73; opposition to 3, 42, 87, 96, 135, 142–44, 187, 175, 187; origins of 32–33, 35–36, 79; and other causes 36, 87–91, 143, 147, 153, 155, 162; and race 3, 82, 146–47, 156, 164, 167; radical and conservative approaches 87, 142–43, 147–48, 153, 160–62, 169, 196; in the states 96–99, 173; unification of 145–48, 169; victory of 146, 150, 154, 169, 201; and women's emancipation 15, 86; and women's support 6, 27, 145, 161–63
Woman's Bible 152–53, 185–98, 203
Woman's Christian Temperance Union 141–43, 150, 160–61, 163
Woman's Journal 173, 175–76
Woman's National Loyal League 79, 92–95
woman's sphere 10–22, 13–14, 18, 21, 24, 27, 30, 35, 52, 62, 75, 157, 159, 186–87, 204
women: Black 2, 32, 67–68, 75–76, 125, 164, 98, 144, 146, 155–66, 163–64; middle-class 32, 85, 121, 141–42, 144; poor 21, 63–64, 171, 174, 94, 122; world 24, 26, 28, 102, 172
women's reform organizations 59, 122, 142–45, 161
women's rights: conventions 14, 16, 19, 52–54; ideas 16, 18, 23–29, 37, 58–64, 142, 151; movement 1, 7, 9–12, 16, 17, 19–22, 32, 43, 46–48, 55, 63, 71, 79–80, 105, 151, 171; *see also* feminism; Seneca Falls
Woodhull, Victoria 87–90, 107
working class 123, 170, 174–76
World's Anti-Slavery Convention 45, 55, 73
Wright, Frances 8, 10, 14, 15
Wright, Martha 14
Wyoming 112

www.ingramcontent.com/pod-product-compliance
Ingram Content Group UK Ltd.
Pitfield, Milton Keynes, MK11 3LW, UK
UKHW041951140426
5217IPUK00015B/754